W9-BWS-945

Fritz Thyssen

I PAID HITLER

by

FRITZ THYSSEN

Published in association with
COOPERATION PUBLISHING CO., INC.,
NEW YORK
HODDER AND STOUGHTON, LTD.
LONDON

First printed November, 1941

---

*Made and Printed in Great Britain for Hodder & Stoughton, Limited, London
by Wyman & Sons Limited, London, Reading and Fakenham*

PUBLISHER'S FOREWORD

THIS extraordinary book has an extraordinary story. And this story must be told.

When, at the outbreak of the war in September, 1939, Fritz Thyssen, the great German industrialist, fled from Germany to Switzerland, almost all the newspapers, magazines, syndicates, and publishers of the world tried to obtain his memoirs, or at least the true story of his rupture with Hitler and his escape from Nazi Germany.

The story of the man who was the greatest industrial power in Germany, who was an ardent German nationalist, who organised the passive resistance in the Ruhr in 1923 ; the man who for more than fifteen years backed Hitler and financed his movement—the story of the great German capitalist who helped the Nazis into power because he believed that they were the people who could save his country from Bolshevism and who have now confiscated all his property—this is indeed one of the most unusual stories of this world crisis.

In this great competition among publishers to obtain Thyssen's memoirs, I have taken part myself and it happened to be that I won. I should like to tell in a few lines, why and how.

During the past ten years I have directed, in Paris, an international newspaper syndicate called COOPERATION. The programme of this organisation was to unite the leading international statesmen and to publish their views on international affairs all over the world. My first contributors were Lord Cecil, Sir Austen Chamberlain, Arthur Henderson, Paul Painlevé, Louis Loucheur, Henri de Jouvenel, and some others. As the organisation grew in the years before the war, it obtained an almost monopolistic position in handling the exclusive world rights of the articles of about a hundred leading statesmen such as Winston Churchill, Anthony Eden, Alfred Duff Cooper, Lord Samuel, Major Attlee, Hugh Dalton, Paul Reynaud, Edouard Herriot, Leon Blum, P. E. Flandin, Yvon Delbos, and many others from England, France, Spain, Belgium, Scandinavia, and the Balkans. These articles, issued almost daily, have been printed all over the world in some four hundred newspapers in about seventy countries. The American public may recall these articles published before the war in the United States by a group of over twenty leading independent newspapers from coast to coast, headed by the New York *Herald Tribune*.

I have tried to present all the conflicting views of Europe and have often published also the articles of the Fascist spokesman, Virginio Gayda, inasmuch as it was possible for us to print also from time to time foreign articles in Italian newspapers. But I have never published Nazi articles. In fact, as the crisis grew, the policy of my organisation became more and more openly anti-Nazi until it was probably the only organisation of this kind fighting Nazi influence and

the Goebbels machine on the European continent.
These publications must have had some effect, as
one day I received the highest tribute from Hitler
himself when, in his first speech after the Munich
agreement at Saarbrücken, he shouted hysterically
that " this propaganda by Churchill, Eden and Duff
Cooper must stop. . . ."

I am obliged to mention this because in connection
with the Thyssen memoirs I shall have to make a few
statements which, under the circumstances, can be
proved only by my past record.

When Thyssen arrived in Locarno he was unable to
reply to any request for publication because he had
given his word of honour to the Swiss government
that, while residing in Swiss territory, he would refrain
from any declaration or publication. Consequently,
I did not think it would be of any use to go to see
him myself and I therefore tried to approach him
through various friends. I received no encouragement
whatsoever. In March, 1940, Thyssen went from
Switzerland to Brussels to visit his dying mother and
I learned that from Brussels he would go to Paris.

On the 3rd of April, I received in my office in Paris
a telephone call from the *Sunday Express* in London
and the *Paris Soir*, newspapers with whom I have long
had business relations, saying that they had been
doing their utmost to obtain the story of Mr. Thyssen
but were unable to approach him. They asked me
whether I could help them.

I immediately went to see M. Paul Reynaud who
was Minister of Foreign Affairs as well as Premier. I
explained to him the political importance of the
publication of Thyssen's memoirs and he emphatically

agreed with me. The problem was how to persuade
Thyssen to write and publish without further delay.
I told M. Reynaud that I knew the man who could
introduce me to Thyssen and who could probably
persuade him to entrust the publication of his memoirs
to me. Unfortunately, this man, who was a friend of
Thyssen, was in London and it was extremely difficult
in view of the existing censorship and prohibition of
international telephone calls to put him in touch with
Thyssen. M. Reynaud instructed one of his attachés
to help me and permitted me to use the telephone line
of the Quai d'Orsay to the French Embassy building
in London.

I spent a most dramatic day and almost a whole
night in the attaché's room at the Quai d'Orsay. I
left M. Reynaud's cabinet at about the same time as
the Paris-Brussels Express on which Thyssen was to
travel left Brussels. As we did not know where
Thyssen was staying in Paris, the Sûreté was charged
to report his movements. We received about half-
hourly messages : " Thyssen crossed the frontier . . .,"
" Thyssen passed St. Quentin . . .," " Thyssen arrived
at the Gare du Nord . . .," and finally, " Mr. and
Mrs. Thyssen arrived at the Crillon Hotel. . . ."

I immediately attempted to arrange a telephone
communication between Thyssen and our mutual
friend in London, but it took almost twenty-four
hours before we succeeded. Finally they were both
on the telephone, talking without censorship inter-
ference on the official line of the French Foreign
Ministry for about half an hour. The following day
I received a note from Mr. Thyssen asking me to come
and see him at the Crillon.

Our first meeting was very cordial and lasted almost two hours. He said that he was prepared to publish immediately the letters which he addressed to Hitler, Goering, and other officials after his rupture with the Nazis and in which he explained why he had left Germany. In fact, he had already sent these letters to a friend of his in America with a view to publishing them. He said he would be glad if these letters could also be printed in England, in France, and in as many other countries as possible, but that he would not like to publish anything more at the moment.

I saw Thyssen every day while he was in Paris. I asked him point-blank, " Do you want to help us destroy Hitler or not ? " When his reply was an unconditional " Yes " I tried to make him agree with me that the things he had to say and the documents and material he possessed must be published during the war and not after if they were to produce their full effect. After the third or fourth conversation he came to understand that in the middle of a war against Hitlerism there was no use having powerful weapons in one's possession and withholding them from instant use.

Once he decided to write his memoirs he was most anxious to proceed as quickly as possible. He wanted his letters to be published without delay, even before the completion of his book. These letters appeared in the United States in *Life* magazine on April 29, 1940. Simultaneously, they were published in London in the *Sunday Express*, and in France in *Paris Soir*.

Thyssen was anxious to have some of his papers which he had deposited in the vaults of a bank at

Lucerne in Switzerland. I discussed the matter at
the Quai d'Orsay and they were prepared to send a
special diplomatic courier to Lucerne in order to
bring the papers to France. After a week's stay in
Paris, Mr. and Mrs. Thyssen left for Monte Carlo.
The papers arrived from Switzerland four days later
and I went down to the Riviera with a collaborator
of mine, who was to help Thyssen in preparing the
book, and a secretary. Thyssen was staying at the
Hotel de Paris in Monte Carlo. I placed my
collaborator near him at the Beau Rivage Hotel, and
in order to evade the attention of the innumerable
Italian spies who were in that region at that time, I
went to stay about ten miles away at the Grand Hotel
at Cap Ferrat, which is one of the quietest places in
the most charming spot of the Riviera. There were
only a few guests in the hotel, among them Sir Nevile
Henderson, the former British Ambassador to
Germany who, at that time, had just finished writing
his book about the failure of his mission in Berlin.
Next to the hotel was the villa of former Premier
Flandin whom I saw often while I was staying at Cap
Ferrat. He was very much interested in the question
why Thyssen had become such an enemy of Hitler.

I spent about three weeks on the Riviera, working
with Thyssen day and night. He usually started work
at about half-past nine in the morning and dictated
without interruption for about three hours. He
dictated rapidly and fluently in German and partly
in French, jumping from one subject to the other,
giving the impression of a man filled to the exploding
point with things to tell, not knowing how to get rid
of them quickest. At one o'clock we usually went to

lunch together, continuing the work in lengthy discussions. The dictation of the morning was typed in the afternoon and submitted to him in the evening. He corrected every page most meticulously, two or three times, until he finally approved the individual chapters.

During our collaboration in Monte Carlo, Thyssen made an unexpected impression on me. I had never met Thyssen before but he was exactly the contrary of the type one would imagine to be a steel king and leading armament manufacturer, and the backer of Nazism. He was a charming old gentleman, unusually witty, with a perfect sense of humour. He loved good food and the best wines, and our luncheons rarely took less than three hours. I drove him to all the famous restaurants of the Riviera—to the Château Madrid up in the mountains, the Bonne Auberge near Antibes, the Colombe d'Or in romantic St. Paul, and all the other places of the highest gastronomic culture. During these luncheons Thyssen told one story after another, some of them unbelievable. Not one of the Nazi leaders and very few of his industrial colleagues escaped his most malicious remarks. He told dozens of stories about the private lives of the German leaders which, unfortunately, cannot be printed in this book.

When talking about the serious problems and of his experiences, he would interrupt his monologue almost daily, pounding his fist against his forehead and exclaiming to himself, " Ein Dummkopf war ich . . . ! Ein Dummkopf war ich . . . ! " (" What a fool I have been . . . ! What a fool I have been . . . ! ") He would then repeat the express hope that his book would be published quickly in America. " I wish

I could tell American industrialists about my experiences," was one of the remarks he made to me many times.

I had the definite impression that his feeling against Hitler was not only sincere, but passionately sincere. He answered every question I put to him and told everything he knew—with one exception. He did not want to tell me what were the *exact* amounts he had given to the Nazis, although he told me that he had somewhere in a safe place the receipts of all the monies paid by him. I was rather anxious to get a photostatic copy of these receipts in order to illustrate the book. But he was unwilling to tell me where they were.

On May the 10th, at 8 o'clock in the morning, I turned on the radio and heard the voice of the French Minister of Information, M. Frossard, announcing that at dawn the German army had crossed the frontiers of Holland, Belgium and Luxemburg, and that the war in the west had started. At 10 a.m. I brought the news to Thyssen. His reaction was very peculiar. He became pale and simply did not want to believe it. He said he knew that the German General Staff had always been against an attack on the west, and the only reason he could offer to explain it was that by this means the army High Command wanted to get rid of the Nazis, driving them to sure defeat. He said he knew the exact production figures of the German heavy industry, the shortage of certain raw materials, and the bad quality of steel used in some armoured divisions, and that this war could not possibly be won by Germany. I was never able to understand whether the explanation of the striking

German success was the extraordinary weakness of the French army or the ultra-efficiency of the Nazi war lords who had been able to hide even from the Chairman of the German Steel Trust what they were producing.

By the end of May we had almost finished the work. More than half the book was completed, corrected, and approved for publication by Thyssen. The remaining chapters had all been dictated, but before the final editing it was necessary to check up some dates and facts which could not be done in Monte Carlo. So I went back to Paris with the understanding that I should return to Monte Carlo about the beginning of June in order to get the book ready for immediate publication.

When I arrived back in Paris the German army had already broken through at Sedan. What happened during the following days and what life during that period in Paris was like, everybody knows. The situation became more and more dangerous by the hour and I could not think of leaving my office for another trip to Monte Carlo without knowing whether the German army would be stopped somewhere or whether we should have to flee from Paris.

I left Paris on the 11th of June, at night by motor-car, and after an unbelievable drive of fourteen hours, under conditions which have already been described in so many books, I arrived in Tours. I was able to take with me only very little in the way of personal belongings but I had with me the Thyssen manuscript. Two days later I was again on the road to Bordeaux, and after the capitulation of France an English destroyer took me out to sea where I was transferred to a British cargo ship which brought me to England. I left my car and most of the things I had been able to save from Paris in the harbour at Bordeaux, but I was able to save Thyssen's manuscript.

After my arrival in London, political friends, newspapers, and publishers urged me to publish the Thyssen book ; but I had a feeling that I could not do so without knowing what had happened to Thyssen and whether or not he was in a safe place. I tried for months to trace him, but it was impossible to obtain any authentic information. Some sources said he had escaped to America, others that he was still on the Riviera, and others that he had been delivered by the French to the Gestapo. Under these circumstances I felt unable to publish any part of Thyssen's memoirs.

I came over from England to the United States in February, 1941, hoping I would be able to find out exactly what had happened to Thyssen and where he was. Unfortunately, nobody knew anything except that he must be in the hands of the Gestapo ; otherwise his family in South America or his friends in the United States would have heard from him in the course of an entire year. I had to accept, therefore, as a given situation that he had been unable to escape after the collapse of France and that he is probably in a concentration camp in the hands of the Gestapo. I felt for many months that under such circumstances this book could not be published as the publication almost certainly would cause Thyssen's assassination.

I wish to make myself clear and to avoid any misunderstanding. I did not intend to defend Thyssen or to protect him. I was always aware that

restes du roi de Germanie, Henri l'Oiseleur. Il est toujours utile
de cultiver l'amitié du chef tout puissant de la police secrète,
surtout lorsque celui-ci est le rival politique du dictateur de
l'économie allemande.

Pour moi, je ne ferai aucune concession contre ma conscience.
Je ne rentrerai pas en Allemagne tant que Hitler et ses hommes
seront au pouvoir. C'est cela que j'ai voulu dire à Goering.

Aussitôt après le départ de Vögler, j'ai rédigé cette lettre, qu'on
ne désirait pas recevoir en haut lieu:

A characteristic page of the manuscript " I Paid Hitler," with Fritz Thyssen's
original handwriting in French.

he was one of the men most responsible for the rise
of Hitler and for the seeking of power by the National
Socialists in Germany. I also knew that he was
probably the man most responsible for Germany's
torpedoing of the Disarmament Conference, and that
he and some of his friends were probably more
responsible even than Hitler for the miseries unleashed
by the Nazis on the world. For about twenty years
Fritz Thyssen played a very big and very dangerous
political game and I do not believe that before the
judgment seat of History his confession, " What a fool
I have been," is sufficient defence for acquittal.

But I had nothing to do with Thyssen on the public
forum. I met him when he was a refugee. I made
with him an agreement as between author and
publisher and I have had a very strong feeling that I
could not publish his memoirs until I was sure either
that he was free or that he was dead.

But as the months passed and the war spread, more
and more people, public men and publishers, were
trying to persuade me that there was no place for
personal consideration in this matter. That this
manuscript was far too important a political and
historical document. And that I could not take the
responsibility of withholding it from publication.
They pointed out that if Thyssen had been put in a
concentration camp, he was almost certainly dead ;
and if he was still alive, nothing could save him. If
he had met the fate of the other enemies of Nazism in
a concentration camp, he certainly must have had the
hope that his memoirs would be published, as this
was the only weapon with which he could strike back
at Hitler. But whatever his personal fate, it cannot

be taken into consideration when the free peoples of the world are fighting a desperate war against Hitlerism, and when the publication of this unique document may enlighten the democracies and may help them to act in time to prevent Nazism from spreading to the Western Hemisphere.

After fourteen months of scruples and hesitations, I finally came to the conclusion that this book could not be withheld any longer from the public. I now believe that if Thyssen is in a concentration camp and if he is still alive, the further postponement of the publication of his memoirs would certainly not save him. On the contrary, I even believe and hope the publication might give him some satisfaction.

But quite apart from the effect this publication might have on his personal life, we are engaged in a life and death struggle against Hitlerism and whatever hurts Hitler is right for us. I think we should not have the weakness to yield to that old and horrible Gestapo blackmail of paralysing the activities of free people by torturing friends and relatives in concentration camps. I think we should have the strength to sacrifice those who are in the hands of the Gestapo, however near they are personally to us, and to keep on fighting under all circumstances. We shall never be able to destroy this monstrous system of human slavery if in dealing with it we let ourselves be guided by sentiment and not by the coldest reasoning.

It was Hitler's attack on Russia that decided me and that provided the final argument for the decision to publish this book. Immediately after the start of the Russo-German war we heard the voices of people in highest positions saying that Hitler had returned to his old programme and that he is the man who will save us from Communism. It had been in order to prove that this last was the greatest possible misjudgment of Nazism that Fritz Thyssen had decided to appeal to the world and to tell to the free nations his experiences. The fate of Fritz Thyssen, the great German nationalist, the mightiest German industrialist, and the devoted Catholic, is the outstanding example of how Hitler is protecting the patriots, the industrialists, and the Christians from Communism.

EMERY REVES,
PRESIDENT,
Cooperation Publishing Co., Inc.

*   *   *

The Author's Foreword, all of Part I, Chapters 1, 2 and 3 of Part II, Chapters 3, 5, 6, and 7 of Part III, and Chapter 3 in Part IV have been revised, corrected, and finally approved for publication by Fritz Thyssen.

The remaining chapters have been dictated by him, but have not been corrected or revised. Some of these chapters contain repetitions ; some paragraphs are not in the right place. It would have been easy to edit these chapters and to avoid the lack of smoothness in some sections, but we thought they should remain in the form in which they were left by Thyssen.

In some places where it was inevitable we have added some explanatory notes in order to make clear

B

problems and circumstances, but all of this additional material is marked either with " Publisher's Note," or with " Historical Note."

There is also appended at the back of the book a series of short biographical sketches of the principal people mentioned by Thyssen.

E. R.

AUTHOR'S FOREWORD

THIS book aims to be something more than the story of an error of whose tragic consequences I am as well aware as anybody else. It is not enough to regret the past ; one must profit from the lessons one has learned. The war into which Hitler has precipitated the world demands of all men worthy of the name that they should gird their loins and fight.

For ten years before he came to power I supported Hitler and his party. I myself was a National Socialist, and I shall explain why. To-day, exiled and fugitive because I did my duty in counselling against war, I wish to contribute to the fall of Adolf Hitler by enlightening public opinion in Germany and the world in general concerning the Führer and the lesser so-called leaders of contemporary Germany.

Hitler deceived me, as he has deceived the German people as a whole and all men of good will. It may perhaps be said—to me and to all Germans—that we should not have allowed ourselves to be deceived. For my part I accept the validity of this charge. I plead guilty. I was completely mistaken regarding Hitler and his party. I believed in his promises, in his loyalty, in his political genius. The same mistake has been made by professional politicians. Hitler was trusted by the Catholics and even by the Jews. Of this I could give many examples.

Hitler has deceived us all. But after his accession to power he succeeded in misleading foreign statesmen, just as he misled the Germans before 1933.

If I wished to attempt to justify myself, I might say that people outside Germany were better informed concerning the initial crime of the regime than we were in Germany. I speak of the burning of the Reichstag. Nevertheless, the great nations of Europe continued to maintain normal diplomatic relations with the Nazi incendiaries and assassins. Their ambassadors and ministers broke bread with them, received them in their embassies and legations, and shook hands with them as with honest men. We in Germany can at least proffer the excuse that we did not know the truth.

Hitler rearmed Germany to an incredible degree and at an unheard-of speed. The Great Powers closed their eyes to this fact. Did they really not recognise the danger, or did they wish to ignore it? Whichever it may be, they took no measures to prevent Germany's illegal rearmament. They did not even arm themselves to meet the danger in time. From the very outset the military effort put forth by the Nazi regime seemed entirely disproportionate to the resources of the country. Even in the early stages, therefore, I had the presentiment that it must inevitably lead to a catastrophe.

But Hitler carried off one outstanding diplomatic victory after the other—successes which neither the Weimar Republic nor Imperial Germany would have ever dared to hope for. He was able to reintroduce compulsory military service ; he secured the military reoccupation and the fortification of the Rhineland, the Anschluss of Austria, the annexation of the Sudeten region of Czechoslovakia, the entry into Prague—three years of victory without striking a blow ! At the very moment when doubt and dis-affection were gaining ground in the country, the leader of the New Germany was in a position to checkmate his opponents in Germany by demonstrating —which he never failed to do—the historical grandeur of the results achieved. And he had himself pro-claimed to be the greatest German of all time.

The Munich Pact was mainly responsible for the historical glamour which surrounded the National Socialist regime. In the eyes of the masses it con-firmed Hitler's reputation of infallibility and enabled the new leaders of Germany to pursue, during the next year, a policy that has plunged the German people into a war which it did not desire and did not foresee.

It may be asked why, in post-war Germany, a dis-organised country menaced by incessant economic and social crises, and burdened by a heavy external debt, an industrialist like me should have seen fit to contribute to a recovery which, by consolidating the State, would have enabled his country to maintain its position as a Great Power in the pacific community of human civilisation ? The following pages may give the answer to this question.

Hitler—at least, so I and many other Germans believed—contributed to the recovery of Germany, the rebirth of a national will and a modern social programme. Undeniably also, his effort was supported by the masses who were behind him. And, in a country which at one time had seven million unemployed, it was necessary to distract these masses from the vain promises of the radical Socialists. For these Left-Wing Socialists had gained the upper hand during the economic depression, just as they had almost triumphed during the revolutionary period following the debacle of 1918. But my hope of saving Germany from this second danger was soon followed by disillusionment. This disillusionment dates almost from the beginning of the Nazi regime. During the seven years which have elapsed since then I intervened on several occasions with attempts to stop excesses that were a defiance to the conscience of mankind. On September 1st, 1939, I protested with all my energy against the impending war, and I informed the German leaders of my intention to appeal to world opinion against their acts.

But the main object of this book is not a negative one. A business man must be optimistic ; otherwise he would never undertake anything. Twice in twenty-five years Europe has been plunged into war. The present German regime bears the immediate responsibility for the catastrophe, which was brought about by a policy at once frivolous and criminal. Nevertheless it is quite certain that the more remote and profounder causes of this must be sought in the conflict of 1914–1918, and in a peace conference which proved incapable of resolving it. For, notwithstanding certain deserving efforts, Versailles did not succeed in establishing a political and economic order which would have insured the world against a new disaster.

If human civilisation is not to perish, everything that is possible must be done to make war impossible in Europe. But the violent solution dreamed of by Hitler, a primitive person obsessed by ill-digested memories, is a romantic folly and a barbarous and bloody anachronism.

Europe must definitely be given political security such as exists, for instance, in America. Otherwise this will be the end of our old continent and of the civilisation of which Europe is the cradle. If the present ordeal is to have any meaning whatever, it must lead to the foundation of the United States of Europe, in one form or another. That is my conviction.

The reawakening of imperialism in the heart of Europe, for which Hitler's Germany bears the responsibility, must compel all German patriots to reflect. In 1923 I was able to save the Rhine and the Ruhr, and preserve German unity. I was imprisoned and condemned by the court-martial of the enemy. This perhaps gives me the right to speak to-day.

By an act of criminal folly, Hitler has imperilled the existence of a German Empire whose precarious character was well recognised by Bismarck, its founder and creator. During almost twenty years of his chancellorship, following a victorious campaign against France, his constant preoccupation was to pursue a cautious policy designed to reassure the other Powers. The wisdom of the founder of the German Empire was soon forgotten. The experiences of 1914, 1938 and 1939 have shown that the existence in Europe of a state of sixty to eighty million inhabitants, ruled by imperialistic politicians commanding the formidable war potential of modern industry, is a permanent danger for the safety of the continent.

In 1871, the genius of a great statesman enlisted Western culture and technique in the service of the spirit of Prussianism. To-day I see in this combination the fundamental cause of political instability in Europe. Prussianised eastern Germany has never succeeded in casting off its colonial mentality as the conqueror of the Slavs. In her hands, Western technique becomes an instrument of war and is no longer a weapon of civilisation.

Moreover, seven years of Nazi tyranny have painfully impressed me with the total incompatibility of the two Germanies—the colonial, servile Germany of the east, originally peopled by Slavs who became the Prussians' serfs, and the Germany of the west, where Christian and Roman humanism was the main civilising force. The persecution of the Christian religion, the sadistic anti-semitism of the Prussians, so foreign to our Rhineland population, the attempts to revive a barbaric paganism which is inhuman in its moral conceptions, have convinced me and many others that the salvation of Germany and of Europe demand the restoration of the former barrier between these two peoples with so widely divergent mentalities. The freedom, culture, and Christianity of western and Catholic Germany—a country belonging definitely to western Europe—must be safeguarded.

The spirit of western and southern Germany is directed toward the west. Its industrial and technical development urges it on toward the great ocean routes of the world. The Nazi conception of Lebensraum, in the form of territories to be conquered, has no meaning for a great industrial country which should have the universe for its pacific domain.

Such a political reorganisation is of course not an end in itself. The post-war world must be able to live and to resume its suspended development. The economic chaos and ruin which already exist will doubtless increase as the result of the present war. They will raise once again the question of collaboration between all well-intentioned peoples for purposes of reconstruction. Do the democratic governments realise the gravity of these problems? Valuable encouragement has been received from America. It would be mad folly to revert to the economic errors that followed upon the last war. What must be done is to combine the resources and the good will of the nations of Europe and of the United States of America in order to repair the ruins, and to begin again. At the end of this war there can be no question, as in 1918, of a suit for damages. Punishment, I hope, will be meted out to the assassins, the criminals, and the forgers by the German people themselves. But may the peace be constructive; may resentment be banished for all time! May we work for the future and forget the past!

In this book I have attempted to set forth certain ideas to which I am deeply attached. They are not the result of improvisation. As head of one of the greatest industrial enterprises of Germany, I have had to cope for twenty years with the consequences of an abortive peace. The leisures of exile have afforded me time to reflect upon an experience which was sometimes merely painful, sometimes tragic. The result of my meditations is consigned to these pages. May they be the contribution of one man of good will to the peace which is to come.!

FRITZ THYSSEN

Monte Carlo, May, 1940.

CONTENTS

ILLUSTRATIONS

PART ONE

MY RUPTURE WITH HITLER'S GERMANY

CHAPTER ONE

MY ESCAPE FROM GERMANY

ON August 15th, 1939, I arrived with my wife at Bad Gastein in the Austrian Alps. We needed a rest. It had been a particularly worrying and strenuous year.

It has been said that I went to Gastein to prepare my escape from Germany. This is untrue. In fact, I had left Germany early that August to visit the Zürich exhibition. Had I wanted to escape I could have remained in Switzerland then. But I did not believe that war would come. The German generals were against it. Moreover, I had been told of statements made by one of Hermann Goering's intimate friends, Gauleiter Terboven of Essen, from which it appeared that all this was purely and simply a diplomatic game and that no one in office dreamed of embarking upon an armed adventure. Terboven's remarks most certainly reflected Goering's own opinion. At the beginning of August Goering was opposed to war ; his subsequent change of mind came only at the eleventh hour. I was therefore quite reassured when I left for Gastein.

On August 23rd I received the surprising news of

Hitler's pact with Stalin. Negotiations had been proceeding for a long time, but I never imagined that they would go so far. Without this agreement with Russia, Hitler could never have embarked upon the Polish campaign. He had been definitely warned by the French and British ambassadors that their countries would not tolerate an aggression against Poland. Our ambassador in Paris, Count Welczek, had solemnly informed his government on several occasions that a German attack on Poland would be the signal for a general outbreak of war.

The situation, moreover, was perfectly clear. Neither France nor Great Britain could accept a second Munich. How was it that Hitler and Ribbentrop did not realise this fact? A year earlier, the British Prime Minister, a man of seventy, had taken an aeroplane for the first time in his life to fly to Germany and negotiate with Hitler. The French Premier had come to Munich for the same purpose. A solution was reached by which Germany received all that she wanted. This was an unprecedented success. No German emperor had achieved anything comparable to this. A great statesman like Bismarck would have realised that Munich was an exceptional gift of the gods. He would have done all in his power to prevent the two great western countries from feeling that they had been humiliated. Above all, he would have applied himself to the pacific consolidation of the results so easily obtained.

But what was Hitler's line? On March 13th, 1939, he invaded Czechoslovakia, whose remaining territory he had promised to respect. This seemed to me monstrous. To break his solemn word in such conditions, to insult two great nations, might perhaps appear to the Nazis as a stroke of genius on the part of the greatest politician the world has ever known (for this is the light in which Hitler sees himself). To me and to many other Germans, it seemed sheer madness—a bound forward on the road to catastrophe. I was therefore sceptical as to the possibility of settling the dispute with Poland by a second Munich. Two great Powers, joined in alliance and disposing of immense resources, do not allow themselves to be deceived twice in the same way.

The news of the signature of the agreement with Stalin caused me anxiety. However, relying—perhaps too strongly—on my knowledge of the situation, I still believed that this was just another of those spectacular episodes which were characteristic of the regime. So far as I could judge, it made almost no impression in Paris and London, for the German-Russian pact did not shake the resolution of the two democracies to oppose any further act of violence by the force of arms. I was not surprised. Any other policy would have amounted to abdication of the Western Powers —a veritable suicide. But still I did not believe that war would come.

On August 25th I was advised that I would have to go to Berlin for a meeting of the Reichstag. The suddenness of such convocations is symptomatic of the rôle to which that assembly has been reduced. In the earlier days, matters were given serious study, they were reported on by committees, and a working session of the Reichstag was then convened. To-day things are different. Members are summoned from one day to the next to hear a declaration by Hitler. That is what is called " good theatre," the sole purpose being propaganda. The members play the part of walkers-on in cheap drama. For my own part, I have always considered that my position as member of the Reichstag carried with it a certain responsibility and the duty to express one's opinion. The meeting summoned for August 25th was cancelled. Once more I endeavoured to reassure myself.

Meanwhile my son-in-law, Count Zichy, had come to see us at Gastein with my daughter Anita and my two-and-a-half-year-old grandson. They intended to stay with us a week. Their visit was entirely unforeseen. Straubing in South Bavaria, where they reside, is only a few hours' distance by car from Gastein. I still felt that there was no special cause for worry.

But in the evening of August 31st I received a telegram from the Gauleiter of Essen, instructing me to travel to Berlin and attend a Reichstag meeting fixed for the next morning at the Kroll Opera. I suddenly realised the gravity of the situation. It was materially impossible for me to get to Berlin in that time. I should have had to travel by car and by night in order to catch the first morning plane from Munich, which might perhaps have enabled me to arrive just in time to see the end of the meeting. In any case, the state of my health did not permit such exertions. If I could have been in Berlin in time, I should certainly have protested publicly against any decision to go to war. I therefore decided to send my excuses for being unable to attend, and at the same time to express my opinion in no uncertain terms. About nine o'clock in the evening I addressed to Goering, as president of the Reichstag, the following urgent telegram :

"Received from the Essen Provincial Administration (Gauleitung) invitation to be ready to fly to Berlin. Unable to act on this suggestion owing to unsatisfactory state of health.

"In my opinion it would be possible to agree upon a kind of truce in order to gain time for negotiation. I am against war. A war will make Germany dependent on Russia for raw materials and Germany will thus forego her position as a world power.

(Signed)   "THYSSEN."

In this way, notwithstanding the material obstacle, I felt I had done my duty as a free man and as a responsible member of the Reichstag. I had informed the government of my absolute opposition to war. I must add that at that moment I had no intention of leaving Germany. I was at once appalled and disgusted by the prospect of an act of folly on the part of Hitler which neither the generals nor anyone else had been able to prevent.

The next morning my son-in-law proposed that we listen-in to the so-called "historic meeting" which I should have attended. I refused quite definitely to hear the reasons by which Hitler would seek to justify his madness.

The previous afternoon I had received a telegram from my sister announcing that her son-in-law and my nephew, von Remnitz, had just died in the Dachau concentration camp. I was ignorant of the conditions under which this had happened. Before the Anschluss, Remnitz had been the chief of the Austrian Legitimists (i.e. Hapsburg monarchists) in the province of Salzburg. After the annexation of Austria the Salzburg Nazis had tried to blackmail him. "Pay a contribution to the party," they had said, "and you will not have to suffer the consequences of your legitimist activity." My nephew had refused, saying that in independent Austria his political activity had been considered perfectly legal. The next day he was arrested and taken to Dachau. I had tried to intervene at Vienna with Gauleiter Bürckel, commissioner of the Reich for Austria, with a view to his release. Bürckel had not even troubled to answer my appeal. I was deeply affected by the news of my nephew's death. It was another tangible proof of the criminal illegality which prevailed in Germany and against which I had several times protested to the responsible leaders.

I was meditating on all this while my son-in-law was listening to Hitler on the radio. Some minutes later he came in, quite overcome. " Hitler," he said, " announces that the German army has entered Poland. This means war. And Hitler also says, ' Whoever is not with me is a traitor and shall be treated as such.' "

This ominous phrase was the reply to my telegram. What it meant was clearly shown by the miserable end of my nephew at Dachau.

There was no possibility of my remaining in Germany without exposing my own life and that of those dear to me. In agreement with my wife and my son-in-law I decided that we must leave the country. Providence had willed it that we should all be together at this critical moment, for I should never have gone if I had had to abandon my children as hostages to the Gestapo.

We started on September 2nd at seven o'clock in the morning. I had my own car, and my children had come to see me with theirs. We left without luggage, as if we were making an excursion. One of the usual drives around Gastein is to take the new Alpine road built by the former Austrian government, to cross the Glockner pass into Italy, and to return by the Brenner pass. On leaving Gastein we were held up by a landslide which barred the way. There had been a violent storm in the region on the previous night ; masses of mud and stones had made the road impassable, and men were at work clearing it. The foreman told us that traffic would soon be re-established. We waited three hours, feigning the most complete indifference. Finally there was just enough room for us to pass. At the frontier the chauffeur, who had no inkling of our plans, presented my papers, including my Reichstag deputy's card, saying that we were making the usual excursion. I did not get out of my car. The frontier police allowed us to pass, saying that we must be back in German territory within three hours. On arriving at the turning which leads to the Brenner, we took the left instead of the right and drove on toward Italy and Switzerland. I did not wish to linger in Italian territory, for everyone expected Italy to join in the war. We stopped at the first Swiss village, Le Prese. We were saved.

On my arrival I drafted the following memorandum, intending to send it to Goering at the first opportunity :

MEMORANDUM

1. On August 31st I sent the following urgent telegram to Marshal Goering at 9 p.m. [*The telegram is quoted on page* 37.]

2. In the Reichstag meeting of September 1st, Hitler said : " He who is not for me is a traitor and will be treated as such."

3. I regard this remark not only as a threat but also as an encroachment upon the rights of a member of the Reichstag to which I am entitled under our Constitution.

4. I have not only the right to express my opinion, but it is my duty to do so when I am convinced that Germany is being ruthlessly plunged into great danger. Hitler has no right to threaten me when I express my opinion.

5. Now, as before, I am against war. Since war has now broken out, Germany should do her best to bring it to an end as soon as possible, for the longer it lasts the harder the peace terms for Germany.

6. The pact with Germany was not broken by Poland—that pact which Hitler himself has repeatedly described as a guarantee of peace. [*Concerning this, reference should be made to Hitler's speech of September 26th, 1938.*]

7. In order to have peace it will be necessary for Germany to respect her Constitution in every way. Non-observance of the Constitution amounts, after all, to anarchy. The allegiance sworn by the individual citizen is valid only if the leaders also act in accordance with their obligations.

8. One hundred members were absent at the Reichstag meeting on September 1st. The seats of the absentees were occupied by officials of the Nazi party. This I consider as grossly unconstitutional, and I protest.

9. I demand that the German public be informed of the fact that I, as a member of the Reichstag, voted against war. If other members acted similarly, the public should also be informed of it.

10. On August 31st, shortly before sending the above-mentioned telegram to Field Marshal Goering, I was advised by telegram that a certain Herr von Remnitz had died suddenly in Dachau. Herr von Remnitz is the son in-law of my sister, Baroness Berg, who lives in Munich. He was interned immediately after the Anschluss, apparently because he had taken part in the activity of Legitimists before the Anschluss. Immediately after his

arrest I approached Gauleiter Bürckel in Vienna, but received no kind of answer. This is characteristic of present German conditions. I demand information as to whether Herr von Remnitz died a natural death or not. In the latter case, I reserve my right to take further steps.

I intended to despatch the memorandum by messenger in order to be sure that it really reached Marshal Goering. The opportunity to do so did not arise until twenty days later, when one of my employees arrived in Le Prese to see me on business. I completed my memorandum and entrusted it to him, asking him to take it to Berlin and to hand it to Marshal Goering in person. But he did not dare to undertake this. All he consented to do was to carry a sealed letter for Herr Terboven, Gauleiter of Essen. The latter was then to forward it to Marshal Goering.

The following week, on September 26th, Dr. Albert Vögler, vice-chairman of the board of the United Steel Works, of which I was the chairman, came to see me in Zürich. The news of my departure had spread in Germany. The French broadcasting services were the first to announce it, about September 12th. Goebbels issued a denial : " What is more natural," he said to his questioners, " than that an industrialist who has suffered from the intense overwork of the past few years should take a few weeks' leave ? " For a long time official quarters in Berlin attempted to conceal the fact of my departure and the reasons which had led to it.

Dr. Vögler came to me for information, for no one at Düsseldorf and in the industrial region as a whole knew exactly what to think. At the same time he conveyed to me a curious verbal message from Terboven. The Essen Gauleiter, who had received my letter, said that he had been unable to take it upon himself to forward my memorandum to the marshal, since he considered its language too violent. At the same time he assured me in writing that Goering had never received my telegram of August 31st and that the Führer, therefore, could not have intended the phrase in which he threatened a traitor's punishment to all who were not of his opinion to apply to me.

Terboven added that Marshal Goering guaranteed that, if I came back to Germany immediately, I should suffer no personal or economic consequences. But I was instructed to bring with me to Germany all the authentic copies of the above memorandum of September 20th. These would then be destroyed with the original.

Thus I was offered an opportunity of making a political recantation, in exchange for which I would be given in Germany the personal immunity which I already enjoyed abroad and which should in any case have been guaranteed to me at home, by virtue of my position as member of the Reichstag. I had further been given to understand that material penalties would be applied if I did not return.

This was a curious communication. On the one hand, Terboven assured me that Goering had received neither letter nor telegram. On the other hand, he transmitted the marshal's reply to a memorandum of which he was presumed to have no cognisance.

Vögler adduced all sorts of arguments of a personal character. Our conversation lasted three hours. I spoke of my nephew's death at Dachau. "After that," I said, "you will realise that I am in no hurry to return. First, let them publish my memorandum and furnish the explanations requested in respect of Herr von Remnitz. Further, if desired, I will prepare a second letter to Goering, stating my point of view. Ask what they think of this in Berlin." Vögler telephoned and informed me that they did not wish to receive another letter from me. I wrote all the same. This letter will be reproduced later on.*

For a moment I thought of suggesting that the Nazi leaders should get into touch with France and England with a view to peace negotiations. My radical opposition to the war might have justified me in taking the part of an intermediary. I gave up the idea, however, fearing to be duped by the Nazis. I told Vögler, therefore, that my return to Germany would depend upon the publication of my memorandum. Also, I asked him to do what he could to find out how my nephew had met his death.

Later I learned that at the end of September, after the presentation of my memorandum to Goering, the Gestapo had made a search of my house in Mühlheim. Naturally they found nothing (except, perhaps, letters from Goering assuring me of his eternal gratitude and friendship). It is common knowledge in Germany that it is unhealthy to keep too many papers. Meanwhile, one fine day, a German arrived in Zürich in a particularly agitated state of mind. "The Gestapo hint that they have found in your house papers compromising other industrialists," he said when he saw me. "Tell me, I beg of you, if this is true!" I reassured him, saying that it could not be true and that, knowing what might happen, I had taken every precaution. The poor fellow seemed relieved. He shall remain anonymous, for he has returned to Germany.

* See page 45.

FINAL RUPTURE WITH HITLER

VÖGLER left for Berlin. I heard no more of him, although he had promised to inform me of the results of his inquiries into the mysterious death of my nephew in the notorious Dachau camp. Before his departure he had entreated me to return to Germany, and my reply was that I would return if the German government published the memorandum I had addressed to Marshal Goering on September 20th. No reply ever reached me, and I am still awaiting the publication of my memorandum in Germany. . . .

Vögler was not the only person to put pressure on me. After the declaration of war several people, who took no trouble to conceal their lack of enthusiasm for the regime, came to see me in Switzerland. They said, " Now that war is declared, everyone must rally behind Hitler, for he represents Germany." To all such attempts to make me reverse my decision I replied, " No ; for this man will plunge the German people into disaster. My resolution is unshakable."

The Nazi leaders expected me to commit an act of cowardice ; to renounce my conviction as a free man. But I refused to return to Germany. I refused

44

to forswear my political convictions. What, after all, was Goering's word and his " guarantee " of my security worth ? Goering, all-powerful as he is, was unable to protect one of his own prefects against a mere Nazi Gauleiter. He abandoned to the miserable vengeance of Himmler and of the Gestapo the German pastor, Martin Niemöller, after he had been acquitted in a court of law. Goering did this although his own sister, Frau Rigle, was one of Niemöller's followers, and after he had protected him as long as he thought he could. For years Niemöller, commander of a submarine in the last war, has languished in secret confinement in the concentration camp of Oranienburg.

I shall therefore make no concession contrary to my conscience. As long as Hitler and his men are in power, my foot shall not pass the threshold of Germany. This is what I intended to tell Goering in reply to his invitation and to his questionable guarantees. Immediately after Vögler's departure I drafted this letter—the communication which, as I have said, the authorities did not wish to receive.

" Zürich, October 1st, 1939.

" DEAR SIR,

" I refer to my letter to you of September 22nd, 1939,[1] together with enclosure, both sent by messenger to Gauleiter Terboven to be forwarded. I hereupon received the following statement from the Gauleiter :

' I declare on behalf of Field Marshal Goering that neither a letter nor a telegram has been received by him personally, nor has any such document been received by his office. This is sufficient to prove that the final sentence of the Führer's speech can in no way be

---

[1] *Author's Note :* This letter to Goering was the covering letter of the memorandum of September 20th, 1939.

intended to refer to any special person. If the writer returns at once, the Marshal guarantees that no personal or economic consequences will ensue.'

" My observations regarding this statement are as follows :

" 1. It is quite impossible that my urgent telegram of August 31st from Bad Gastein should not have arrived. It is to be hoped that a telegram addressed to Marshal Goering is always delivered in Germany. Furthermore, my letter must have reached its destination, otherwise the Gauletier could not have sent the answer as above given.

" 2. It may be that my telegram did not arrive in time, despite the fact that it was sent the moment I was invited to hold myself in readiness for a meeting of the Reichstag. Though it may be possible that this telegram did not influence Chancellor Hitler's speech, the circumstances were, nevertheless, such as to convince me that this was the case, since I believe that I alone, of all the members, had dared to express a dissenting opinion.

" 3. I never requested you to protect me from the personal or economic consequences of my political action. I do not see how you arrived at this conclusion.

" It is true that since 1923 I have supported the party first at the request of General Ludendorff, and that since then I have invariably carried out the wishes expressed by yourself, Hitler, Hess, and others. But I have never on any occasion negotiated either with you or with the others concerning my own decisions in the economic field. On three occasions only—unfortunately too few—have I reproached you, as follows :

" First, when President Weitzel, of the Düsseldorf police whom you promoted to a state councillorship, disseminated an indecent and scandalous pamphlet against the Catholic Church, the Church to which I shall now more faithfully than ever adhere. The steps I then took were in vain.

" Secondly, when on November 9th, 1938, the Jew

were despoiled and martyrised in the most cowardly and brutal fashion, when the first magistrate of Düsseldorf, whom you had yourself appointed, was nearly murdered and driven away.

"My reproaches were in vain. I then resigned, in protest, my post as councillor of state. I requested the Prussian finance minister to stop paying the salary attached to this office. This had no effect. The payments have continued, but they have been deposited in a special account at the Thyssen Bank and are available.

"Now for the third time, when the worst has come to the worst, and Germany is once more plunged into war, without any kind of reference to the parliament or the state council, I inform you quite definitely I am opposed to this policy, and shall maintain this opinion even though I am accused of being a traitor. This accusation—remembering that in 1923 I, an unarmed man, not protected by ninety billion marks' worth of armaments, organised the passive resistance in the regions occupied by the enemy, and thus saved the Rhine and the Ruhr—is almost as grotesque as the fact that National Socialism has suddenly discarded its doctrines in order to hobnob with Communism.

"Even from the standpoint of practical politics this policy amounts to suicide, for the sole person to benefit from it is the Nazis' mortal enemy of yesterday, transformed into the friend of to-day—Russia, the country of which the Führer's most intimate adviser, Keppler, speaking at a board meeting of the Reichsbank a few months ago, said, 'It must be Germanised as far as the Ural Mountains.'

"All I can do now is to appeal most urgently to you and to the Führer to stop pursuing a policy which, if successful, will cast Germany into the arms of Communism ; and, if unsuccessful, will mean the end of Germany. Try to discover how the catastrophe can still be avoided.

"At all events, Germany will have to reinstate consti-

tutional conditions, so that treaties and agreements, law
and order, may once again have a meaning.

"In conclusion, I wish to express my regret that, in
order to speak frankly to you, I have to write from abroad.
But you will see that for me it would be deliberate stupidity
to act otherwise in view of the fate meted out to political
adversaries, as, for instance, in 1934. That these methods
have not changed is unfortunately demonstrated by the
case of Remnitz, who, as stated in the enclosure of my
letter of September 22nd, died in Dachau, without anyone
being notified of the cause of his death. What is new to
me is that Herr von Ribbentrop did not hesitate to annex
the property of the dead man.

"With my regards, I remain,

(Signed)   "FRITZ THYSSEN"
"Member of the Reichstag."

This letter was posted at Heidelberg and registered
in my name by one of my acquaintances.

This was the final rupture. Henceforth, as I frankly
informed Goering, I would be the political adversary
of that National Socialist regime which I had supported in its efforts to seize the power in Germany.
I shall remain abroad in order to retain my freedom
of opinion and my liberty of action.

Goering never acknowledged the receipt of my
letter. But this time I had reason to know that he
received it, for on October 13th, 1939, the Gestapo
distrained on the whole of my property in Germany.
This was, most certainly, his reply. Mr. Reinhardt,
manager of the Commercial and Private Bank, and
head of the Association of German Private Banks
within the Nazi organisation, despatched to all German
banks a secret circular, the text of which was com-
municated to me. It read :

" In virtue of a letter addressed to me by the secret police of the state from its headquarters in Berlin, on October 13th, I draw the attention of all our members to the following order issued by the state police of Düsseldorf.

" In execution of an order issued by Marshal Goering to the Commissioner for National Defence of the Fourth Military District, Gauleiter and Senior President Terboven, the entire fortune of Dr. juris h.c. Fritz Thyssen, Mühlheim-Ruhr, Speldorf, is placed under state control pursuant to Paragraph 1 of the decree of February 28th, 1933, and Paragraph 1 of the law concerning the secret police. The sole person authorised to dispose of these goods is the mandatory accredited to Marshal Goering, to wit, the Commissioner for National Defence, Gauleiter and Senior President Terboven.

" Since it has been impossible to form an exact estimate of the property of Herr Thyssen and his wife, I request you to instruct all banks by confidential circular to communicate, within five days following the receipt of this letter, information as to all accounts, deposits, and safe deposit boxes held in the name of Fritz Thyssen and of his wife, born Amalie zur Helle on December 9th, 1877, at Mühlheim-Ruhr. This communication to be addressed to the headquarters of the state police at Düsseldorf, inscribed with the name of Senior Councillor Dr. Hasselbacher or of his deputy.

" Heil Hitler !

" Chief of the Economic Association
of the German Private Banks :
(signed) " Reinhardt."

Gauleiter Terboven then appointed as trustee the Nazi banker Kurt von Schröder of the Stein Bank at Cologne. Schröder accepted.

The text of this order of distraint is not quite clear in its legal phraseology. It may further be questioned why this measure was extended to the property of my wife, who had committed no crime of *lèse majesté* against the regime. The order, in fact, is based upon a law conferring upon the Gestapo powers which are unlimited and arbitrary. No court in Germany is competent to entertain an appeal against a measure taken by the sinister Gestapo, even when it affects personal liberty.

In reality, this distraint, commonly a preliminary to confiscation, was intended to bring pressure to bear on me. The Nazi authorities wanted to wait before taking irrevocable steps. I might perhaps prove more manageable. I did not stir.

Two months later, on December 14th, 1939, the German Official *Gazette* (*Reichsanzeiger*) published a notice to the effect that my fortune had been confiscated by the state of Prussia. This measure was based upon the law of May 26th, 1933, prescribing *confiscation of the property of the Communist party*! This was the limit of effrontery.

The notice, signed by the Regierungspräsident of Düsseldorf (chief of the provincial government), was final, not subject to legal appeal. The press received formal instructions not to mention it. The foreign journalists in Berlin, who nevertheless gave some attention to my affair, let this sensation pass.

In all this business one detail was astonishing. The confiscation had been executed by the state of Prussia, not by the government of the Reich. Yet, as a matter of fact, the property consisted mainly of shares in important industrial enterprises, smelting and steel works, which were of the greatest importance for national defence. Normally, if confiscated, they should have been acquired by the Reich. But this would have been counting without Goering. Goering, besides being president of the Reichstag, is prime minister of the state of Prussia! Now Goering had often been my guest in my house at Speldorf-Mühlheim.[1] On these occasions the marshal had admired a small but fairly valuable collection of paintings and engravings, some of which were presents I had made to my wife since our marriage, forty years ago. Goering is like a child; he wants everything he sees. By having my property confiscated in the name of the Prussian state, he made sure that these paintings, engravings of the eighteenth century, and other objects of art, would not escape his grasp. For Goering is virtual sovereign of Prussia. All that is Prussian property is his. He has proved this on various occasions. This time he was not content with unhooking the paintings from the walls of my Mühlheim home and carrying them off. He also made an expedition to my son-in-law's place at Straubing, in Bavaria. There he possessed himself of the pictures which belonged to my daughter and her husband. And this notwithstanding the fact that the latter is a Hungarian subject.

These little stories may seem somewhat ridiculous. Nevertheless they are very significant from the economic point of view. For my financial interest in the greatest metallurgical concern in Germany, the United Steel Works, instead of being transferred to the Reich, has been seized by Prussia. Goering may have certain ideas in this connection. Indeed, a large share ownership in these steel works might save the

---

[1] *Author's Note :* In searching my residence, the Gestapo must have found numerous letters from Goering assuring me of his eternal gratitude and friendship. I am certain that Heinrich Himmler, as head of the Gestapo, has carefully filed these letters under the name Goering, a dossier which he keeps strictly up to date;

Hermann Goering Works from bankruptcy. I shall have more to say about this metallurgical enterprise later on.

The foregoing notice was published in the Official *Gazette* on December 14th. I was not informed of it until about Christmas. I immediately decided to write direct to Hitler as German Chief of State, to protest against this further illegal act and to explain to him personally the reasons for my conduct and what I thought of his policy. The text of my letter was as follows :

" Lucerne, December 28th, 1939.

" SIR,

" I have just read in the Official *Gazette*, No. 293, December 14th, 1939, the following notice :—

' In execution of the law of May 26th, 1933, concerning the confiscation of Communist property (sic) (*Reich Statutes Bulletin*, No. 1, page 293) and in connection with Paragraph 1 of the Decree of May 31st, 1933 (Law No. 39) and with the Law of July 14th, 1933, concerning the Confiscation of Property of Enemies of the People and the State (*Reich Statutes Bulletin*, No. 1, page 479) the entire movable property of Dr. Fritz Thyssen, formerly resident at Mühlheim-Ruhr, now abroad, together with his estate is confiscated by the state of Prussia, and that with the publication of this decree in the German Official *Gazette* and in the Prussian State *Gazette*, the said property enters into the possession of the state of Prussia. No legal remedy is provided against the effects of this decree.

' Düsseldorf, December 11th, 1939,

' REGIERUNGSPRÄSIDENT REEDER.'

" No reason is given for this measure. I note that neither legal nor administrative proceedings of any kind have been initiated against me. To this very day I have received no communication from the German government, apart from that brought to me by Dr. A. Vögler, on behalf of the Gauleiter in Essen, in which I was asked to withdraw the memorandum presented by me as member of the Reichstag and to destroy the copies, whereby all personal and economic consequences would be averted. It is known that I rejected this peace offer, because my political opinion as a member of the Reichstag is not for sale. Moreover, I have never been requested to answer for my personal or political attitude or for anything else. Your propaganda ministry had in fact opposed any action against me. Therefore, the confiscation of my property as ordered in the Official *Gazette*, especially as it was directed against a privileged member of the Reichstag, is an open and brutal breach of the law, illegal and unconstitutional. I protest sharply against this measure, and declare that the Reich government, and more particularly all those who took part in this confiscation, or are still involved in it, above all the appointed trustee, Baron von Schröder of Cologne, are personally responsible and liable. The time will come when I shall have to defend my rights. In particular, I warn you not to lay hands upon the property of my wife, my children, Count and Countess Zichy, and upon the bequest of my father, August Thyssen, who was one of the first founders of Germany's great industry.

" My conscience is clear. I know that I have committed no crime. My sole mistake is to have believed in you, our leader, Adolf Hitler, and in the movement initiated by you—to have believed with the enthusiasm of a passionate lover of my native Germany. Since 1923 I have made the greatest sacrifices for the National Socialist cause, have fought with word and deed, without asking any reward for myself, merely inspired by the hope that our unfortunate German people would finally recover. The initial events after the National Socialists came to power seemed to justify this hope, at least as long as Herr von Papen was vice-chancellor—Herr von Papen, who sponsored Hindenburg's appointment of yourself as chancellor. Before him you took a solemn oath in the Garrison Church at Potsdam to respect the Constitution. Do not forget that you owe your rise not to a great revolutionary uprising but to the liberal order which you have sworn to sustain.

" A sinister development followed these events. The persecution of the Christian religion, taking the form of cruel measures against the priests and insults to the Churches, led me to protest in the early days, for instance when the police president of Düsseldorf issued a protest to Marshal Goering. It was in vain.

" When, on November 9th, 1938, the Jews were despoiled and martyrised in the most cowardly and brutal manner, and their temples razed to the ground throughout Germany, I also protested. To reinforce this protest, I resigned my office as state councillor. This, too, was in vain.

" Now you have compounded with Communism. Your propaganda ministry even dares to proclaim that the honest Germans, who voted for you as the opponent of Communism, are in essentials identical with the bloody revolutionaries who plunged Russia into misery and whom you yourself denounced (p. 750, *Mein Kampf*) as ' vulgar blood-stained criminals.'

" When the great catastrophe became an accomplished fact, and Germany was again involved in a war, without seeking the assent of parliament or the council, I emphatically declared that I was firmly opposed to this policy.

" As a member of the Reichstag, it is my duty to state my opinion and to abide by it. It is a crime against the German people if its men and in particular its representatives, who are held responsible by other countries, are no longer allowed to express their views. I cannot bow to this yoke. I refuse to lend my name to your acts, notwithstanding your declaration in the Reichstag meeting of

September 1st, 1939 : ' He who is not with me is a traitor and shall be treated as such.'

" I denounce the policy of the last few years ; I denounce above all the war into which you have frivolously thrust the German people, and for which you and your advisers must bear the responsibility. My past shields me from the accusation of treachery. In 1923 I, an unarmed man, organised the passive resistance in the occupied territories, at great danger to myself, and thus saved the Rhine and the Ruhr. I appeared before the enemy's court-martial and fearlessly proclaimed my opinion as a German. But it is precisely this conviction which makes it impossible for me to renounce the real ideals and the original doctrine of National Socialism which, as you yourself explained in my house, are in essentials identical with the principles of German monarchy and designed to lead to social appeasement and a stable order. I allow myself to recall that you instructed me to continue the *Institut für Ständewesen* in Düsseldorf in this sense. A year later, it is true, you left me very much to my own devices ; and you approved the internment of the director of the institute, appointed by me in agreement with Herr Hess, in the ill-famed concentration camp of Dachau. In Dachau, my chancellor, where my nephew came to a sudden death. His Schloss Fuschl, near Salzburg, was thrown as a sop to Herr von Ribbentrop, who was shameless enough to receive in it the foreign minister of Italy and envoy of Mussolini.

" I further remind you that Goering was certainly not sent to Rome to see the Holy Father and to Doorn to interview the former Kaiser, in order to prepare them for the forthcoming alliance with Communism. And yet you have suddenly concluded such an alliance with Russia, an act which no one has denounced more strongly than yourself in your book *Mein Kampf* (earlier edition, pp. 740-750). There you say : ' The very fact of an agreement with Russia contains the premises of the next war. Its end would be the end of Germany.' Or again : ' The present leaders of Russia have no intention of concluding a pact on an honest basis, or of keeping to it.' Or again : ' One concludes no treaty with a partner whose sole interest lies in the destruction of the other.'

" Your new policy is suicide. Who will benefit by it ? If the courageous Finns, with their faith in God, do not bring this enterprise to naught, the former mortal enemy of the Nazis and their present ' friend ' Bolshevik Russia, certainly will—the same Russia, of which your closest adviser, Herr Keppler, secretary of state in the ministry for foreign affairs and a skilled diplomat, declared in May, 1939, at a board meeting of the Reichstag that it must be Germanised to the Ural Mountains. I earnestly hope that these frankly spoken words of your confidential adviser will not weaken the effect of the telegram of congratulations which you addressed to your friend Stalin on his birthday.

" Your new policy, Herr Hitler, is pushing Germany into the abyss and the German people into ruin. Reverse the machine while there is still time ! Your policy means at long last, ' *Finis Germaniae*.' Remember your oath at Potsdam. Give the Reich a free parliament, give the German people freedom of conscience, thought, and speech. Provide the necessary guarantees for the reinstatement of law and order, so that treaties and agreements can once again be made in faith and confidence. For if further evil and further useless bloodshed are averted, it may then be possible to achieve for Germany an honourable peace and the maintenance of her unity.

" International public opinion urges me to explain why I have left Germany. So far I have been silent. All the documents and written evidence of my fifteen years of combat are still unrevealed. At a time when my Fatherland is fighting a hard battle I do not wish to present its enemies with further moral weapons. I am a German and remain so with every fibre of my being. I am proud of my nationality and will be so to my last breath. Just because I am a German I cannot and will not speak during the sore distress of my people as one day it may be necessary in the interest of the truth. But I feel in me that stifled voice of the German people which calls : ' Turn back and restore freedom, law and humanity in the German Reich.'

" I shall await your acts in silence. But I start with the assumption that this letter shall not be withheld from the German people. I shall wait. If my words, the words of a free and sincere German, are concealed from the people, I propose to appeal to the conscience and the judgment of the rest of the world. I wait.

" Heil Deutschland !

(Signed) " FRITZ THYSSEN."

" P.S.—I am handing this letter to the German embassy in Berne to be forwarded, and I have further sent a registered copy to the Chancellery in Berlin and to your personal address in Obersalzberg near Berchtesgaden. I am compelled to take these measures since I am officially advised that my letters and telegrams to Field Marshal Goering never arrived.

" Copies were also sent to Field Marshal Goering and Regierungspräsident Reeder in Düsseldorf, who ordered the confiscation of my property. Copy of the first paragraph of this letter was also sent to Baron Kurt von Schröder of Cologne, presumably the present administrator of my property."

This letter to Hitler meant not merely a rupture. It meant that I would no longer confine myself to theoretical opposition to the Nazi leaders. I intended to declare war upon them. I hope that my attitude may not be misinterpreted. As a member of the Reichstag it was my right and my duty to protest against war if it was my conviction that the war was wrong. I would, however, have bowed to a valid decision of the legislature, if such a decision had been taken. I would have admitted that in a war it is the common duty of a citizen to support a government which is truly representative of the will of the nation. I would also have avoided a rupture, or active opposition, if the government had published my memorandum to Goering, as I requested in my message sent through Vögler. But I never even received a reply to this request. Berlin continued to conceal the fact that the bellicose policy of the National Socialist government had aroused the formal opposition of at least one German patriot.

I have taken note of this silence and I have decided to act. For some time the international public has been interested in the reasons for my departure from Germany. I am constantly asked why I have broken with National Socialism. So long as I enjoyed the right of refuge on Swiss territory, I held my peace. The Swiss federal authorities granted me permission to remain in their country until March 31st, 1940. But this authorisation implied for me the obligation to abstain from any kind of political activity while residing in Switzerland.

Some time after the despatch of my letter to Hitler I learned that the government of the Reich had issued a warrant for my arrest on a charge of embezzlement, or something of the kind. This was a clumsy device to obtain my extradition and to get me handed over to the German authorities. The Swiss government, informed of the reasons for my departure, refused even to consider the request. I take this opportunity of once more conveying to the Swiss government my admiration and gratitude.

Faced by the failure of its attempts to attach my

person, the government of the Reich decided, as a last resource, to deprive me of my German nationality. On February 4th, 1940, the German Official *Gazette* published a decision of the minister of the interior withdrawing the rights of German citizenship from me and my wife. Thus I was first pursued as a criminal and, when this failed, the government saw fit to proclaim that I was no longer a German. This incoherent procedure is as symptomatic of the Nazis' embarrassment as is the silence which continues to prevail in Germany in respect of the whole affair.

I deny that there is any kind of justification for this last act, as I have already done in the case of the others. I merely exercised the rights conferred upon me as a member of the Reichstag. I based—and still base—my actions on a parliamentary mandate for which I am responsible to the German people alone. As for the withdrawal of German nationality from my wife, who has never joined in any political demonstration against the regime, I can only explain it by the sordid motives to which I have already referred.

On receiving information of the measures taken against me by the minister of the interior, I despatched to him the following letter of protest :

" Locarno, February 16th, 1940.
" Sir,
" I see from the papers that you have officially declared that my wife and myself have forfeited all right to our German nationality.

" I herewith protest in due form. I have done my duty as a member of the Reichstag in opposing the present policy of the government of the Reich. I have left Germany because the immunity assured to members by the Constitution seemed to me no longer guaranteed.

Neither the confiscation of my property, nor a warrant of arrest, nor the loss of my nationality will prevent me from doing my duty as a member of the Reichstag, an office in which I feel myself responsible to the German people.

(Signed) " FRITZ THYSSEN,"
" Member of the Reichstag."

Several months have elapsed since my first protest, and since my request to the German leaders to communicate it to the nation. I now accuse the German chancellor of disloyalty and of violating his solemn oath ; I summon him to restore Constitution, law, and justice in Germany ; and I appeal to world public opinion by laying before it the documents in the case.

CHAPTER III

THE END OF A POLITICAL ERROR

"THE republic we had under the Empire was a delight." This was a common saying in France when the Empire of Napoleon III had been supplanted by the Third Republic—after 1871. How many National Socialists in Germany and Austria to-day may have similar, melancholy reflections ! For " National Socialism " under Brüning and Schuschnigg was indeed a delight.

This has in fact been my own feeling for some years. But my rupture with the regime is not merely the result of this disillusionment. Things were brought to a head by the war, for which Hitler is responsible. It is often said that an industrialist, particularly an iron master, is always in favour of war, since it is supposed to be remunerative to heavy industry. My own attitude may perhaps serve as a defence against accusations of this sort.

To-day I have broken with a long past, and a certain line of conduct. This line of conduct was at all times, and especially after the defeat of 1918, actuated by the ardent desire to promote the greatness and the prosperity of an empire into which I was born two

years after its foundation, and for which I have worked
throughout my life.

I am not a politician, but an industrialist, and an
industrialist is always inclined to consider politics a
kind of second string to his bow—the preparation for
his own particular activity. In a well-ordered country,
where the administration is sound, where taxes are
reasonable, and the police well organised, he can
afford to abstain from politics and to devote himself
entirely to business. But in a crisis-ridden state, as
Germany was from 1918 to 1933, an industrialist is
drawn, willy-nilly, into the vortex of politics. After
1930 the aspirations of German industry may be
summed up in one phrase : " a sound economy in a
strong state." This was, I remember, the slogan of
a meeting of the Ruhr industrialists in 1931. It was
at the height of the economic and social crisis. During
that winter there were six or seven million unemployed, that is, about one-third of the entire
German labouring population. The Weimar Republic
was torn asunder by party and other strife, and the
ship of state was at the point of foundering. The
government was incapable of assuring a proper
administration, or just plain everyday order. Even
the police were unable to cope with the daily riots and
the political disturbances in the streets.

I, too, approved this slogan. To surmount the
crisis it was necessary to reinforce the authority of the
state. That is why I was in favour of the restoration
of the monarchy, for the German people had clearly
shown that it was not fitted for a republic. But I
also believed that by backing Hitler and his party
I could contribute to the reinstatement of real government and of orderly conditions, which would enable

all branches of activity—and especially business—to function normally once again.

But it is no use crying over spilled milk. The strong state of which I then dreamed had nothing in common with the totalitarian state or, rather, caricature of a state, erected by Hitler and his minions. Not for an instant did I imagine that it was possible, one hundred and fifty years after the French Revolution and the proclamation of the Rights of Man, to substitute arbitrary action for law in a great modern country, to strangle the most elementary rights of the citizen, to establish an Asiatic tyranny in the heart of Europe, and to foster anachronistic aspirations of conquest and world dominion.

As a Catholic, born on the shores of that mighty Rhine where the influences of Western culture and Roman law had always been stronger than in other parts of Germany, where Christianity had been implanted very early, and where the French Revolution had left its indelible trace, I found it impossible to believe that in our time we could destroy all the normal conditions of human and political life. In 1930 I should have been astonished if anyone had called me a liberal. But this was in all probability my real conviction, although I did not realise it. My desire to re-establish order in the state and to restore authority and discipline was in complete accordance with the dignity of the individual with respect for the fundamental liberties. Indeed, the exercising of these liberties seemed to me as natural as breathing.

Germany after 1918 was over-industrialised. This was the logical consequence of a development which had taken place since 1870 and of which my father was one of the pioneers. The whole character of the country had been profoundly modified. The problems

raised by the existence of an industry which has to
feed two-thirds of the population is not always fully
understood in countries like France or the United
States. Before the war of 1914, the monarchy of
Prussia and the German Empire, though absolute in
the political and administrative domains, had been quite
liberal in the social and economic fields. Notwithstanding certain mistakes, the political personnel of the imperial regime and, in particular, its very efficient civil
servants, had almost always been equal to their tasks.

Of this system the very foundations had been
destroyed by the national defeat and the revolution
of 1918. Germany, exhausted by the war, demoralised
by defeat, starved by the blockade, had to make a
tremendous effort merely to assure the material
existence of her population. Instead of straining
every nerve to achieve recovery, it yielded to a tide
of anarchy and radicalism which definitely precluded
any attempt at genuine reconstruction.

The internal crisis was aggravated by the pressure
exercised by the victors. It made itself felt not only
in the political field but also in business, which it
burdened with a formidable mortgage, namely the
war reparations. The political circles which had
governed the country for well-nigh a century, and
the competent and trusted officials who had officered
the staff of a sound and correct administration, had
almost all disappeared in the upheaval following the war.

Associated with my father at the head of a great
industrial enterprise I faced the terrible problem of
providing the working population with labour and
bread. This was no longer merely a question of
technical and economic organisation. It was indispensable that Germany should once more be able

COOPERATION

PRESS SERVICE

CABLE COOPERATION PARIS

TEL. BALZAC 51 00

33, CHAMPS-ÉLYSÉES, PARIS

ARRANGEMENT

entre :

Monsieur Fritz THYSSEN, d'une part,

et

Monsieur E. REVES, 37, 'venue des Champs-Élysées, Paris (VIIème), d'autre part.

I.- M. Thyssen transfert à M. Reves les droits exclusifs de publication dans le monde entier de ses "Mémoires" actuellement 'en préparation, dont le titre est à déterminer.

Monte-Carlo, le 29. IV. 40

F. Thyssen

E. Reves

Facsimile of the contract signed by Fritz Thyssen and Emery Reves for the publication of his memoirs.

to export, to re-establish her credit, and to restore order at home, so as to permit the resumption of work.

To cope with pressure from our late enemies, I organised Germany's passive resistance during the occupation of the Ruhr in 1923. To combat political radicalism and the anarchical tendencies which became rife in the early years of the Weimar Republic, I supported various semi-military patriotic formations, among them the National Socialist party. Later, after the initial crises, when developments appeared to have resumed a more normal course, I turned my attention to business. My subsequent political activity was confined to membership in a parliamentary opposition group, the German National party, headed by Count Westarp and later by Alfred Hugenberg. The German Nationals were conservative and monarchistic.

The modification of the reparations system in 1929, consummated by Germany's acceptance of the Young Plan in the following year, appeared to me as a vital economic error. At that moment I therefore resumed a more active opposition. I attached myself to those groups which offered resistance to the Reich's policy of far-fetched compliance. This seemed to me a proper response to the situation at the moment, and to clear the way for the establishment of sounder economic conditions, first in Germany and then in the world as a whole. I was not in close touch with the daily party wrangles ; but, like many belonging to the Right Wing, I was under the impression that Hitler was an active factor in Germany's recovery, and this was why I gave him an ever-increasing support.

In January, 1933, the National Socialist party, to which I had belonged for two years, came into office. I thought, like everyone else, that it would succeed

E

in re-establishing the political equilibrium and, at the cost of a hard initial effort, in promoting the recovery of the country. I even hoped that it would finally lead to a restoration of the monarchy, a system which conforms to the German people's traditional respect for authority. The monarchy, I thought, would have guaranteed a more or less normal evolution and thus would have averted a revolutionary crisis.

My disappointment dates almost from the very beginning of the Nazi regime. Hitler's eviction of the conservative elements from the government, of which he was the head, gave me some cause for anxiety. But I was inhibited by the impression produced by the burning of the Reichstag. To-day I know that this crime was staged by the National Socialists themselves, in order to gain more power. Throughout Germany, they spread the fear of armed Communist rebellion. They induced the belief that this arson, organised by themselves, was the signal for a second Red revolution which would have precipitated the country into the bloody convulsions of civil war. I then believed that by their energy Hitler and Goering had saved the country. To-day I know that I, like millions of others, was deceived. But almost all Germans are still in the same state of deception, if so be they inhabit the Reich. In order to learn the truth I had to go abroad.

The burning of the Reichstag, organised by Hitler and Goering, was the first step in a colossal political swindle. With the argument of this alleged Communist crime, the leaders of the Nazi party extorted from President Hindenburg a so-called " Law of Suspects,' authorising summary execution and enabling the Nazis to silence all political opponents.

The same law, " for the protection of the people and the state," was adduced by the Gestapo as a pretext for illegally confiscating my own property. The so-called law suspended all the fundamental constitutional guarantees of personal liberty, freedom of conscience and of opinion. These guarantees are still in abeyance. Thus an emergency measure has become a regular instrument of government.

One month later a trembling Reichstag, one hundred of whose members had been arrested and imprisoned, voted the law conferring full powers on the government, which law lies at the root of all the arbitrary acts committed by the regime since 1933. Thus began a series of revolutionary acts which theoretically observed the forms of legality, but were in fact based upon a crime and a lie. Public opinion in foreign countries has never protested against these acts.

To-day, I can no longer hesitate : I say that all the " laws," all the decrees enacted by the National Socialist government, are illegal. In law, they are null and void, since they are based upon a crime and an abuse of confidence.

Hitler achieved power by engineering a political combination. The National Socialist government owes its being to no revolutionary event comparable to Mussolini's march on Rome. Hitler swore before Field Marshal von Hindenburg a solemn oath to respect a constitution which guaranteed the rights of man and political freedom in Germany. The burning of the Reichstag is the criminal act by which he perjured himself and usurped the power to rule.

To-day this is my conviction ; but for six years I was deluded. Goering, an officer of the former Imperial army, holder of the Order " Pour le mérite,"

showed me the smoking ruins of the Reichstag on
March 1st : " This," he said, " is a Communist
crime ; yesterday, I myself nearly arrested one of the
criminals." Two months earlier he had telephoned
to my house to warn me that a rebellion was about
to break out in the Ruhr and that I headed the list
of the proposed hostages. He said that he had been
informed by his spies in the Communist party. How
could I have doubted his word ?

I therefore began to collaborate openly with the
regime. The rowdy anti-Semitism of the early period
produced no immediate practical consequences. I
considered this as a not particularly dangerous concession to public feeling. In my native country, the
Rhine provinces, where the population is not anti-
Jewish, such stupidity had aroused ironical laughter
at the expense of the Nazis. Politically I was absorbed
by the task which had been entrusted to me by the head
of the government to prepare plans for the economic
organisation of Germany on " corporative " lines.

The fateful day of June 30th, 1934, when Hitler
ordered the brutal murder of his revolutionary com-
panions, revolted and terrified me. There was something absolutely un-German in such a massacre. It
was sheer barbarity. Some months later I went to
South America for several months to attend to some
business. On my return I found the regime solidly
established. It had launched that policy of building
and rearmament which was to lead to Dr. Hjalmar
Schacht's resignation as German minister of economy
and as president of the Reichsbank. From that moment
I entered into open conflict with the National Socialists.

The first incident took place in 1935. An infamous
anti-Catholic tract had been disseminated at Düssel-

dorf. It reproduced the most ridiculous fables from the outworn catalogue of the adversaries of the Church. It attacked Christian morals and dogmas, the Pope, the priests, and the religious orders. One of the leaflets distributed at Düsseldorf was brought to me. To my great astonishment it was signed by Weitzel, the chief constable of Düsseldorf. He had signed his name without stating his office. But this tract could only have been distributed with his connivance and help.

The National Socialist government had signed with the Catholic Church a concordat by which the latter was to be protected against such attacks, especially on the part of official persons. In a state where laws are really enforced, the author of this scandalous document would have been denounced and immediately prosecuted. But in National Socialist Germany this would have been superfluous, for no judge would have dared to apply the law. I was a councillor of state. I wrote to Goering, drawing his attention to what I considered an intolerable example of disorder. Goering did not reply, but some time later he told me that he had ordered an inquiry. The question was not further pursued.

The persecution of the Catholics was merely a beginning. From that date disorder, illegality, and arbitrariness were the main weapons in the National Socialist arsenal.

In September, 1935, I was summoned to Nuremberg to attend an extraordinary meeting of the Reichstag. Before the meeting I heard that the Reichstag, at the request of Hitler and in agreement with the commander-in-chief of the army, General von Blomberg, would have to vote a law replacing the former black, white and red flag of the empire by the swastika of National Socialism, I returned by train

immediately, without waiting for the meeting. Hence
I did not vote the infamous laws enacted at Nuremberg,
which elevated anti-Semitism to the rank of a government policy. Since then, even in the most solemn
circumstances, such as the marriage of my daughter,
which was attended by the Archbishop of Cologne
(I invited Goering, but he did not come), I have never
raised the swastika over my dwelling at Speldorf,
even when we were ordered to hang out flags.

Some time later my wife met General von Blomberg
and voiced her surprise : " How could you do a thing
like that ? " " Sad to relate," Blomberg replied, " the
army had to make that concession to the Führer." The
Nazis had, in fact, extorted the consent of the army,
alleging that rearmament might be compromised over
the flag issue. They had skilfully exploited the fact
that in many regions, and particularly the Rhine provinces, the population, in order to express its dissatisfaction with the regime, rarely flew the flag with the
swastika, but almost invariably the old black, white
and red. The Nazis had, more or less correctly, con-
strued this as political agitation against their party.

For four years I was the melancholy and powerless
witness of the incoherence, futility, and corruption
of the National Socialist leaders. Only on one more
occasion did I protest formally and in writing, and
that was at the time of the anti-Semitic excesses of
November, 1938. But neither Hitler nor Goering
were unaware of my feelings with regard to their
policy. I had expressed them publicly in the council
of state and in the economic meetings which I
attended. However, what use was opposition under
a dictatorship ? Even a general to whom I remarked
that " this cannot go on " shrugged his shoulders and

replied, " What can you do ? " An industrialist is even more powerless than a general. He can be arrested on any charge.

The important events of 1938 left me sceptical. Next year the occupation of Prague and of Czecho-slovakia, despite the solemn promises made to the governments of three great countries, seemed to me criminal and shameful. At the same time I regarded it as a dangerous political mistake. Then came the provocation of Poland. For five years Hitler had constantly extolled the friendship between Germany and Poland. His change of face with regard to the Poles can, in my opinion, be explained by the irritation which he experienced when the Polish govern-ment refused to join him in the great projected thrust towards the east—an operation which was expected to give Germany the whole of European Russia, up to the Ural Mountains. This plan was, in fact, re-vealed just before the quarrel with Poland by the Führer's accredited confidant and economist, Wilhelm Keppler, at a meeting of the board of directors of the Reichsbank, which I attended.

I was already at Gastein when, on August 23rd, 1939, I was informed of the conclusion of the pact between Stalin and Hitler. I had attentively followed the development of the international situation. I still reckoned with the success of the National Socialist move in the diplomatic game that was being played. The further course of events gave me food for anxiety ; yet I never imagined that Hitler would commit the supreme folly of precipitating Germany into a Euro-pean war. Some days before, I had received from Albert Vögler a letter which had caused me to reflect seriously. Vögler had met the director of a factory who had been one of a delegation of German industrialists just returned from Russia. At a farewell dinner offered by some Russian commissar for industry, the latter had raised his glass to the "friendship between Russia and Germany." I must confess that, on receiving his letter, I wondered what was in the wind. The very possibility of an agreement between Soviet Russia and National Socialist Germany seemed beyond belief.

I had always warned industrialists, as well as military circles, against a *rapprochement* with Communist Russia. For me this regime was the enemy of Germany and of Europe as a whole. To deal with Russia seemed to me as great a crime as the treason of the German Protestant princes who had allied themselves with Richelieu against the Emperor of the Holy Roman Empire in the Thirty Years' War.

Hitler shared my aversion. At least, so I believed. His book, *Mein Kampf*, contains whole pages of imprecations against the Russian regime. All of a sudden, for reasons of political convenience, he abandoned his earlier convictions and concluded an alliance with a country which he had on other occasions described as Enemy No. 1 of Europe. Such cavalier tactics may have been regarded as excellent diplomacy by Hitler and Ribbentrop ; to me they were appalling. They meant a complete reversal of the traditional home and foreign policy of Germany. The National Socialist government had fought Bolshevism on the inner and on the outer front. Anti-Communist pacts had been concluded with Italy, Japan, Hungary, and Spain. Hitler had preached the crusade against Bolshevik Russia as the enemy of the human race. And suddenly he had allied himself with the monster. He had the insolence to ask serious-minded people to support him in this adventure. For my part, I should never have been cowardly or imbecile enough to do so.

But the Germans—who as a race have never had much political acumen—were completely confused by the innumerable lies poured into their ears. They thought that an alliance with Stalin was just like any other alliance. Had not Bismarck himself concluded an alliance with the Czar ? One of the most grotesque features in the case is that certain Germans who actually fear Bolshevism, instead of protesting against Hitler, have accused me of encouraging the advent of Bolshevism in Germany. They say it was my protest against Hitler's policy that led to the confiscation of my private fortune. And this creates a dangerous precedent. That is the point at which they have arrived !

On the Russian side, apart from the political interests involved, I can explain the change of face by two psychological arguments. Stalin, it is said, expressed his admiration for Hitler after the events of June 30th, 1934. By murdering his political opponents, Hitler had shown Moscow that he had the makings of a real dictator. From that moment Stalin took Hitler seriously. Further, the Russians had been extremely impressed by the attitude of the Western Powers on the occasion of the occupation of Czechoslovakia. In 1939 their sense of political realism showed them how they could divert the Hitler menace from Russia and, at the same time, to recoup their former frontiers. The conclusion of the pact was Stalin's master stroke. By means of it he rid himself, for a certain time, of the very real menace represented by a German army —an army infinitely superior to the Red Army— equipped and trained mainly for war in the East. To me, in those days of August, 1939, the pact with

Moscow seemed abominable from two points of view : first, because it was an unnatural alliance with the enemy of Western civilisation ; and secondly, because it was an immediate preliminary to war.

As recounted above, I addressed a formal protest to the National Socialist leaders on September 1st. The events which followed have justified this action. The violation of the neutral countries, Denmark, Norway, Holland, Belgium, and Luxemburg has erased the Third Reich from the roll of the civilised states. It is quite possible that in the country itself the immense majority of Germans, dazzled by one-day victories and duped by lying propaganda, are unable to realise this fact.

Up to the eleventh hour I thought that it would be possible to avoid war. I consoled myself by imagining that the responsible generals would succeed in restraining Hitler. Before the *blitzkrieg* of 1940 on the Western front I still hoped that it would be possible to prevent the assault on the West. That is why I asked the Nazi leaders to publish the memorandum in which I had set forth the reasons for my opposition to the war.

But Hitler and his advisers turned a deaf ear. They think that they can force Fate to fight on their side. The outrage which they have perpetrated on Europe will fall back upon them and—unfortunately—on their blind tool, the unseeing and unhearing German people.

For my own part I have drawn my conclusions and I have acted accordingly. But I hope and believe that the peace which will follow Hitler's downfall will be concluded in the light of the experience gained since 1918. This story of the political error which led me to believe in Hitler, and of my awakening, is my contribution to a better future.

PART TWO
THE ROAD TO THE THIRD REICH

CHAPTER ONE

DEFEAT AND REVOLUTION

Germany Threatened by Anarchy

I WAS an officer in the first World War. Until the last day I shared the sufferings and the hopes that animated all the soldiers at the front. I had known for a long time that the civilian population at home was tired of the gigantic effort it had put forth. In our Rhenish-Westphalian industrial region, where my father's factories were located, the fires of revolt had been smouldering for a long time. In 1917–1918 there had been strikes, accompanied by such grave disorders that a great many people had to be arrested in the industrial cities of the Rhine. These strikes were motivated by the lack of food and the consequent sufferings of the workers' families, but political agitation aggravated their nature.

At Kiel the naval crews, under the influence of Socialist propaganda, had refused obedience and made an attempt at mutiny.* From 1918 onwards extremist agitation took on an even more revolutionary character. The example set by the Russian Revolu-

* See Historical Notes at end of chapter, page 87.

tion, surreptitiously promoted by the German High Command, had serious repercussions in Germany. The Bolsheviks, who had seized power at Moscow during the October revolution, sent their most dangerous agents across the frontier. Incidents occurred everywhere ; women and children demonstrated against food shortage or in favour of peace. At the front Ludendorff made a last attempt at forcing a military decision. The success of the offensive of 1918 at first raised the morale of the German people. Final defeat made it fall all the lower.

Neither the officers of the army nor even the great mass of the soldiers were affected by defeatist and revolutionary propaganda. The army succumbed, exhausted by its effort, to the crushing superiority of the opposing forces.

In October, 1918, the revolution began to take shape. The Socialists of the extreme Left had formed a group named Spartacus,* after the Roman gladiator who started the Third Servile War in 73 B.C. The Spartacus group later on became the German Communist party (K.P.D.). Radical elements, inspired by the Russian example, were preparing the formation of workers' and soldiers' councils, i.e. " Soviets." The storm was near.

It was at Kiel that the lightning struck first. The mutiny in the Imperial Navy, early in November, marked the beginning of the German Revolution. It spread rapidly through all the cities of northern Germany. In Cologne, Socialist parades were held in the streets even before the armistice was signed. The soldiers who returned from the front were disarmed as they arrived at the stations. Most of them sympathised with the crowd. In the Rhenish cities the moderate Socialist leaders at first succeeded in

* See Historical Notes at end of chapter, page 88.

preventing disorder. But the arrival of delegates of
the Kiel mutineers, accompanied by professional agitators, carried the day. In the great industrial cities—in
Hamborn, Mühlheim and Essen—workers' and soldiers'
soviets were formed and these quickly seized power.

The great Rhenish industrialist, Hugo Stinnes, in
order to avoid disorder and sabotage in the Rhenish-
Westphalian region, negotiated with the unions. He
secured promises which guaranteed order and social
peace in the region. But already a part of the workers,
influenced by revolutionary propaganda, had abandoned the leadership of the Social Democratic party.
The workers' and soldiers' councils opened the prison
gates and the political prisoners of the past two years
were freed. Along with them were set at large many
persons of doubtful past, who might be either sincere
revolutionaries or common-law criminals.

At Mühlheim we spent a painful five weeks. The
workers' and soldiers' councils which held the power
had signs posted everywhere to the effect that excesses
and looting were punishable. Yet the streets were
no longer safe. In the councils the moderate elements,
which at first held the majority, had yielded to radical
agitators.

In the evening of December 7, a group of men,
armed with rifles and pistols, presented themselves at
my door. They had come to arrest me. They also
took my father with them, despite his seventy-six
years. We were escorted to the prison of Mühlheim,
where four other industrialists soon arrived to join
us. In the middle of the night we were awakened, and a
dozen rowdy-looking individuals carrying guns ordered
us into the courtyard. I thought they were going to
execute us. However, they simply took us to Berlin.

Our guards led us into third-class carriages and sat down near the doors, no doubt to prevent any attempt at escape. It was cold. Fortunately, my father had been able to take a blanket with him. The train arrived at the Potsdam station in Berlin on the following evening. On the platform a military detachment awaited us. Our escort handed us over to them and jeered as they left us. My father, who had left his blanket in the train, addressed himself to one of the guards and asked him, very politely, to go and fetch it. "What are you taking me for?" the other asked indignantly, "I am the Chief of Police of Berlin!"

I learnt later on that he was Emil Eichhorn, a dangerous Communist agitator in the service of Soviet Russia who had had himself nominated chief of the Berlin police during the revolution. He had transformed the central police station at the Alexanderplatz, commonly known as the "Red House," into a fortress and had picked his personal bodyguard from the most obscure elements of the Berlin proletariat. Most of them were fugitives from jail. It was said that Eichhorn had ordered the arrest of many political enemies and officials of the old regime, and that he had had them executed in the courtyard of police headquarters without trial. A month later, this strange chief of police organised the riots in the streets of Berlin and the Social Democratic government had to appeal to the army to dislodge him from the Red House, where he withstood a regular siege.

Such was the man into whose hands we had now been delivered. He took us to police headquarters and examined us.

"You are accused," he said, "of treason and anti-revolutionary activities. You are enemies of the

Fritz Thyssen showing Hitler an industrial plant. From left to right, Albert Vögler (Vice-President United Steel Works), Hitler, Thyssen, Dr. Borbel, another director United Steel Works.

people and have asked for the intervention of French troops in order to prevent the Socialist revolution."

None of us had had the slightest contact with the French army of occupation. We all protested.

Eichhorn went on insolently :

" Don't try to deny it. I am well informed. The day before yesterday you had a conference at Dortmund with other industrialists and you have decided to send a delegation to the French general to ask him to occupy the Ruhr. This is treason. What have you to say, gentlemen ? "

We looked at each other in astonishment. None of us had gone to Dortmund. So far as I was concerned, I knew nothing of such a decision. Later on I learned that the alleged conference had never taken place. My father and I could produce an alibi. We had not left Mühlheim for a week ; numerous witnesses could affirm it. Eichhorn answered brutally :

" Those witnesses ! All bourgeois ! Their statements have no value whatever. Take 'em away."

We were led out of the chief's office. We did not feel reassured. Had we escaped death at Mühlheim only to be shot here ? After a short interval an employee came to inform our guards that there was no more room left for prisoners at police headquarters.

" Take them to Moabit," he said.

That was the main prison of Berlin. At the gate of police headquarters a prison car awaited us. Through the bars we could see the agitation in the Berlin streets ; near the Alexanderplatz a machine-gun car was on patrol. After twenty minutes our car entered the prison yard. The director came to meet us and said :

" I don't know anything about this affair. At any

F

rate, it is perhaps much better for you to be here. With me at least you are safe."

This seemed to confirm the sinister rumours about the executions at police headquarters. The director of the Moabit prison was an old official who was responsible to the Prussian state administration, and not to the redoubtable chief of police.

My father was interned at the infirmary, by reason of his old age. He endured this adventure with the utmost calm. " Never mind," he said, " at my age no great accident can befall me." The other industrialists and myself were confined in the cells for prisoners under investigation, and not in the section for convicted prisoners. We lived an almost luxurious life. We had our daily walks in the prison yard. Later on I received numerous letters from prisoners who reminded me of the time we had spent together at Moabit.

Next morning the Protestant prison chaplain entered my cell. He came to bestow upon me the consolations of his faith. I told him I was a Catholic. He left without even saying good-bye. I was outside his competency. Several minutes passed and the Catholic chaplain arrived. He made a little speech that I shall remember all my life.

" Yes, I know," he said to me, " it's always the same story : the first day you pretend to be full of courage, and you don't believe anything will happen to you. But wait for the third day—you'll see what will happen when you know what is awaiting you. Then you will be crushed." The good man thought we had already been condemned to death. He applied to me the method which he used with common-law prisoners. In order to persuade them to accept his ministrations and make them repent their crimes, he frightened them with visions of dire punishments that were supposed to be awaiting them.

On the fourth day I was freed with the others. Eichhorn, it seems, had had our declarations verified and could not hold anything against us. Such was my first personal contact with the Revolution of 1918.

On the 19th of November I had witnessed the return of the troops in Cologne. They were the 6th and the 17th armies, who crossed the Rhine bridges at dawn and in good order. The city was full of flags and the population cheered the soldiers and offered them coffee and cigarettes.

The Jäger (i.e. Rifles) Division paraded on the Cathedral Square before General von Dassel. They were preceded by the black-white-and-red flag of the Reich, the black-and-white Prussian flag, and the green banner of the Jägers. Marching at the head of each battalion the bands played military marches. They all marched in goose step ; it was a comforting spectacle of order and discipline in the midst of the revolutionary upheaval that was spreading further and further.

The Mühlheim regiment returned three weeks later, acclaimed by the population. But the calm did not last for long. At Mühlheim all the workers knew my father and respected him. At Hamborn, however, where we also owned a factory, the radical elements held the power. In the entire industrial district the revolution was organised by the Communist Karl Radek, delegate at Essen of the Russian soviets. It is interesting to note, however, that at Essen itself he had come to some agreement with the mayor, Hans Luther, who later became Chancellor of the Reich, then president of the Reichsbank, and finally ambassador to Washington. Luther has always been more successful as a politician than as a financial expert. I do not happen to know by what means he succeeded in softening up Radek, the Russian revolutionary ; yet it is a fact that the latter abstained from provoking any disorders at Essen. He was all the more active in other cities.

On Christmas Eve, a strike was proclaimed at Hamborn. Alarmed, the mayor called me on the telephone to ask me to come over. However, as I said, Hugo Stinnes had managed to negotiate, right after the armistice, an agreement with the unions in the name of the entire industry of the district. This agreement had not been denounced. I recalled this to the mayor, adding that I could not conclude any separate arrangement. That was that. But early on the following morning, a delegation of five Communist workers came to my home at Mülhheim. They came to take me to Hamborn by force. I did not fancy the prospect of repeating my recent Berlin experience.

I told the butler to let them know that I was dressing and to ask them to come in and take some coffee while I was getting ready. While they were drinking coffee, I warned my wife and asked her to go with my little daughter to Duisburg, which was occupied by Belgian troops. In the meantime, we arranged, I was to go and warn my father. He was living at about eight miles' distance from Mühlheim at the Castle of Landsberg on the Ruhr. I left by a hidden door and proceeded to Landsberg. My father and I left immediately, afoot, along the road. But soon we were given a lift in a car, which saved my old father a painful walk of about seven miles. We had good reason to fear that we would be arrested once more. Already the rumour was spreading that well-known personalities had been shot by Communist bands. The best known of those executions of hostages is the one that took place at Munich, where the revolutionary government ordered the notables of the city who had been arrested to be executed without trial.

The impressions which those agitated days have left upon me have never been blotted out. I have spent my life among workers. My father had worked with them at the beginning of his career. Never have the workers of our factories shown us any kind of hostility, still less of hatred—not even the Communists. All disorders and excesses have almost always been due to foreigners.

Hamborn has always been the "reddest" town of the industrial district. Several years after the revolution the German National party, to which I belonged, invited me to attend an electoral meeting in that Communist citadel. All along the way there were demonstrations against the presence at Hamborn of a reactionary candidate, which the crowd considered to be a provocation. Out of caution, I had left my car some distance from the meeting place. The party committee had been clumsy enough to organise its electoral meeting in premises usually employed for Communist demonstrations. As I arrived at the door of the hall I found the place occupied to a large extent by people wearing the Communist party insignia. The atmosphere was stormy. However, the candidate made his speech without being interrupted. Then the opposition replied. A local Communist leader passed all the industrialists of the district in review, passing judgment on one after the other. I was sitting in the front row and he certainly had seen me. His speech was violent. I expected him to attack me and thus provoke a hostile demonstration. Nothing of the kind happened. During the entire critical period that preceded

Hitler's accession to power I often had to deal with Communists who were working in our factories. As I spoke to them I realised that many of them were animated by a good deal of idealism. They believed in that false doctrine, fancying that it would secure happiness to the proletariat. But at the time the revolution took place, those who committed excesses were not found among local workers. The organisers of strikes and riots were professional political agitators, many of whom were in the pay of the revolutionaries at Moscow : these were the men responsible for riots and murders. The Social Democratic party consisted of reasonable and moderate people. When the miners struck in January, 1919, I took part in the negotiations with the strikers. They understood the difficult position of the industrialists. The latter, for their part, tried their very best to remedy the food shortage which resulted from the continuation of the Allied blockade. We came to an agreement, and this agreement would always have been respected had it not been for the intervention of the radicals and the anarchists, whose only function it is to create or to encourage disorder in times of crises.

During an entire year, 1918-1919, I felt that Germany was going to sink into anarchy. Strikes followed one another without either motives or results, since the feeding of the working population did not depend on the employers. It was impossible to reorganise industrial production. The mining of coal diminished day by day. We ever feared that saboteurs might destroy the machinery. No one was any longer assured of his individual freedom, or even of the safety of his life. A man could be arrested and shot without any reason.

It was then that I realised the necessity—if Germany was not to sink into anarchy—of fighting all this radical agitation which, far from giving happiness to the workers, only created disorder. The Social Democratic party endeavoured to maintain order, but it was too weak. The memory of those days did much to dispose me, later on, to offer my help to National Socialism, which I believed to be capable of solving in a new manner the pressing industrial and social problems of the great industrial country which is Germany.

Historical Notes

The Kiel Mutinies

The German Revolution began in October, 1918, with the mutiny of the sailors of the navy stationed at Kiel. The immediate cause was the sailors' dissatisfaction with the bad food which began to be served aboard the warships in the summer of 1918. A number of marines and sailors who had participated in the disorders were arrested by their superiors and were threatened with severe punishment. Many naval officers distinguished themselves by their cruelty in making arrests. The secret revolutionary organisations, which then already covered the whole country, exploited these incidents for agitation among the naval crews. When an armistice seemed almost certain, some members of the admiralty were still preparing for the sailing of certain battleships and cruisers of the German fleet, in the hope of fighting a decisive battle on the sea. Among the sailors, however, and also among the lower naval officers, a strong feeling of opposition began to spread. In the early days of November, scores of sailors left their ships and organised parades through the city, waving the red flag ; they were joined by a large number of workers and of soldiers on furlough. Shops had to be closed after several stores had been looted. Noske, a Social Democratic member of the Reichstag, was sent to Kiel ; he succeeded in directing the Kiel movement into orderly channels, especially after it was learned that the Republic had been proclaimed in Berlin.

THE SPARTACUS LEAGUE

After the Social Democratic Party had split, during the War, over the question of war credits, radical agitation began to spread among socialist workers. It was at first directed mainly against the government and its conduct of the War. After the triumph of the Bolshevist revolution in Russia, however, the agitation took on a more revolutionary character and was pointed particularly against the leadership of the Social Democratic Party. A particularly important role was played in this propaganda by a series of letters signed " Spartacus," in imitation of the name of the leader of a historic slave revolt in ancient Rome. No doubt these letters contributed much towards the kindling of the German Revolution. They were assiduously read, although the domestic police as well as the military police at the front confiscated all the copies of which they could get hold. It has never been possible to establish who belonged to the " Spartacus League," by which the letters were distributed. It appeared later on that the leader of the League was an old member of the Reichstag, Ledebour, and that Karl Liebknecht and Rosa Luxemburg were his close collaborators.

THE GOVERNMENT OF PEOPLE'S COMMISSARIES

Immediately after the proclamation of the German Republic, Germany was governed by a " Council of the People's Commissaries " which consisted of three members of the older majority wing of the Social Democratic party, and three members of the " Independent Socialists," who had seceded from the Social Democratic party after it had voted for the war credits during the first part of the World War. Friedrich Ebert, chairman of the Social Democratic party, presided over the Council.

NATICONAL HUMILIATION

Versailles and the Ruhr

MY family has always been Catholic. My ancestors came from the left bank of the Rhine, after having been settled as peasants in the frontier region between Liége and Aix-la-Chapelle. My father and I belonged, until after the World War, to the Catholic Centre party,* my father being very close to Matthias Erzberger, the party's leader. We were almost the only Catholics among the industrialists of the district ; most of them were Protestants. To be a prominent Catholic in a region administered by the Prussians was not always without disadvantages. We had had an example of this under Bismarck, at the time of the famous _Kulturkampf_. That was the reason we gave our support to the Centre party, a party which defended the rights of Catholics against the policy of the government, often excessively Prussian and Protestant. But after the war the Centre party, and especially its president, Erzberger, lost all sense of national pride. At the time of the

* See Historical Notes at the end of chapter, page 103.

Armistice and the signing of the Treaty of Versailles*
my father and I were deeply saddened by the
spectacle of Germany's abject humiliation. We
resigned from the Centre party after it had participated
in the signing of the Treaty.

In the spring of 1919 I went to Paris with one of the
members of the German Peace Delegation, Postal
Minister Johann Giesberts. Giesberts held his membership in the delegation primarily as the mandatory of
the important Catholic party. I myself held no
official appointment. I had hoped, however, to be of
service to the German delegation in the discussion of
the economic questions which were to be settled by
the Peace Treaty, by making use of the numerous
contacts I had made in France before the war. But
it was absolutely impossible for me to renew these
relations. I made several trips from Versailles to
Paris, but always under close police surveillance.

It is not necessary to retrace the painful history of
the negotiations at Versailles. To-day it is clear to
everybody that the treaty there imposed on Germany
was nefarious. But I should like to pay tribute to
the memory of Count Brockdorff-Rantzau. The
Socialist government of Germany, availing itself of
his diplomatic experience, had appointed him minister
of foreign affairs and chief of the delegation to
negotiate the peace. Brockdorff had accepted this
trust in the hope of being able to discuss and conclude
a treaty founded on law. The attitude of the Allies
dispelled this hope. Clemenceau imposed on
Germany a treaty which charged her with the
responsibility for the war, condemned her to pay
reparations which were absurd from the point of view

* See Historical Notes at end of chapter, page 104.

of economics, mutilated her frontiers, and deprived the German nation of the right to dispose of its own affairs. Brockdorff, with whom I was well acquainted, was opposed to the signing of the treaty. The economic experts designated to study the conditions pertaining to reparations (to whom I was unofficially attached) declared these conditions to be unfulfillable.*

I stayed nearly three months at Versailles. I left on June 16th, 1919, to accompany the German ministers belonging to the Peace Delegation to Weimar, where the government and the National Assembly were then in session. Brockdorff did his best to persuade the German government not to sign the Treaty. I myself tried to convince the Catholic deputies whom I knew that it would be an error to accept the Draconian conditions of the Allies. Almost all of them were of the opinion that the Treaty could not be fulfilled, but that a refusal to sign was out of the question.

This was a capital political mistake. By signing, we engaged ourselves to fulfil. Yet we knew fulfilment to be impossible. It is my opinion that the great political lie which has poisoned Europe for over twenty years began on the day of the signature of the Treaty of Versailles.

Brockdorff had insisted, in arguing with the government, that signature should be refused. He did this in the full realisation of the consequences which would result for Germany. Field Marshal von Hindenburg, when consulted as to the possibility of military resistance, declared that resistance in the west would be useless in the face of the opponents' superior means. But he added : "My duty as a soldier is to choose

* See Historical Notes at end of chapter, page 106.

death in preference to a dishonourable peace."
Brockdorff's advice was to let the Allies overrun
Germany and let them take all the responsibility for
a military action against a people which would not
defend itself. He envisaged the prospect of foreign
domination, of occupation, of famine. . . .

"Can we at this moment demand such sacrifices
from the German people ? " he said to the German
chancellor, Friedrich Ebert. "I believe that we
must," he added proudly, "for these are the last
sacrifices which the war demands of our people."

Ebert understood the internal situation. He knew
that the refusal which Brockdorff demanded might
result in revolution. He was afraid to see Germany
plunged into Communism and anarchy. In my
opinion Ebert exaggerated the danger. The magnificent behaviour of the entire population later on,
during the occupation of the Ruhr, has borne me out.

In a moving letter addressed to the Socialist
chancellor, Brockdorff admitted, however, that Ebert's
reasons were plausible. "But," he added, "if that
is the state of things I cannot pursue the foreign
policy which I had intended to follow." And he
offered his resignation.

The dilemma in which the German leaders thus
found themselves was a tragic one. They knew that
acceptance of the treaty in the proposed form constituted a lie to the Allies and a lie to the German
people, because the treaty was not fulfillable. Rejection,
on the other hand, meant surrendering the country
to immediate foreign occupation and revolutionary
upheaval. Ebert had said in November, 1918, "I
detest revolution as I detest sin." He decided to
accept. He was supported in his attitude by the

leader of the Centre party, Matthias Erzberger, whose political temperament favoured compromise and subtle manœuvring. To him nothing was ever final; all you needed, in his opinion, was patience and ability in order to change the course of events and re-establish a situation.

For my father and myself the refusal to sign would have resulted in consequences of the gravest kind. For the Rhenish-Westphalian industry would have been the first to feel the Allies' heavy hand. This became obvious a few years later, when Poincaré ordered the occupation of the Ruhr. But this hostile foreign pressure inevitably provoked a sudden re-crudescence of patriotism. Perhaps this would have come in any case. Be that as it may, my father and I were in favour of rejecting obligations which manifestly could not be fulfilled. It was at this point that we broke with Erzberger, in spite of the deep friendship which existed between him and my father. Thus we left the party to which our family traditionally belonged, of which my father had been a member from its foundation—the Catholic Centre.

The extremist excesses of 1918 and 1919 threatened Germany's destruction through fire and blood. The signature of a humiliating treaty condemned a whole nation to a sort of economic slavery, which on top of everything had been rendered insulting by extorting from the German people a confession of guilt. The surrender forced on the so-called " war criminals " was resented as a humiliation by all the veterans of the war. The revolutionary danger and the humiliation of Versailles gave rise to the violent nationalistic and anti-Socialistic reaction which soon gathered momentum throughout Germany.

Groups commanded by former army officers were being formed here and there as a check to the elements of disorder. They were called " free corps." The government more or less tolerated them, for the Socialist members of the government of the Reich, and especially Gustav Noske, the Reichswehr minister, were convinced that it was necessary to erect a solid barrier against the rising flood of anarchy if the country was to be brought back to work. Ebert himself, destined to become President of the German Republic later on, was far from being an extremist. It was due to his personal influence and the complete harmony existing between him and Field Marshal von Hindenburg (his eventual successor as president), throughout these difficult years, that the army was able to contribute to the rebirth of discipline and the sense of order in Germany.

It was the military and conservative elements in Germany that staged the first post-war *coup d'état* in 1920. Even at the time of the signature of the Versailles Treaty, in June, 1919, a party of officers wanted to set up a military dictatorship and appealed to their chief, Gustav Noske, the Socialist minister of defence. The *coup* of March, 1920, was in fact a revival of that project. Only this time the generals wanted to be absolutely rid of Left-Wing radicalism : they had pushed Noske aside in favour of Dr. Wolfgang Kapp, a conservative official from East Prussia, founder of the Fatherland party, which during the war had protested against the peace resolution voted by the Reichstag, in 1917.

General Ludendorff supported the new project. That the general was a great soldier had been amply demonstrated during the war. But he had never possessed any political sense. The greatest mistake of his career was to ask to be relieved of his command in the fall of 1918. I am persuaded that if he had remained at his post, he could have prevented the Kaiser's abdication and flight to the Netherlands. In that event the history of post-war Germany would have taken quite a different turn.

Politically the *coup d'état* of 1920, afterwards known as the Kapp Putsch, had been badly prepared. The conspirators had no genuine support except that of Captain Ehrhardt's Marine Brigade, and several other military units. But the army as a whole had not been definitely won over. Nevertheless the putschists succeeded in taking possession of Berlin and its government offices. Whereupon the government proclaimed a general strike.

In the industrial district the consequence of this clumsy attempt at counter-revolution was a new revolutionary movement. At Essen, at Duisburg, at Düsseldorf, and at Mühlheim, revolutionary committees reminiscent of the councils of workmen and soldiers of 1918 seized political power under the pretext of the general strike proclaimed by the Ebert government. The situation was rendered the more critical when the workers learned that General Watter, who commanded the Reichswehr at Münster, sympathised with the counter-revolutionaries at Berlin and was preparing to enter the Ruhr. The workmen immediately organised a militia of which a large part was armed with the rifles retained after the war.

As soon as the trouble began, I left Mühlheim with my family in order to go to Krefeld, on the left bank of the Rhine. The bridge over the Rhine was guarded by Belgians, who allowed me to pass. The

German industrialists watched the new revolutionary movement with apprehension, for it disorganised the whole economic life of the district anew. The disorders lasted a fortnight. Finally the Reichswehr was obliged to intervene in order to re-establish order, and veritable battles took place at Duisburg and at Wesel between the workers' militia and the army.

The abortive Kapp Putsch and the wave of radicalism that followed it had powerful repercussions in our industrial region. Agitated spirits could no longer be calmed. During the following year new strikes and street battles occurred in many industrial cities of the Ruhr. Only gradually could quiet be re-established. And hardly had the revolutionary danger been overcome when the weight of reparations began to disorganise economic life.

The flood of currency inflation* rose steadily and slowly ruined the German middle class, which did not understand the monetary mechanism. Even my father no longer understood it. One day, returning from a trip, he told me with indignation that the hotel where he habitually stopped wanted to double the price of his room. He had refused to pay the new price and had taken another room, one which cost what he usually paid. But it was, he said, a miserable attic under the roof of the hotel! All the same, at another time he ordered a parcel of securities to be sold at a price which seemed advantageous. In reality, of course, the sum in paper marks had only a fictitious value.

The most serious consequence of the inflation was that it made it impossible to adapt wages to the constant rise in the cost of living. A workman's

* See Historical Notes at end of chapter, page 106.

family could no longer obtain the prime necessities of life ; for the weekly wage, whose value diminished from day to day, made it impossible to apportion the purchases of daily necessities through the week which followed any given pay day. To remedy this state of things the Ruhr industry finally issued a kind of emergency money with stable value, with the object of enabling housewives to do their marketing regularly at the workers' co-operative stores.

While we were discussing ways and means in the midst of these difficulties, the French government under Poincaré decided, at the beginning of 1923, to occupy the industrial region.* On January 11th, French and Belgian troops entered Essen and Gelsenkirchen. On the following day the occupation was extended to Bochum, to Dortmund, and the entire basin of the Ruhr. In several cities incidents of a sanguinary character between the troops and the population took place. Workmen were killed.

It was my opinion that Poincaré's *coup de force* might have given us the chance to denounce the Treaty of Versailles. In effect, in deciding to take so grave a measure as the military occupation of a whole German region under the pretext that certain deliveries, of minimal importance, had not been made on time, the Belgian and French governments had become the first to violate a treaty whose execution they wanted ostensibly to assure. Indeed, the crown attorneys of Great Britain have never admitted the existence of a legal basis for the occupation of the Ruhr.

The German coal syndicate presently met at Hamburg. I attended the meeting, together with

* See Historical Notes at end of chapter, page 107.

G

such other industrialists as Kirdorf, Krupp von Bohlen, Klöckner, and Hugo Stinnes. I was of the opinion that, since we had not taken advantage of the occupation by denouncing the Treaty violated by Poincaré, we should now resist.

A second session was held several days later at Essen. The other industrialists adopted my opinion and asked me to be their spokesman. The meeting passed a resolution declaring that the industrialists would deliver coal to the Allies in accordance with the Berlin government's consent. At the same time we sent an emissary to Berlin to ask the government to cover us by forbidding the deliveries. Not everybody had supported our intransigent attitude. Two days after the occupation the French engineers arrived and got in touch with the mine-owners. A few of these operators entered into negotiation. In order to enforce respect for the resolution voted at Essen, we then decided to institute a secret tribunal which was to punish the refractory owners.

It was a very critical moment for Germany. If France had succeeded in getting possession of the Ruhr industry, the country would never have been able to recover. Two years later I met, in Paris, a section chief in the foreign ministry of which Briand was the head. He said : " During the war the Germans wanted to destroy France in order to get hold of its mineral deposits. During the Ruhr occupation it was France which wanted to destroy Germany in order to get its coal." That was true. But how much better it would have been for the two countries to have come to an agreement !

Several days after the entry of the French troops

I was summoned by the French general. He received me very correctly and asked, " Have the industrialists decided to effect the deliveries which Germany has agreed to make under the Treaty ? " I replied that the occupation of the territory was considered by the German government to be a violation of the Treaty and that in consequence we had received orders not to effect these deliveries. In that case, the general told us, the industrialists themselves would have to take the consequences of their refusal.

On January 20th I and several other mine-owners were arrested and tranferred to the military prison of Mainz. I stayed there three days.

When they heard the news of my imprisonment the workmen of our factories became agitated. There had already occurred a grave incident between the people and the army of occupation at Bochum. In the face of this unrest among the workers, the French government decided not to have me condemned to prison for five years, as I had expected they would. The court-martial merely imposed a fine of 300,000 gold marks. I was set at liberty at once, before having paid the fine.

As I left the court-martial, the population of Mainz and delegations of workmen who had come from the Ruhr staged a great demonstration in our honour. We were carried to the railway station as in triumph. My father, who had attended the session of the court-martial, had been treated with great courtesy by the French authorities.

When I returned to Mühlheim I organised the passive resistance which was Germany's answer to the occupation. In view of his advanced age, my father took no part in the movement whatsoever. The government had forbidden the coal deliveries. The officials had been instructed to refuse to obey the order of the occupation authorities. The railway employees went on strike. Navigation on the Rhine was stopped. The French themselves had to provide the means of transporting passengers and goods by rail, road and water. The army occupied the mouths of the mine pits belonging to the Prussian state. When this happened, the miners quitted work. In the other collieries the work continued, but the coal accumulated in great heaps on the surface. No train, no boat transported any of it to Belgium or France.

In order to break the resistance, the occupation authorities established a customs cordon between the occupied territories and the rest. of Germany. No merchandise was allowed to leave. Nevertheless, we succeeded, in several cases, in shipping whole train-loads. The August Thyssen foundries at Mühlheim had their own freight stations. These were guarded by Belgian officials. In order to distract the soldiers' attention, we sent them pleasant and pretty young girls, who performed their mission very well. During such a period of distraction perhaps four trains could be loaded and dispatched. Unfortunately one of the loads was too heavy and the couplings of the cars broke. We were caught in the act, and an inquiry uncovered the secret.

The passive resistance was organised in its entirety by me. But in my task I had the absolute co-operation of the population. The Catholic clergy, particularly the Cardinal Archbishop of Cologne, supported our efforts with the greatest devotion. It is thanks to them that there could be accomplished in the Ruhr a real national union which made it possible to save the integrity of the Reich.

It is necessary to-day to emphasise this attitude of the Catholic clergy. The Prussian minister of labour, Herr Brauns, was a cleric. It was he who took all the measures to prevent work in the mines of the Prussian state domain. The Vatican was the only power which dared to send a diplomatic representative into the Ruhr during this trying time. The American ambassador, whom I had approached in order to get the help of the Quakers in feeding the working population, did not dare to come himself, or even to be represented.

The National Socialists had nothing to do with the passive resistance. They have since then boasted of having organised acts of sabotage. That is absolutely untrue. Their " hero," Schlageter, who was arrested and condemned to death by the French war council, was not a Nazi at all ; he belonged to a good Catholic family.

Hitler has never understood the national importance of the fight which we then carried on along the Rhine. Already during that time he was dreaming of seizing power, and he was preparing his famous Munich Putsch.

The highly patriotic attitude of the Catholic clergy and population during the occupation of the Ruhr has been rewarded by Hitler with the blackest ingratitude. Ten years later the Nazi regime even flagrantly reproached the Catholics with not being good Germans. He has arrested our priests, has falsely accused them in the most odious manner ; he has dragged bishops before his tribunals, where they have been insulted. I shall tell later on what conclusions the Rhenish Catholics are prepared to draw from such ingratitude and such indignity.

Historical Notes

THE PARTIES IN THE GERMAN LEGISLATIVE NATIONAL ASSEMBLY AND IN THE GERMAN REICHSTAG

Immediately after the outbreak of the German Revolution there existed only two Socialist parties—the Social Democratic party, which was the older majority wing, and the Independent Socialist party. The Communist party came into existence only considerably later, when the Independent Socialist party split ; the Communists took over the majority of the defunct party, while the rest joined the Social Democrats.

As for the non-Socialists, it seemed for some time as though there was no bourgeoisie capable of organising itself in a party system. This situation changed only when it became certain that the German Republic would endorse the parliamentary form of government. First of the non-Socialists to enter the political stage was the German Democratic party. It recruited its members from the adherents of the former German Progressive party and the National Liberal party, both of which had played an important part in the Imperial Reichstag. The new party's platform was republican and pacifistic ; it advocated the reconstruction of German economy by collaborating with all European nations ; it favoured an economical financial policy and the extension of the existing social legislation, and wished to prepare for Germany's entry into the League of Nations.

As the founders of the Democratic party refused to give a representative position within the new party to Gustav Stresemann, who had been one of the National Liberal party's leaders, Stresemann was prevailed upon by other members of the former National Liberal party to accept the leadership of another new party—the German People's party. Its membership consisted mainly of the upper commercial class, university professors, and, above all, industrialists whose interest lay principally in the revival of purchasing power in the German home market. The programme of the German People's party recognised the Republic as a *fait accompli*. It demanded the re-establishment of the German people's self-respect, it advocated reasonable concessions in social welfare legislation, so as to secure a peaceful understanding with Labour, and it provided for the reconstruction of German agriculture.

Immediately after the foundation of the German Democratic party, the Catholic Centre party began to resume activity. It did not think it worth while to change its name. The Centre party had been founded in 1875, when Bismarck had engaged in the Kulturkampf, the politico-religious struggle against the alleged interferences of the Pope in German affairs. The harsh measures used by Bismarck against religious orders and against priests caused an ever-growing percentage of Germany's Catholic voters—almost half of the total constituency—to join the Centre party. Partly as an opposition party, partly as a government coalition party (during the World War), the Centre constantly increased in importance. The revolution changed nothing in the composition of its membership ; as before the war it comprised all economic strata—Catholic workers as well as Catholic aristocrats. Naturally, as in Germany as a whole, so within the Centre party, the conservative elements found mostly among the representatives of the nobility, heavy industry, and big business, were now willing to agree to all concessions made necessary by the conditions of the time. The programme of the Centre also approved of the republican form of government ; it advocated a pacifistic policy, demanded the reconstruction of agriculture, and favoured the raising of the standard of living of the middle classes.

The newly founded German National party represented a modernised version of the old conservative pre-war parties. Its membership comprised the large landowners, a large part of heavy industry, several groups of workers organised as Protestant Christian bodies, and certain elements of the middle classes who were bound to the Imperial family and the former German monarchs by sentimental ties or by material interests. A large number of German university professors also signed up as members. The programme of the German National party was moderate in its form ; but its content was as nationalistic as was possible at the time. Its economic demands centred around the maintenance of the working capacity and efficiency of Germany's middle class and the agricultural communities.

The National Socialist German Labour party made a comparatively late appearance in the Reichstag. It was at first represented by a very small number of deputies who, moreover, split into several groups. Eventually it became the second largest party in the Reichstag ; shortly before Hitler seized power, it succeeded in depriving the Social Democratic party of its rank as the largest single party of the Reichstag.

Among the more important splinter parties, which often played a decisive part by holding the balance of power, there were the Bavarian People's party (a Bavarian version of the Catholic Centre party) and the German Economic party, whose following consisted mainly of artisans and small shopkeepers, convinced of their economic importance and the futility of securing due consideration from the more powerful political groups.

The Signing of the Peace Treaty

The Legislative National Assembly at Weimar found it a difficult task to reach a decision as to the acceptance or rejection of the Versailles Peace Treaty. The result of the vote remained uncertain up to the very last moment. The Social Democrats and the German Democratic party agreed in voting for the Treaty. The German People's party and the German National party rejected it. The final decision depended on the Catholic Centre party ; though the votes of several representatives of the People's party also hung in the balance. The position of those who, in their minds at least, desired the signing of the Peace, was weakened by the fact that Count Brockdorff-Rantzau, the minister of foreign affairs, had resigned, because, as he explained in his letter to President Ebert, in the interest of the German people, he felt he could not sign the Versailles peace terms. They were further weakened by the rumour that in case Germany refused to sign the Peace, the then latent differences between the Allies would become acute and create an opportunity for Germany to secure more favourable terms. On the other hand, there were reliable sources of information to the effect that in the event of non-acceptance, considerable military forces were ready to march into Germany. Now, the consequences of a possible Allied occupation of further German territories were viewed with considerable apprehension. It was feared not only that new revolutionary movements might spread over the country, but also that the individual governments of the German federal states might be ready to make separate peace offers to the Allies. The government of Württemberg, it was rumoured, was already firmly resolved to take such a step. The fear of such possibilities eventually consolidated the majority by which the National Assembly declared itself in favour of accepting the Peace, despite the total uncertainty of the situation.

THE " POLICY OF FULFILMENT "

Throughout many years, the harsh economic conditions imposed by the Treaty of Versailles, which found their expression in the payment of the war reparations, created dissension among the German people. From the very start, one section of public opinion advocated utmost resistance to the reparation terms, while the other section demanded the fulfilment of the treaty obligations. Both sections agreed that the demands imposed by the treaty

could not possibly be fulfilled. The partisans of " fulfilment," however, urged the view that it was necessary to
prove to the Allies that the fulfilment of Germany's
obligations was impossible, not only because Germany
was incapable of making the deliveries, but also because a
fulfilment of Germany's obligations would have the
immediate result of creating disorder in the world market
and in international finance—and this very much to the
disadvantage of the Allies. In this way it was to be made
clear, especially to Great Britain and the United States,
that German payments would not suffice to reimburse
them for loans made to their allies and associates in the
late war. The partisans of fulfilment fully realised that
their method would impose certain sacrifices upon the
German people ; but they firmly believed that they would
gradually bring about the abrogation of the harsh terms
of the Treaty by peaceful and legal methods.

THE GERMAN INFLATION

Germany had financed her war almost entirely by
means of loans ; consequently, even before the end of the
war, inflation had taken on enormous proportions. The
currency issued amounted to something like ninety billion
marks, whereas the gold cover was not more than three
billions. The revolutionary government of the People's
Commissaries increased the circulation of the currency still
further, since foreign countries continued to accept German
bank-notes as payment for the shipments of foodstuffs and
raw materials. Although a federal income tax was introduced soon after the National Assembly had convened, the
circulation of bank-notes was further increased because
the capital for industrial stocks needed by German industrial enterprises could best be raised on the credit of the
Reichsbank. Indeed, German industry was very busy, as
it could throw its products on the world market at low
prices, owing to the devaluation of German currency.
This procedure found the support of Dr. Havenstein, the

president of the German Reichsbank. He clearly recognised that the value of the mark would thus be constantly lowered ; but he considered this to be the best method of convincing the world of Germany's inability to pay war reparations. Numerous industrialists took advantage of this opportunity by discounting enormous bills of exchange at the Reichsbank, and paying them back in more and more devalued notes. With their profits they not only bought raw materials and paid their workers, but they also acquired new enterprises, either by extending their own factories or by buying up shares ; whereupon they merged their enterprises into larger concerns. Private banks, and also the German Reichsbank, in this way lost ever-increasing amounts of their gold cover. At the beginning of the organised " passive resistance " to the occupation of the Ruhr by French and Belgian troops, the German currency received its final blow. Indeed, the enormous cost of this struggle was by no means covered by taxation, but by the printing of new bank-notes. Even before the end of the resistance labour began to rebel, as the workers' wives could buy practically no food in the markets with the money their husbands had brought home on the preceding evening. Industrial plants and municipalities were obliged to create emergency currencies on a fictitious gold basis, in order to prevent the workers from setting the factories on fire. Thus the government was forced to proceed to a stabilisation of the currency, in which it succeeded with the help of foreign governments. In November, 1923, the official value of the American dollar was fixed at forty-two billion marks !

The Occupation of the Ruhr

Germany had engaged herself to render to the Allies war reparations in the form of cash payments as well as deliveries of goods. From the very beginning most Germans were convinced that it would be practically impossible to fulfil all of Germany's obligations, so far as payments in goods were concerned. Chancellor Cuno and his cabinet had made it their aim to reach a new agreement with regard to Germany's obligations. The French government was already threatening that in case Germany should delay her payments, France would make use of her right given her by the Peace Treaty and occupy the Ruhr district, Germany's most important industrial region. The offers made by the Cuno cabinet were all rejected. The conviction that a " terrible end," in the form of the occupation of the Ruhr, was preferable to an " endless terror," i.e., the status quo, gradually grew within the cabinet. Moreover, the members thought themselves reliably informed to the effect that England would not permit France to resort to violent military measures. Eventually the Reparations Commission actually declared that Germany was delaying her obligations because she had not delivered some one hundred thousand wooden telegraph poles. Despite the unimportance of the direct cause, French and Belgian troops marched into the Ruhr district late in 1922, without being opposed by the other Allies. The German government supported the population's resistance to the occupation— a decision which found the support of all parties, the Communists as well as the Catholics and the German Nationalists. In the summer of 1923 the resistance in the Ruhr collapsed and the Cuno cabinet was replaced by a government headed by Stresemann.

CHAPTER THREE

MY FIRST MEETING WITH HITLER

IN October, 1923, after the end of the passive
resistance, I made a trip to Munich. I paid a
call on General Erich Ludendorff, whose acquaintance I had made at my father's house during the war.
I have always had a great admiration for Ludendorff.
Under the influence of his second wife he adopted
in later years an attitude violently opposed to Catholicism, and he almost played the part of the founder of
a new religion. During his last illness, however, he
was under the care of nuns in a Catholic hospital at
Munich. I have been told that he had flowers
purchased every day in order to decorate the altar.

After the revolution of 1918, General Ludendorff
enjoyed a great reputation among patriots. Although
he was a Prussian, he moved to the Bavarian capital
two years after the war, where he took up residence
with his sister and where he continued to work on
his memoirs without abandoning his close contact
with political life. As the Ruhr was being occupied,
Hugo Stinnes established relations with him, and
Ludendorff went to Berlin with a view to organising
military resistance to the occupation with the help of

the government and General von Seeckt. But both General von Seeckt, who was then commander-in-chief of the German army, and the Reich government side-stepped this project—not without reason, it seems to me, for considering the state in which Germany found herself, military resistance would only have increased the disaster.

The experiment in passive resistance which I organised and, later on, the experiences of the Nazis in Czechoslovakia have shown that a population which systematically opposes violence by defenceless passivity deprives the military of all their means of action. They can kill, but they cannot force into obedience a population which does not resist them.

Just after the Ruhr incident, I was asked to become the head of a Reich government to replace the cabinet headed by Wilhelm Cuno, which was universally regarded as too weak. Dr. Class, the head of the Pan-German League, approached me on the subject. He asked me to take advantage of the prestige I had acquired by virtue of my activities during the Ruhr occupation, and thus to revive successfully the national counter-revolution in which Kapp had failed in 1920. My answer to Dr. Class was this : " I am an industrialist. As an industrialist and a patriot I have organised the passive resistance. I am not a politician. I wish to serve my country only by doing my duty."

I went to see Ludendorff chiefly to pay him a call of courtesy, but also in order to discuss with him the great national questions which then preoccupied his mind as much as mine. I deplored the fact that there were not at that time men in Germany whom an energetic national spirit would inspire to improve the situation.

" There is but one hope," Ludendorff said to me, " and this hope is embodied in the national groups which desire our recovery." He recommended to me in particular the Oberland League and, above all, the National Socialist party of Adolf Hitler. All these were leagues of young people and World War veterans who were resolved to fight Socialism as the cause of all disorder. Ludendorff greatly admired Hitler. " He is the only man," he said, " who has any political sense. Go and listen to him one day."

I followed his advice. I attended several public meetings organised by Hitler. It was then that I realised his oratorial gifts and his ability to lead the masses. What impressed me most, however, was the order that reigned in his meetings, the almost military discipline of his followers.

Several days later I made his acquaintance at the house of Dr. Max Erwin von Scheubner-Richter, a young Baltic nobleman who had taken refuge in Germany after the Bolshevik revolution. He was a very engaging person. He served as go-between for Hitler and Ludendorff, the latter of whom had arranged this interview. The conversation ran on political topics.

We were at the worst time of the inflation. The money issued by the Reich, the individual states, and the municipalities sank in value from one day to the next. In Berlin the government was in distress. It was ruined financially. Authority was crumbling. In Saxony a Communist government had been formed and the Red terror, organised by Max Hoelz, reigned through the countryside. In Hamburg a Communist revolt had broken out. Hundreds were said to have been killed. After Saxony, Thuringia had given itself a Communist government. In the Rhineland, Separatist revolts, more or less openly sponsored by the Allied army of occupation, had taken place at Düsseldorf, Aix-la-Chapelle, Mainz, and in the Palatinate. The German Reich, which had resisted the ordeals of war and of defeat, was now about to crumble.

Amidst all this chaos, Bavaria seemed to be the last fortress of order and patriotism. It was in Munich that the revolution of 1918 had caused the greatest ravages. The government of Kurt Eisner,[1] the Red terror, and the execution of hostages had left a profound impression on the population. But Bavaria, among all the German states, had recovered first. A Catholic government, supported by the majority of Bavarians, had succeeded in liquidating the revolution. Munich had become the centre of all those who desired to re-establish discipline and authority. In Berlin, Gustav Stresemann had succeeded Chancellor Cuno ; he put an end to passive resistance and sought an agreement with France. His policy was severely criticised. The patriotic leagues held it to be treacherous to the German cause. As for the Conservatives and Catholics in Bavaria, they apprehensively watched the progress of radicalism throughout Germany.

Little by little a new policy began to take shape at Munich. If Germany should break into pieces, it was said, Bavaria would remain the nucleus of order whence recovery would come to the whole country. The Bavarian government declared publicly that they did not recognise any longer, so far as they were concerned, the Treaty of Versailles, which had

[1] *Publisher's Note :* Kurt Eisner was the Independent Socialist premier of Bavaria who in 1919 was murdered in cold blood by Count von Arco, a young nationalistic " patriot."

been broken by Poincaré. They proclaimed a state of emergency in Bavaria.

The army corps which was stationed in Bavaria and commanded by General von Lossow, a Bavarian, refused to execute the orders of Berlin and put itself at the service of the Bavarian government. As an answer to the measures taken by the Berlin government, Bavaria gave itself a kind of chief of state in the person of Gustav von Kahr, who took the title of Commissioner General of the State. This was almost open rebellion against Berlin. The old Field Marshal von Hindenburg, who happened to be spending his holidays in his estate of Dietramszell in the Bavarian Alps, sent a cable to the Bavarian government warning it not to commit any irremediable acts and advising it to consider the unity of the Reich. Several days later the Bavarian government declared, in a proclamation, that the Bavarians were the most loyal of all Germans, but that they had broken off diplomatic relations with Communist Saxony.

Such was the atmosphere in which my first meeting with Hitler took place. I cannot recall with certainty the exact part which each of us took in the conversation. Yet I remember the general content. Ludendorff and Hitler agreed to undertake a military expedition against Saxony in order to depose the Communist government of Dr. Zeigener. The ultimate aim of the proposed expedition was to overthrow the Weimar democracy, whose weakness was leading Germany into anarchy.

Funds were lacking. Ludendorff accepted fees for the interviews which he gave to American newspaper correspondents. However, as he told me, this did not get him very far. He had already solicited and

H

obtained the help of several industrialists, particularly
that of Herr Minnoux of the Stinnes firm. For my
part, I gave him about one hundred thousand gold
marks. This was my first contribution to the National
Socialist party. These funds, however, I delivered
neither to Hitler, nor to Scheubner-Richter, the
treasurer of the *Kampfbund* (the patriotic military
organisation under the political leadership of Hitler),
but to Ludendorff, whom I desired to use it as best
he could. I did not examine the details of the plans
evolved by Ludendorff and Hitler. I have already
said that I did not wish to mix in politics. I took
advantage of my stay at Munich also to visit Herr
von Kahr, who was to all practical purposes the
Bavarian chief of state.

Being the confidant of Crown Prince Rupprecht,
Kahr held that the Wittelsbach dynasty should be
re-established on the Bavarian throne as quickly as
possible. The Bavarian dynasty had never abdi-
cated. When the revolution of 1918 broke out, King
Ludwig III had left his country after authorising
the officers and officials to support the new order of
things. After the excesses committed by the Red
government the majority of Bavarians had again
become monarchists. Kahr contemplated the restoration of the Wittelsbachs first of all. And then, perhaps, a Wittelsbach might one day become emperor
of Germany or at least of a Catholic Germany to
which might be joined the western provinces of Austria.
Vienna, the Red citadel, where the Socialists were in
power, would be left outside.

Such was the atmosphere which I found in Munich
in the autumn of 1923. Political imagination was
given free rein. Infinite possibilities loomed every-

where. So far as I was concerned, I had no ambition to play any part in this movement. My duty as an industrialist came first. It was a heavy duty in itself. As soon as we might free ourselves from disorder, the ruins which war and revolution had left behind had to be mended : Germany had to be put back to work.

Ludendorff and his allies, the patriotic leagues, had undertaken Germany's political recovery. I gave them material assistance, but I did not wish to enter political life.

Besides, I was unaware at the time of the importance of Adolf Hitler, the National Socialist leader. No doubt he was a good speaker—a political agitator who knew how to carry the masses by his words, but nothing more than just that. For me, Ludendorff and Kahr were the two decisive figures. I knew nothing of the deep disagreement that separated them on the question of the restoration of the Bavarian monarchy. Ludendorff was a personal enemy of Crown Prince Rupprecht for reasons that went back to the World War. But all this I only learned much later.

The true facts about the Hitler Putsch of November 9th, 1923, have never been entirely revealed. It seems that the leading characters of that abortive revolution—Ludendorff, Kahr, Hitler, and General von Lossow—each had different intentions. This accounts perhaps for the complete lack of agreement on the day of the execution of the Putsch. I remember, however, a very revealing detail that might possibly interest future historians.

General von Seeckt, who still was chief of the Reichswehr in Berlin, had sent his wife to Munich during these critical weeks. She returned to Berlin only after the 9th of November. However, Seeckt had protested to the Bavarian government when the latter assumed authority over the troops stationed in Bavaria under General von Lossow. Was he playing a double game? He had not supported the *coup* attempted by Kapp in 1920, which had failed through the default of the army. Was he now—in 1923—planning to execute his own *coup* by seeking the support of the Bavarians? The presence at Munich of Frau von Seeckt seems to corroborate this explanation. If this was so, the hasty action precipitated by Hitler caused the failure of the entire scheme.

An expedition of the Bavarian army and of the armed political leagues against Communist Thuringia and Saxony was decided upon in Munich. But it was Berlin that executed the decision. The army corps stationed in Saxony received the order to march on Dresden and to depose the Zeigener government. The army carried out this mission with eagerness. After Saxony came Thuringia's turn. The two Red governments resigned. The great political project evolved at Munich had no further *raison d'être*.

Hitler decided to march, nevertheless. Kahr and Ludendorff opposed his plan. It is known in what circumstances Hitler forced the Commissioner General of the Bavarian State to give his consent—at the point of the revolver. Ludendorff was informed only at the last minute, but he placed himself at the head of the parade that marched through the streets of Munich on the following morning. The adventure ended badly. The police fired on the demonstrators, fourteen of whom were killed and in particular Scheubner-Richter, whom I had met a few days before. Ludendorff marched erect among the bullets that were whistling around his head. Hitler fled to

Uffing, near Munich, where he was arrested two days later.

On the following day I went to see Ludendorff. He was surprised. "What gives you the courage to come to me after what happened yesterday?" he said as he received me. "Everybody accuses me of high treason."

Ludendorff has never explained to me how he came to be involved in the action, of which he personally disapproved. I am convinced that he did not withdraw from it only because he had given his officer's oath and therefore considered himself bound. Besides, the Munich tribunal, which judged the conspirators of the 9th of November, acquitted Ludendorff, because his responsibility in preparing the plot could not be established.

General von Seeckt, General von Lossow, Commissioner General von Kahr, and the Bavarian government desired a Right-Wing government in Germany. No doubt they did not entirely agree on the details of the execution of their plan. On the whole, however, it was a question of attempting all over again what Kapp had tried in Berlin. Only this time failure was to be averted by starting the *coup* in Munich, where the population was monarchist. Hitler, however, desired only one thing—to seize the power for himself.

Never again did Ludendorff mention Hitler to me. I have never known for what reason he broke with the Nazi leader, of whose praise he was full when I saw him before the Munich Putsch. As for Herr von Kahr, he subsequently retired from political life. Yet Hitler had him assassinated at the age of seventy-two years on the 30th of June, 1934.

CHAPTER FOUR

THE FIGHT AGAINST THE YOUNG PLAN

My Advocacy of Franco-German Understanding

I FINANCED the National Socialist party for a single, definite reason : I financed it because I believed that the Young Plan spelled catastrophe for Germany. I was convinced of the necessity of uniting all parties of the Right, and I believed it possible to reach agreement on a reasonable basis. With that end in view I directed the negotiations with the " Steel Helmet " (an organisation of patriotic World War veterans) and with the Young Men's Groups of the German National People's party—directed them at the instigation of Hitler and Goering. Hermann Goering declared his willingness to place the National Socialist Storm Troops (known as the SA) under the leadership of the Steel Helmet. He always feared that one day the SA would experience a great misfortune.

The co-founder and chief organiser of the SA formations was Ernst Röhm, a former officer of the Imperial Army, who afterwards became the chief of

staff of the SA, in closest association with Adolf Hitler
himself. Röhm was a military adventurer. He had
spent a long time in South America, where he was
particularly occupied with the re-organisation of the
Bolivian army. The impressions and experiences
which he gathered in South America furnished the
ideological basis on which the SA troops were constructed. Thus they became armed mercenaries
whose main purpose was to be ready for action in
the expected revolutionary upheavals. Goering feared
that the spirit of the SA men would prove an obstacle
in the pursuit of any constructive policy.

I turned to the National Socialist party only after
I became convinced that the fight against the Young
Plan* was unavoidable if a complete collapse of
Germany was to be prevented. In no sense had I
been an opponent of the Dawes Plan,* since the
Dawes Plan envisaged a system of reparation payments to be made chiefly in goods. But under the
Young Plan the German reparation deliveries were
superseded entirely by money payments. In my
judgment the financial debt thus created was bound
to disrupt the entire economy of the Reich. Walter
Rathenau,[1] too, had regarded this as a misfortune :
he had always maintained the view that Germany
could pay only in the goods it produced.

One of our representatives in the committee of

* See Historical Notes at end of chapter, page 125.

[1] *Publisher's Note :* Walter Rathenau, a leading Liberal German
Jewish statesman and economist, the head of one of Germany's
greatest electrical concerns, the A. E. G., had devised Germany's war
rationing system and organised the conservation of war materials
as the answer to the British blockade. It is generally conceded that
this saved Germany from an early surrender. After the war, as
Foreign Minister, he was brutally murdered by nationalistic
desperadoes.

experts which conducted the preliminary negotiations concerning the revision of the Dawes Plan in Paris was Director General Vögler, of the Gelsenkirchen iron and steel concern. These Paris negotiations were interrupted, and both Vögler and Dr. Hjalmar Schacht, the president of the Reichsbank, returned to Germany because they had misgivings about the proposed Plan. In the end, too, Vögler did not sign the new proposals which became the basis of the Young Plan ; and I must admit that I had done all I could to convince him of the correctness of his misgivings.

My position was largely determined by what an American banker told me and Vögler. I refer to Mr. Clarence Dillon, of the firm of Dillon, Read & Co., a Jew with whom we were in very friendly relations. Mr. Dillon expressly said, " If I may give you a piece of advice, don't sign." I have never forgotten this, and I have always remained particularly grateful for his advice, for he gave it against his own interests, and for the good of Germany.

Anybody with the power of clear judgment saw that the Young Plan meant the pledging of Germany's entire wealth as a pawn for Germany's obligations. As a result, American capital was bound to flood Germany. Isolated groups in Germany attempted, in good time, to free their particular property from this huge mortgage. In this connection I remember particularly the following undertakings, forming part of the electrical industry : the A.E.G. (one of the two leading German electrical concerns), the S.O.F.I.N.A., and the electrical works of the Felten and Guillaume concern. The stock of these companies was at this juncture sold to a Franco-Belgian holding company, which has been holding them ever since. It was wrong to do this, for it meant the beginning of a financial liquidation of Germany. It would have been far better for the industrialists concerned to have opposed on principle the whole Versailles system, and the Young Plan in particular.

It must be said, moreover, that the whole American idea, which had such great influence on the details of the Young Plan, has had pretty bad results in America as well. For there, too, many German concerns were converted into corporations whose stock was sold to the public. To-day the shares of these American companies are worth only a quarter of the purchase price. It was a good piece of business for the bankers, but in reality it constituted a money inflation which far exceeded the normal earnings of industrial operation. This was a time when people had lost all sense of the normal in figures. It must not be forgotten that the Young agreements themselves comprised the astronomical sum of twenty billion dollars.

The Young Plan was one of the principal causes of the upsurge of National Socialism in Germany. Of course, Alfred Hugenberg helped it along considerably with his radical agitation ; it is true, too, that the appointment of Hitler as chancellor of the Reich would not have occurred—at least not so soon —without the intrigues of Franz von Papen. But the more profound causes were, nevertheless, the danger of Communism in Germany, the occupation of the Ruhr by the French and the Belgians, and finally the Young Plan.

Soon after the liquidation of the Ruhr affair, I went to Paris. This was long before Locarno, in the days when the intransigent Raymond Poincaré was still premier of France. I talked repeatedly with several French ministers, including especially Aristide Briand, who became foreign minister in 1925. My first impression was that my mission would have a favourable issue, although the French minister of commerce kept me waiting for half an hour. Briand, on the contrary, was very cordial and always received me without delay. Unfortunately, however, the situation as a whole was still very strained. And the word went round Paris that the French General Staff was opposed to Briand's policy of *rapprochement*.

Nevertheless I took pains to further the cause of understanding through the Franco-German Society, of which I was one of the founders. But the strain continued and a violent incident at Germersheim in the Palatinate ruffled people's nerves anew. Some further conferences were to be arranged, but that proved no longer possible. All this was before the Locarno Conference began a fresh series of negotiations, which was hailed as the beginning of a new era of good will.

If the German government of the day had not accepted the Young Plan, some progress could surely have been made, and more favourable results could have been achieved. The trouble at that time, however, was caused by a serious psychological error on the German side. I agree that Germany found itself in a difficult situation just then, but it is precisely in difficult situations that one must not compromise on fundamental issues. It would have been easy to resist when even the Americans said " For God's sake, don't ! " Payment in money was simply not possible, for money cannot be produced like goods.

The rise of the National Socialists was also furthered

through the maladroitness of the other parties. I
have already mentioned how I was induced by the
National Socialists to negotiate with the Steel Helmet,
with a view to placing the SA troops under the Steel
Helmet's supreme command. I talked with Major
Düsterberg, the chief of the Steel Helmet organisation, for a whole night. In the end, the offer of the
National Socialists was rejected by his side. A similarly accommodating offer had been made by the
National Socialists to the cabinet of Chancellor Brüning. They were willing to tolerate Brüning, without
being represented in his cabinet, if the chancellor
would be prepared to say that he would part company with the Socialists. Josef Goebbels at that time
said, " If Brüning breaks with the Socialists we will
support him without entering the cabinet." That
should have been done, but the offer was refused.

By means of his great adroitness Hitler was able
to harness the injured nationalism of the German
people for his own purposes. A people with the
traditions of the Germans cannot be transformed
into docile sheep. If the Social Democrats had been
a little more nationalistic they could have made their
party the strongest in the country. One Social Democratic minister of the Reich, Gustav Noske, was a
nationalist. If Otto Braun, the Social Democratic
premier of Prussia, had only been a little cleverer !

Already the Versailles Treaty, from the economic
point of view, was wrong. And the Young Plan was
a consistent development of the very principles underlying the Treaty of Peace that were wrong. It was
for that reason that I joined a committee which aimed
to bring about a plebiscite on the question of the
Young Plan before it was adopted. I know that wide

circles hold the opinion that this radical agitation
against the Young Plan enabled Hitler to give his
party the necessary impetus to swing it into power.
And I know, too, that in certain French circles the
anti-Young Plan movement was regarded as a renas-
cence of the spirit of revenge, But no thought of
revenge ever occurred to me in this connection. Nor
could it have occurred to me, in view of the declarations made again and again by Hitler at that time.

To-day it has become clear that Hitler was playing
a perfidious game. But in those earlier years he
emphasised constantly that he had given up the idea
of revenge against France. Despite everything he had
written in his book, *Mein Kampf* (which incidentally
was of no importance then), he repeatedly said this :
" With France there is no longer any conflict. We
want to bury all that. It is absurd always to remind
people of Alsace and Lorraine. Alsace certainly has
a German-speaking population ; but it is conceivable
that one can renounce Alsace-Lorraine on high
political grounds." (Exactly as Hitler, out of consideration for Italian susceptibility, later on renounced
South Tyrol, which is mainly inhabited by Germans.)

Personally I have always held that a Franco-German
rapprochement was more important than an Anglo-
German one, at least for the pacification of Europe.
England's traditional policy persistently aimed at
keeping the countries of the European continent on
opposite sides. I was always guided by the idea of
Napoleon, who in my estimation desired—like Charle-
magne—a united Europe. In German history books,
it is true, Napoleon is always represented as one who
wanted to dominate Europe. I, however, believe he
was animated by a higher thought.

Historical Notes

THE DAWES PLAN

After the resistance in the Ruhr had collapsed, and after inflation had caused the complete ruin of German currency, Chancellor Stresemann obtained the consent of the Reparations Commission to accept foreign help in order to rehabilitate the German Reichsbank and the German currency. Moreover he obtained the promise that the whole of Germany's financial obligations would be converted into another form. In November, 1923, a commission of experts, headed by an American, Charles G. Dawes, was set up with the aim of examining Germany's situation and of suggesting a new mode of payment. The result was the so-called " Dawes Plan," which was accepted by the Reich on April 16th, 1924. According to this plan a foreign gold credit of 800,000,000 marks was opened for Germany, so as to create a new gold basis for the Reichsbank. The Reichsbank, thus based on a secure foundation, was placed under the control of foreign finance. The foreign loan was secured by a mortgage on the German Railways and on the securities of certain German industries ; also by a transport tax, and by other taxes. A permanent foreign control commission, residing in Berlin, was to supervise Germany's budgets and the functioning of the mortgaged enterprises. The Dawes Plan did not fix the sum of Germany's total obligation, and it would indeed have been difficult to agree on any sum. The Dawes Plan merely decided on the mode of payment. It was decided that for five years Germany would have to make annual payments, beginning with one billion gold marks and gradually increasing to two and a half billions in the fifth year. If, after 1928, the value of gold should be either raised or lowered by 10 per cent. Germany's obligations were to be re-examined. Each year Germany's obligations would be considered as fulfilled whenever the annual payments were handed to the agent-general of the Reparations Commission in Berlin. His duty was then to convert the sums paid by Germany into foreign currencies and distribute them among the Allied nations. After the Dawes Plan was accepted by an international conference in London, and after Germany had adopted the necessary legislation, the Dawes loan was issued—100 million dollars in the United States, the rest in Europe.

THE YOUNG PLAN

The conditions of the Dawes Plan were fulfilled up to 1928, the first year of the economic world crisis which greatly affected the German economic situation. Under a provision of the Dawes agreements Germany was entitled to request a revision of the Plan. Accordingly, at Germany's behest, another committee of experts convened in Paris, in the summer of 1928, again under the chairmanship of an American, Owen D. Young. He proposed a new plan, the " Young Plan," which was accepted on August 31st, 1929, at an international conference at The Hague. Germany's annual payments were considerably reduced ; but henceforth they were to be effected entirely in cash. The essential difference between the Dawes Plan and the Young Plan was that the latter disregarded the political aspects of the agreements and heeded only economic necessities. Above all, the international control of Germany's budget and the pledges given by Germany was discontinued. The mortgaged enterprises were freed and the agent general of the Reparations Commission was replaced by the " Bank of International Settlements " in Basle, Switzerland. This bank was founded by the government banks of all the Allied nations and the German Reichsbank.

When the Young Plan began to be enforced, a number of German private banks had to suspend payment because they were not in a position to fulfil the demands of American banks for repayment of the loans which had been granted them. Germany's economic situation seemed to be so much worse that further payments of war reparations were not to be thought of, for the time being. President Hoover yielded to Germany's demand and proclaimed a moratorium for one year, which was accepted by the other Powers involved. One year later, in 1932, Chancellor von Papen, at an international conference in Lausanne, secured a further concession—namely that Germany's obligations were to cease after a final payment of one billion gold marks.

There is a considerable difference of opinion as to the total sums paid by Germany for war reparations. The lowest estimate, made outside Germany, amounts to 12,000,000,000 marks whereas the highest German estimate amounts to 44,000,000,000 marks. The German estimate, however, comprises not only the actual payments made, but also the expression in money terms of the cession of Alsace-Lorraine, Upper Silesia, the German colonies, the ships, and also the estimated value of German private property abroad, Germany's interest in which was forfeited under the Treaty of Versailles.

CHAPTER FIVE

MY PERSONAL AND FINANCIAL RELATIONS WITH THE NAZI PARTY

The Support of the Party by Heavy Industry

I DID not become a member of the National Socialist party until December, 1931. This was after my collaboration in a great mass meeting in Harzburg, at which Alfred Hugenberg, as leader of the German National People's party, and Hitler, as leader of the German National Socialist Labour party, announced the co-operation of the two parties. The German National People's party was the heir of the old Imperial Conservative party. The German National Socialist Labour party is, of course, the official title of the National Socialists, commonly known as Nazis. That this partnership in principle did not become a real union, which might long have survived the appointment of Hitler as chancellor of the Reich, was probably due more to Hugenberg than to Hitler. I personally had worked zealously for the German Nationals, but finally had fallen out with their leader. Even while I was a member of the German National party, the National Socialists were congenial to me. I considered them to be sensible and rational.

As I have already mentioned, I came to know Adolf Hitler in Munich, when I was still a member of the German National party. I did not enter into closer relationship with him until sometime later on, and even then we never became very intimate.

Rudolf Hess was instrumental in bringing about a closer personal association between the Nazis and myself. He came to me sometime during 1928, on the initiative of old Geheimrat Kirdorf, for many years the director general of the Rhenish-Westphalian Coal Syndicate, with whom I was on friendly terms. Hess explained to me that the Nazis had bought the Brown House in Munich and had great difficulty in paying for it. I placed Hess in possession of the required funds on conditions which, however, he has never fulfilled. For by no means did I want to make the Nazis a present ; I merely arranged a foreign loan for the National Socialist party through the banks. At that time Hess received the money, which he was obligated to pay back. But he returned only a small part of it ; for the rest I myself simply had to " acknowledge receipt."

Geheimrat Kirdorf had been a member of the National Socialist party long before me. His importance in Germany had always been rather exaggerated. Even the creation of the Coal Syndicate, which made his name known far beyond the borders of Germany, is not to be credited to him alone, but jointly to him and his colleague, Unkel. But Kirdorf was its first president, and he always assumed a very domineering manner *vis-à-vis* the outside world. As far back as the time when Kaiser Wilhelm II brought

I

out his first social welfare laws, Kirdorf was aroused
to violent opposition to the emperor. For at bottom
he was a reactionary, although he was by no means
unkind. He simply had the bad habit of making a
quick decision whenever he was in anger. During
his famous quarrel with the Kaiser he named the
little castle in which he lived the " Battle Yard."

Nor did he always remain on good terms with
Hitler, the party's chief. One day he wrote Hitler
a letter, which he gave me to deliver personally.
He was afraid that otherwise the missive might not
reach its destination, because Hitler's staff often held
back letters which contained disagreeable matter.
In this letter Kirdorf protested against the persecutions of the Jews which went on in Germany in 1933.
For it happened that Kirdorf was much beholden to
the Jews for the success of his career. In spite of
this he then became the great financial backer of the
Nazis. Also he had renounced his membership in
the state Church—even before the Nazis came to
power. But as he was afraid of death, he allowed
himself to be converted by Mathilde von Ludendorff
(wife of the general) and entered the neo-pagan
church, " At the Fountain-head of German Strength,"
which she had founded.

Kirdorf died at the age of almost ninety years, and
I attended his funeral. It was terrible. The coffin
had been set on a Nazi flag, which made a beautiful
effect. But then the Reich minister of economics,
Dr. Walther Funk, made a very bad speech ; it
consisted entirely of flattering tributes to Hitler, who
was present. At the end the Horst Wessel Song was
sung. I left immediately at the end of the ceremony,
Hitler left at the same time. I hid behind a tree.

so he wouldn't see me. But I was able to see how the Führer stood up in his automobile, obviously in expectation of an ovation from the assembled workmen. But as nobody was prepared for a demonstration, this made a painful impression, not to mention the tastelessness of Hitler's posture. I was sorry for old Kirdorf because of this burial; he deserved a better one.

Hermann Goering I came to know in the following manner. One day the son of one of the directors of my coal mining companies, a certain Herr Tengelmann, came to me. "Listen to me," he said, "there exists in Berlin a Herr Goering. He is trying very hard to do some good for the German people, but he is finding little encouragement on the part of German industrialists. Wouldn't you like to make his acquaintance?" In consequence of this suggestion I met Goering in due course. He lived in a very small apartment in those days, and he was anxious to enlarge it in order to cut a better figure. I paid the cost of this improvement.

At that time Goering seemed a most agreeable person. In political matters he was very sensible. I also came to know his first wife, Karin, who was a Swedish countess by birth. She was an exceedingly charming woman and showed no signs of the mental derangement which clouded her life before she died. Goering idolised her, and she was the only woman who was able to guide him—as though he were a young lion. She also had a great influence on him. Sometime after her death Goering made his estate, Karin Hall, into a fantastic memorial to his first wife.

As for Hitler, I saw him again in Munich, at a meeting concerning the Young Plan. Later I met him occasionally at Goering's house, but I have never visited him at Obersalzberg and I have never been inside the Brown House. On one occasion Hitler, Hess and Röhm slept at my late father's house. That was about the extent of our acquaintance.

But I did in fact bring about the connection between Hitler and the entire body of Rhenish-Westphalian industrialists. It is common knowledge that on January 27th, 1932—almost a year before he seized power—Adolf Hitler made a speech lasting about two and a half hours before the Industry Club of Düsseldorf. The speech made a deep impression on the assembled industrialists, and in consequence of this a number of large contributions flowed from the resources of heavy industry into the treasuries of the National Socialist party.

The preliminaries to this "historic" speech are worth noting. It was not my original intention to let Hitler speak to this gathering. In fact, no provision had been made for the delivery of a National Socialist address. On the contrary, the committee of the Industry Club had given permission to a Social Democrat to make a speech, with the result that the members became greatly excited, and many threatened to resign. At a very stormy session of the committee I said there was only one way of making good this mistake, and that was to invite a National Socialist to address the assembly as well. This proposal was adopted.

However, in making it I had certainly not immediately thought of Adolf Hitler, but rather of Gregor Strasser, as the man to make the speech. For Strasser was in those days the most popular figure among the National Socialist representatives in the

Rhineland. He was an educated man, a pharmacist by profession ; and generally people took him seriously, despite his National Socialist leanings. That was because one could argue with Strasser, and because he made not nearly so disagreeable an impression as, for instance, Dr. Robert Ley, who at that time published a paper in Cologne and who is to-day the head of the German Labour Front.   So I asked Gregor Strasser to make the speech at the Düsseldorf Club. But shortly after this I accidentally met Adolf Hitler in Berlin. When I mentioned to him the projected address before the Düsseldorf Industry Club he said, " I think it would be better if I came myself." I duly agreed ; and it was actually through this invitation that Hitler first became properly known in the Rhineland and in Westphalia.   So far as I was concerned the origin of the invitation had no political significance. But Hitler, no doubt, immediately saw the political value of the opportunity which was thus offered to him.

I have personally given altogether one million marks to the National Socialist party. Not more. My contributions have been very much overestimated, because I have always been rated the richest man in Germany. But after all, what does it mean to own factories ? It does not follow that a man has a lot of cash to spare. In any case, Hitler had other sources of money besides me. In Munich, for instance, there was Herr Bruckmann, the well-known printer ; and in Berlin there was Carl Bechstein, the world-renowned piano manufacturer, who also contributed large sums. Aside from this, Hitler did not receive many subsidies from individual industrialists.

It was during the last years preceding the Nazi

seizure of power that the big industrial corporations began to make their contributions. But they did not give directly to Hitler ; they gave them to Dr. Alfred Hugenberg, who placed about one-fifth of the donated amounts at the disposal of the National Socialist party. All in all, the amounts given by heavy industry to the Nazis may be estimated at two million marks a year. It must be understood, however, that this includes only the voluntary gifts, and not the various sums which the industrial enterprises were obliged to provide for the party's numerous special manifestations.

The fact that I never became specially intimate with Hitler is probably due to the hostility of Rudolf Hess and Josef Goebbels, the propaganda minister. Although Hess knew that I had rescued the party from a great embarrassment arising from the purchase of the Brown House in Munich, both these men worked against me. Belonging to the Left Wing of the party, they were suspicious of me as the representative of heavy industry ; and I know, too, that quite a number of other people resented Hitler's intercourse with heavy industry.

But Hitler's relations did not extend to industrialists in general. In fact, besides old Kirdorf, who was not really an owner of heavy industrial works, I was the only one of that ilk who freely exposed himself in this connection. The case of Herr Krupp von Bohlen und Halbach,* head of the famous munition works, was the reverse of mine. Until Hitler's seizure of power, Herr von Krupp was his violent opponent. As late as the day before President von Hindenburg appointed Adolf Hitler chancellor he urgently warned

* See Historical Notes at end of chapter, page 136.

the old field marshal against such a course. But as soon as Hitler had the power, Herr von Krupp became one of his most loyal party adherents. I am not saying this in order to reflect on Herr von Krupp in any way. In any case, this would not minimise my own mistake. And I candidly confess that I did make a great mistake when I trusted Adolf Hitler. Only it would be much better if Herr von Krupp could get himself to confess his mistake as well.

In making this confession I must emphasise again and again—not as a complete excuse, but by way of extenuation—that the trouble with the Nazis was not the party itself but certain individuals in it. That, of course, is principally the fault of the party chief. He retained all the leading people within the party, regardless of their character, and they could do what they liked. A *Gauleiter*, whose functions within the party organisation roughly correspond to those of a *Regierungspräsident* (county president) within the organisation of the state, is to-day sacrosanct. As soon as the Gauleiters realised which way the wind was blowing they started among themselves a sort of club ; and this club of Gauleiters is what really governs Germany to-day.

This will be the party's ruin ; for no country can flourish under such conditions. In every system, even under Communism, the Leader must be responsible for order. In Russia, Stalin manages to keep order —according to his own particular method, to be sure !

Historical Notes

THE KRUPP PLANTS

The Friedrich Krupp Corporation (*Aktiengesellschaft*) at Essen has always been Germany's most famous arsenal.

As early as the 1860's, when it was still a private firm, it received a subsidy of five million thalers from the Prussian State. All the artillery used by Prussia during the Danish war of 1864, the war with Austria of 1866, and the Franco-Prussian war of 1870-1871, came from the Krupp plants. After the Franco-Prussian war Krupp's establishments grew to such an extent that they occupied entire districts in the city of Essen, whose rapid growth was mainly due to the increase in the number of Krupp workers. The city's administration fell entirely into the hands of the Krupp concern. In order to secure a foreign market, where it had to meet the competition of the French firm of Schneider-Creuzot, the Krupps employed a whole army of agents, mostly chosen from the ranks of former German diplomats and army officers. Krupp's agents interfered in Germany's foreign policy and, as a consequence of the personal influence exerted by the Krupps at the Imperial court, Germany's diplomats were often at the disposal of Krupp's agents. This influence increased after old Fredrich Krupp, the founder's son, committed suicide. Indeed, Kaiser William II took a personal interest in bringing about the marriage of the only daughter of the deceased, and sole heir to the Krupp fortune, to Herr von Bohlen und Halbach, a hitherto unimportant member of the foreign office. Herr von Bohlen und Halbach, who, after his marriage, took the name of Krupp von Bohlen und Halbach, was not sufficiently familiar with the business to manage the enterprise. He transferred it into a limited company ; all the shares, however, remained the family's property and were never sold in the open market. The administration was entrusted to a large board of directors. After the collapse of the monarchy the Krupp plants diminished their scope considerably. A large part of the remaining plants were adapted for the manufacture of peace-time goods. Since Hitler, however, they have again increased in volume, and are now many times larger than they were in the Kaiser's time.

CHAPTER SIX

THE NAZIS' ROAD TO POWER

AFTER December 2, 1932, a new government was formed in Germany, with General Kurt von Schleicher at its head. Schleicher had for many years occupied one of the most important positions in the war ministry and was, moreover, the most intimate adviser of the minister of defence, General Wilhelm Gröner. The latter, originally a citizen of the state of Württemberg, came from the Democratic camp. Schleicher's real intention was to put into practice the main points of the National Socialist programme without letting Hitler seize the power. It was notorious, however, that he would have liked to give a cabinet post to Gregor Strasser, a student of social politics, who sat in the Reichstag as a National Socialist.

Gregor Strasser was, as I have already indicated, very well known in the Rhineland. At that particular time he had several conversations with the leading industrialists, in which I, however, took no part. Strasser lived in Franconia, the northern part of Bavaria ; however, he was not a Franconian but a genuine Bavarian, and as such was particularly popular in the Rhineland and in Westphalia.

Strasser and I maintained outwardly pleasant relations ; but he did not like me very much. Within his party he sided with the extreme Left, and he suspected me on account of my past connection with the German National party. Consequently, I got no direct news of his conversations with the other owners of heavy industry. As to his numerous conversations with General von Schleicher, all I knew of them was through the National Socialist party. The party was very suspicious of these interviews. They were considered to be treacherous toward Adolf Hitler, and I openly shared this opinion.

Whether General von Schleicher might eventually have succeeded in forming a cabinet chiefly by German Labour—this question can no longer be answered. His negotiations with Strasser appear to have been very successful. I was even told that Schleicher counted on the support of a part of the Social Democratic labour unions. His aim apparently was to separate the unions from the parties, which in the case of the National Socialist party would have had the natural consequence of splitting the party in two.

At that time I sent Rudolf Hess a copy of the letter I had addressed to the secretary of a Rhenish industrial enterprise and in which I expressed the opinion that the manner in which Strasser worked against Hitler was contemptible. Hess answered me in a very cordial letter. It is therefore all the less understandable why the National Socialist party did not invite me to attend the afore-mentioned meetings.

To-day I am of the opinion that it would probably have been better if Strasser's negotiations had led to a successful end. It was mainly Herr Krupp von Bohlen und Halbach who then advocated a *rapproche-*

ment between Strasser and General Schleicher. No doubt he was right when he made the attempt, which I have already mentioned, to persuade old President von Hindenburg never to appoint Hitler chancellor of the Reich. I have already said that this enmity to Hitler on Herr von Krupp's part vanished as soon as the former came to power. Indeed, after Hitler was appointed chancellor, Herr von Krupp became a super-Nazi. How closely he sided with the National Socialists was proved to me as late as in 1938. At that time a meeting of industrialists took place at the house of Geheimrat Bosch, director general of the I. G. Farben Industrie, the largest German chemical concern. Several of the industrialists present severely criticised Hitler's behaviour. The meeting was confidential and several instances of monstrous corruption within the party were mentioned in particular. Herr von Krupp rose and said, " I cannot bear hearing those accusations and I am leaving the meeting." Similar meetings, incidentally, frequently took place among industrialists.

In keeping with the " social " character of the policy which General von Schleicher intended to pursue, he brought to light the so-called Osthilfe scandals. The " Osthilfe " (" Aid to the East," meaning chiefly old Prussia) was a large-scale financial measure to salvage agricultural enterprises. It had been originated by the Social Democratic government of Hermann Müller, and was broadened by the Brüning cabinet. It seems that some of the funds of the Osthilfe had been corruptly used ; however, compared with the gigantic graft that now flourishes under the National Socialist regime, these sums appear ridiculously small. Much excitement arose among the large landowners east of the Elbe when a Reichstag investigating commission was to be appointed. The excitement increased when General von Schleicher threatened to make the investigation public, a threat which resulted in creating a violent resentment against him—a resentment shared even by President von Hindenburg.

Herr von Papen took advantage of this situation. A member of the Reichstag, where he represented the Catholic Centre party, he was disliked by a great number of its members on account of his intrigues. In his youth he had been a cavalry officer on active duty ; later he married the daughter of a very wealthy industrialist of the Saar region. During the World War of 1914–1918 he was the military attaché of the German Embassy in Washington. His activity as military attaché has made him notorious throughout the world. Indeed, one of his associates lost a brief case in a New York subway which enabled the United States government to prove that a series of dangerous acts of sabotage had been directly instigated by the government of the Reich, and that Papen himself had played an important part in their execution.

For some reason Herr von Papen had developed an intense hatred of General Schleicher, whom he planned to eliminate as a chancellor of the Reich. His candidate for that post was Adolf Hitler. To further his plan, Herr von Papen arranged an interview between Hitler and the Cologne banker, von Schröder, a cousin of the well-known London banker, Baron Schröder. The interview took place at Cologne, in Herr von Schröder's banking house. Rudolf Hess was also present.

I heard of this interview only a long time after it

had taken place. It seems that Hess, who at first opposed my friendship with Goering, did not keep me informed. Nor had Goering, who perhaps might have informed me, been consulted in the matter. In fact, it was always doubtful whether Goering was party to a secret or not, especially after the Prussian police ministry had been taken from him. The present intimate relationship between Hitler and Goering dates only from the great massacre of June 30, 1934, in which the National Socialist party was purged of all members objectionable to the regime.

I have the impression that Goering had so large a part of the responsibility in this massacre that he no longer dared to oppose the regime. In any case he was much more independent before it took place. It seems that he has made himself guilty of so many crimes on account of his personal jealousies that he has come entirely into the grip of the Gestapo, who know too much about him. Ever since then he has been silent.

It is a well-known fact that Papen was successful in his intrigues. On January 28, 1933, General von Schleicher resigned his chancellorship and on January 30, President von Hindenburg appointed Adolf Hitler to that office. I was well content with the turn of events, especially as I had heard that Alfred Hugenberg (although a German National deputy) had become a member of the Hitler cabinet and had taken into the government with him a number of trusted friends. Besides, Hugenberg had obtained from Hitler a formal promise, given personally to Hindenburg, to the effect that for the following four years nothing would be changed in the composition of the cabinet and the distribution of key posts.

In any case, I thought at the time that Hitler's
taking office as chancellor was merely a transitional
stage leading to the reintroduction of the German
monarchy. My opinion rested on the following
grounds. In September, 1932, I had invited a number
of gentlemen to my house in order to enable them to
put their questions to Hitler. Hitler answered all
questions directed to him to the utmost satisfaction
of all present. On that occasion he said in distinct
and unambiguous terms that he was merely a " peace-
maker to the monarchy." Directors General Kirdorf
and Vögler and other great industrialists were present.
Hitler's monarchistic attitude of those days brought
to his party a large following among industrial circles.
I also wish to recall that in the fall of 1932 Goering
paid a whole week's visit to ex-Kaiser Wilhelm II at
Doorn. The fact that Hitler and Goering were invited to dinner by the Crown Prince seems to prove
that the Hohenzollerns themselves had great hopes
during this time. Truth to tell, Goering subsequently
told me that after he and Hitler had left, the Crown
Prince had made several deprecatory remarks in the
presence of his servants, who immediately carried the
information to the Nazis. This, it is said, put an
end to the friendship Hitler had for the Crown
Prince.

But this did not prevent the Crown Prince from
attending, in the spring of 1933, the first of Goering's
regularly recurrent Opera balls. On the one side of
the tier of boxes sat Goering with his entire staff ;
on the other side, facing them, sat the Crown Prince
—and so ostentatiously that some of the Nazis were
quite vexed. But others were not ; and to the outside
world it indicated that the Hohenzollerns had reason

to be optimistic about their expectations in the early days of the Nazi regime.

To-day I am unfortunately forced to admit that I, too, misjudged the political situation at that time. But I, at least, can claim that I acted in good faith.

Historical Notes

The political situation was indeed somewhat confused in 1932. It is true that Schleicher cherished the thought of setting up a so-called " social " (i.e. social welfare) government. His intention was perhaps to imitate Mussolini's Fascist government, at least in essence, if not in form. His negotiations with Gregor Strasser went very far. At the same time he actually carried on negotiations with several representatives of the important labour unions which, although formally independent, were closely connected with the Social Democratic party. So far as the National Socialists were concerned, the entrance of Gregor Strasser into the cabinet would indeed have resulted in a split, or at least in a struggle between Gregor Strasser and Adolf Hitler which could not have ended otherwise but in a party schism. Indeed, the idea of the Führer's defeat was unthinkable.

The case of the Social Democrats was quite different. The entry into the cabinet of a few Social Democrats would not, at the beginning at least, have bound the party as a whole. The question whether the party should maintain its independent position, or whether it should identify itself with the Schleicher government would be determined by the action of its deputies in the Reichstag, though it risked having to sacrifice the Socialist members of the cabinet. Of course, new parties might possibly have been founded and the Social Democratic party have suffered a severe loss in votes and prestige.

The decisive turn of events at that time is entirely due to Herr von Papen. Up to a short while before the events in question, President von Hindenburg had still refused to trust Hitler. Papen's intrigues were based primarily on Schleicher's threat to make the Osthilfe scandals a public affair. The Osthilfe was not a purely agrarian measure ; certain sums had also been given to the industries. Moreover, several party groups represented in the Reichstag were attempting to widen considerably the geographical concept of the " East." By and by, enterprises in the centre and the south of Germany were also included in the Aid to the East. Finally it included all those enterprises that were endangered by the general economic crisis whose distress was believed to be caused by the post-war changes, notably the inflation and the subsequent revaluation of the currency. The measure as a whole, although it was originally well meant, had eventually taken on an aspect which might be called corrupt by an objective observer. The main " corrupt " feature was the apparent purpose to eliminate all risk inherent in private enterprise, and to shift the burden of all deficits to the community. Conscious corruption on the part of the receivers of the subsidies played only a minor role.

The case of the Agrarian Aid (*Agrarische Nothilfe*) looked quite different. Its original objective was to help out those landowners who had become indebted, not through any fault of their own, but as a result of the peculiar conditions at the time. It was soon discovered that the larger part of the funds which the Agrarian Aid controlled had been granted not to the owners of small or medium-sized estates, but to the big landowners. Indeed, in several cases landowners not only did not use the funds granted them to pay off their debts, or improve their estates, but they spent the money lavishly in Europe's fashionable resorts.

General von Schleicher had played an important part in most of the political intrigues of the past decade. However, he did not recognise the danger to which he exposed himself when he made the Osthilfe affair the decisive issue in his cabinet policy. His real purpose was, of course, to become popular with the masses and to lay the foundations for a good start for the Labour cabinet which he intended to set up.

Herr von Papen saw the situation in quite a different light. Through his middlemen he was exactly informed of the game that was being played in the entourage of President Hindenburg. Shortly before, the great estate of Neudeck, Hindenburg's birthplace, had been presented to the president. The gift was made possible mainly by contributions of industrialists. Thus—very cleverly—the president himself had been raised to the rank of a large landowner, and his son, who at the same time acted as his aide, succeeded in making him see how difficult it was to run a new estate and how little profit there was in it. Thus the president was put into the right frame of mind for lending a sympathetic ear to the insinuations of the other large landowners. Although perhaps he did not oppose the punishment of corrupt acts which had actually taken place, he was convinced that these were not sufficient cause to interfere with the landholding class as a whole, and to create distrust among the population with regard to the ownership of land.

This perhaps would not have been sufficient to deprive Schleicher of the president's confidence. It might have been possible to negotiate and to find agreement by which the affair would have been either made public without creating a scandal, or entirely hushed up. Whoever knew Schleicher sufficiently well never doubted that a simple hint from the president would have sufficed to make him change his course, for he was anxious to keep his premiership. But this is precisely what Herr von Papen feared. Trustworthy information relating to the events immediately preceding Schleicher's resignation point to Herr von Papen as the man who insinuated to the president that Schleicher was preparing a military revolt against him. It is said, at any rate, that the president's final and sudden decision to suggest resignation to

K

General Schleicher had been provoked by a report, received during a certain night, that Schleicher had already concentrated troops in Potsdam, ready to march on Berlin.

Papen's hatred of Schleicher was mainly due to the fact that the latter had played an important part in the overthrow of the Papen cabinet. It is true that Schleicher, who hitherto had been accustomed to pulling the wires from behind the stage, did not now intend to take the stage himself, as chancellor, right after he had overthrown Franz von Papen. It happened, however, that he was left no choice.

Thus it was that General Schleicher was forced to resign, and two days later Hitler, appointed by President von Hindenburg, took office as chancellor. It is known that Hitler had made up his mind to obtain the office of chancellor of the Reich without resorting to a revolutionary act. He wished to follow the legal path until he was in power. He certainly had always had the intention of abandoning the legal way as soon as he had received the desired powers from the Reichstag. Whether he could have succeeded in his legal conquest of the chancellorship without Papen's help is a matter for speculation. At any rate, the prospects of the party at that time were particularly poor. The National Socialists had suffered great losses at the last Reichstag elections, held under the Schleicher government. Moreover, the secession of Gregor Strasser and his group would have weakened not only the party but also the S.A. organisations. It is certain that huge expenditures had completely exhausted the National Socialists' party funds. This is also the reason why Herr von Papen arranged the meeting between Adolf Hitler and the Cologne banker, von Schröder. The party finances, which just at that time were threatening to reduce the party to an unbearable position, had to be remedied. Its subsequent success in obtaining the necessary funds was complete.

PART THREE

MY EXPERIENCES WITH HITLER AND THE NAZI REGIME

CHAPTER ONE

ATTEMPTS AT CO-OPERATION WITH THE NAZIS

*Efforts to Organise the Corporative System—My
Nomination as Member of the Reichstag
and of the Prussian Staatsrat*

I HAVE never really cared for politics. I did not want to be a politician, for I believe that industrialists should keep clear of politics. It is true that on various occasions I have influenced political processes ; but this happened either through a chain of circumstances, as in the case of Hitler's speech before the Industry Club of Düsseldorf, or it concerned purely economic issues, as was the case in the Ruhr struggle and in the fight against the Young Plan. At those times I took the leadership because I enjoyed a certain popularity.

The case of Hermann Rauschning was different. I knew Rauschning, for he frequently came to the Ruhr region, and people there generally considered it fortunate that he was active in the National Socialist ranks. We were especially glad to know that so rational a man as Rauschning occupied the very

important position of president of the Danzig Senate,
when so much depended on the feeling in the League
of Nations.[1] But Rauschning told no one in the
Ruhr that his position was in danger. Now that I
have read his second book, *The Voice of Destruction*,
I do not understand why he has never mentioned this,
to some people at least. To-day, to be sure, after
having experienced what I did, I am inclined to
think that it would not have made much difference.

My activities on behalf of the National Socialist
party, I imagined, would be of the same incidental
nature as those described above. What interested
me primarily was the way in which economic life
should be organised in the National Socialist state
or—as I advocated—under a collaboration of the
National Socialists and the German Nationalists.
Here was a problem of great importance. For the
question to be decided was whether industry and
economic activity in general should be taken over
by the state ; or if not, what was to be the rôle of
the state in relation to economic life.

At the end of the eighteenth and the beginning
of the nineteenth century the generally dominant
idea, derived from Ricardo and Adam Smith, was
that commerce must be entirely unfettered, and that
free trade was fundamentally linked with economic
life. But the Liberals have " emptied the baby with
the bath," with the result that the state, in opposition
to them, has assumed more and more control over
the economic process and has even gone into business
on its own account. In my opinion the results

---

[1] *Author's Note :* The government of the Free City of Danzig
was, until 1939, nominally responsible to the League of Nations,
represented by a High Commissioner.

achieved by the state as business manager have, on
the whole, been bad. Business is based on private
initiative, which is guided on the one hand by the
risk involved, and on the other by the chances of
profit. The function of the state, however, is to
administer ; and administration is something wholly
different from enterprise under business management.

Even in railway operation, which can certainly not
be left entirely in private hands, the conditions under
state ownership are by no means as brilliant as is
often publicly assumed. The German railways are
a case in point. So far as my knowledge of French
railways goes, private operation there, despite many
disadvantages, is to be credited with many things
that are more advanced than in Germany. For
instance, France possesses more mechanised freight
stations, and the French shunting system is far more
mechanised than the German. As the result of
government ownership, a certain lack of flexibility
is inherent in our railway operation. There is a
constant lack of sense of responsibility on the part
of higher officials when there is no private owner
who must make decisions at his own risk—something
which an official can never do to the same extent.

A similar situation exists in gas and electric power
companies. Probably the best managed electricity
establishments to-day are those of the Rhenish-Westphalian Electricity Works. Their management is in
private hands. But here we have an example of an
entirely new form of organised undertaking, the
initiative for which was taken by the late Hugo
Stinnes. A part of the share capital is in the hands
of private capitalists and some sizable economic groups,
and a part is owned by the municipalities or communes

which take their electric power from these works. The representatives of the municipalities and communes sit on the board of directors. The result is that a kind of sparring match takes place between the private economic interests on the one hand and the communal interests of the cities and villages on the other ; but only when these interests are opposed to each other. The object is precisely this : to insure that the private economic interests must not injure the common weal. The final supervision is, of course, the business of the government, that is, so long as we have an economic system in which not absolutely all private enterprises have been taken over by the state.

That, indeed, is the underlying idea in President Roosevelt's New Deal. He wants to harmonise the private economic interests of the United States with the common interests of the people as a whole. Just as the state prevents people from stealing, so it must make it impossible for private business to exploit and injure the public.

This, to be sure, sometimes makes it necessary to prevent the industry from doing things which in the long run are injurious to itself. Let me give only one example. The construction of the German *Autostrassen* (strategic motor highways) caused many industrialists to build factories for the production of cement. Here is a case where the state should have foreseen that this was neither in the interests of business in general nor in that of labour. For the construction of even the most gigantic highway system must some day come to an end, and then there is nothing to do but to close down all these numerous cement works in order to prevent a glut in cement. Here is an extraordinarily difficult problem. For once the state itself begins to do business, it is no longer an unbiased umpire. It has become an *entrepreneur* with special interests of its own.

There are, for instance, the Hermann Goering Works, of which I shall have more to say later on. Being state-owned they have determined the decisions of the Reich as umpire in advance and in a very one-sided sense.

As a medium which would reconcile all interests, I have always imagined a state which recognises the principle of private industrial profit, but which at the same time provides a corporative constitution for the regulation of industry and business. This would mean the separation of politics and business, and would give to business, i.e. both private and state-owned organisations, an autonomous administration above which stands the state, as moderator in the struggle of interests and as champion of the common weal. The creation of a corporative system is necessary also in order to provide a permanent contact with labour. I, for instance, had much less contact with my workmen than was the case in my father's time, and this, no doubt, is true of all large industrial employers of this mechanised age.

My father, August Thyssen, who died at a very advanced age, was wholly absorbed by his work for the factory which he created, and was a great favourite with his workmen. Here was a chief who worked hard and who at the same time had retained his simple ways of living. Whenever he had a free half-hour he went to the works and talked with his men. But this did nothing to change his old-fashioned ideas, which he upheld to the end. He believed, like Adam Smith, that the workers' wages had to be reduced when prices went down, and when business was bad. But he did not believe this because he wanted to profit at the expense of his workers, but because he thought that this was a healthy basis on which to develop his factories and a good way to enable him to employ more labour.

August Thyssen began with a very small factory. That was in 1873, the year in which I was born. My birthplace was a modest house near the factory. The whole property was very small—just sufficient to accommodate the first workshop. My father managed the factory, kept the books, functioned as his own travelling salesman—in short, he did everything himself. It was much the same as the early days at Krupp's.

I had not as much time as my father to occupy myself with the workers, although I watched for every opportunity that presented itself. But perhaps I didn't have my father's way to talk with the men, either, and I did not enjoy their confidence in the same degree. For this reason, if for nothing else, I wanted to bring about the corporative system—in order to establish the contact with the elected representatives of the workers, who were to sit with the representatives of the Council of State, in order to discuss economic problems, wage problems, questions of export, and the like. For it was my firm conviction that a workman will even accept a wage reduction if he is convinced that it is justified. But I consider it impossible to let work-people *participate* in the business. The moment they became joint owners, a private undertaking would be run like a government service ; whereas industrial enterprises must be managed very individually. A business just cannot be administered like the state.

Naturally it is possible for a manufacturer to explain to his co-workers why he conducts the business in the manner which he considers to be necessary. And the corporative system ought to provide the means whereby all broader considerations are taken into account.

The idea of a corporative system is not mine. It was suggested by a well-known professor of national economy in Vienna, Othmar Spann. My acquaintance with it was due to the presence in Düsseldorf of a certain Dr. Klein, who was social welfare secretary in the I. G. Farben Industrie (the great German dye trust). Long before the Nazis came to power Dr. Klein, under the influence of Professor Spann, was preoccupied with the solution of the social problem.

The problem of establishing a corporative economy is of course a very difficult one. Nevertheless, I have always considered it to be the best solution. There are only two other solutions : either to manage our economic life as before—in a reactionary manner, or to do the opposite—abolish private enterprise and let industry be run by the state.

After all, one should not forget all that private enterprise has accomplished in the past century. The disappearance of this motive force, in the event of a system of state ownership, would be an enormous loss. The corporative state, on the other hand, is an attempt to find a middle way—a way which would allow the owner the liberty which he needs in order to manage his business successfully, and which would at the same time avoid excesses.

In the Sudeten region of Bohemia the development of a corporative system was already fairly well advanced ; and the system is a characteristic feature of the Mussolini regime in Italy. In Germany it was I who was chosen by the National Socialist party to found an institute charged with the preparation of the introduction of the corporative order. This was before the party's seizure of power. In reality Professor Othmar Spann would have been the proper man for this task, but Spann had completely fallen out with Hitler, for a very particular cause. Hence Hitler had appointed me and one other person. We therefore founded this institute, or academy, in order to train suitable people. We also organised an experimental Chamber of Corporations which I attended every day. The aim was eventually to form a permanent chamber from among the people who had passed through the academy.

Then came the seizure of power by the National Socialists, at the beginning of 1933. At first everything seemed to go on well enough. My institute and the experimental chamber had gained the sanction of the Reich minister of economy, Dr. Schmidt, who was formerly a leading and well-known insurance director. I had three secretaries. But these secretaries were obliged to spend part of their time in getting people released from prison or from the concentration camps. For in those days everyone came to me to beg for help. And I almost always succeeded in putting things to rights.

But it soon became clear that the idea of a corporative system in general, and our institute in particular, had many opponents. For one thing, many industrialists were against it because I had been made its director. And almost the entire government bureaucracy was against it, as a matter of course. Within the party a meeting took place in which Dr. Robert Ley expressed his views. Hitler took a position opposed to Ley. Opinions clashed violently. And finally Hitler declared solemnly that everything was to be done as I and my friends had proposed ; within eight days we were to establish a corporative system in Germany. In conclusion Hitler remarked, " Just as the political movement originated in Munich, so the economic reform shall originate in Düsseldorf."

One reason why Hitler was for the corporative order, it seemed to me, was that he opposed the idea of fusing the three general federations of labour unions which existed in Germany into one. What he wanted was to divide the Labour Front ; and he was right in seeing the necessity of this. But unfortunately he did not stick to his ideas.

For a time, it is true, Adolf Hitler seemed to maintain his original point of view with regard to the corporative system, particularly under pressure from the radical movement within the party. Gregor Strasser, too, had plans for a sort of corporative system. But it is possible that it was just Strasser's sympathetic attitude toward the corporative idea that eventually contributed to Hitler's change of mind— that is, after Gregor Strasser's " treachery " (recounted in the previous chapter). Ley's prediction was correct : the workers, he said, do not stand behind Strasser ; they stand behind Hitler and Ley.

In order to counter Ley's fight against the corporative system I entered a complaint with Hitler against Ley. I told him that in any case Ley was not the right man for the post which he occupied. Thereupon Hitler became quite wild and challenged me to prove it. And I did so ; at least, I thought I had done so. But nothing happened.

As I have already remarked, I was not close to Hitler in a general way. Nevertheless, I was able to discuss the corporative system with him at various times.

I was frequently in Berlin, and once we talked about the subject while I conducted him around one of my mines. On this occasion, by the way, another matter came up as well, namely, the encounter which Hitler had had with Wilhelm Furtwängler, the orchestral conductor. Hitler told me how he had sent for Furtwängler and told him he simply could not keep on playing pieces by Jewish composers. That was as intolerable as if he, Hitler, were to fall in love with a pretty Jewess. I had to laugh inwardly. For actually, whenever Hitler did go near a woman at all, the woman he ogled would turn out to be a Jewess.

The Nazis not only nominated me a Reichstag deputy, but Goering, as Prussian prime minister, made me Prussian state councillor for life. Besides Field Marshal von Mackensen and Admiral of the Fleet von Raeder there were only two or three people in the party who were state councillors for life. It was, therefore, supposed to be a special honour. In the State Council I attended five sessions, which were not bad. But one day Goering said to me : " I can't continue these sessions behind closed doors, as I had intended, because I have seen the Bishop of Osnabrück, Monsignor Berning, taking notes." So, after four further sessions everything was changed. There was no more listening to the motions of members ; henceforth the worthy state councillors were treated like pupils who were being crammed in a course on National Socialism.

Once even Julius Streicher, editor of the anti-Semitic sheet, *Der Stürmer*, was permitted to give a lecture in this Prussian State Council. Streicher was not even a Prussian but a Franconian from Nuremberg. He spoke on the law. He related something that had happened to him not long ago. He had been indicted on that occasion while the republican government was still in power, and had not been treated impartially—which I for one am quite willing to believe. But that can certainly be no reason for a " statesman's " saying that the law should be abolished ! However, that was the clear meaning of his speech. And it is very significant that this monstrous idea which was being expressed did not even arouse a discussion.

Soon, however, the State Council was as good as forgotten, and so was the corporative order. Ley achieved a complete victory for his point of view. This was just as well, so far as he is concerned. For the corporative system would have made impossible such corruption as that which permeates Ley's own creation—the Labour Front.

I was a fool to believe that Adolf Hitler's intentions were sincere.

Publishers' Note

The " corporative " system of economy (*Ständische Wirtschaftsordnung*) is not, as might appear from Thyssen's account, an invention of Professor Othmar Spann. What might be called corporate organisations existed throughout medieval Europe in connection with various national economics. It will be recalled that all parliamentary governments were similar in origin. The reigning princes, whenever they required large sums of money, summoned the representatives of the various " estates," i.e. social, economic, and vocational groups (in German, *Stände*), in order to get these money grants voted to themselves, or appropriated to their use. These estates consisted of (*a*) the nobles, (*b*) the clerics (or representatives of the Church), and (*c*) the burghers—the merchants of the towns. The struggle to get the workmen and peasants recognised as a " Fourth Estate " is familiar from the history of the French Revolution.

These estates were not artificial creations ; they had developed quite naturally, as the result of economic activity. The noble landowners, as well as the burghers, had organised associations among themselves, and the decisions concurred in by their representatives facilitated the levying of taxes. Although the Third Estate, that of the burghers, was first accorded its rightful place during the French Revolution and in the English parliamentary struggles, the economic power of the bourgeois, or citizens' classes had long before grown far beyond their political status.

Even the medieval artisans or craftsmen had formed vocational groups or guilds in accordance with their various trades. And each of these groups undertook the regulation of its own trade or craft, in a sort of self-governing administration.

The influence of this economic autonomy did not, of course, remain confined to purely economic matters, but extended to public life, and particularly to public morals. In general, the tendency of these vocational bodies was to secure for each member of their trade or craft or profession as great a degree of comfort as possible. This became more and more difficult as economy outgrew its medieval fetters and developed in the direction of free capitalistic enterprise. The vocational organisations—guilds and the like—which in the Middle Ages could easily protect the well-being of the artisan citizens, were eventually forced to take measures to prevent unfair competition, both in the sale of the goods produced, as well as in the labour market. These measures no longer conformed to the modern way of life which national economy had developed in the course of centuries.

The bad features of the supercapitalistic system which has come to flourish since the nineteenth century have been widely criticised, and attacked by many reformers.

On the one hand there were the socialist groups, who wanted to transform the capitalistic system into a collective economy. On the other hand we had the bourgeois social reformers, who desired a greater degree of social justice and a fairer division of the national income, while recognising the right of the capitalist system to exist. But there was also a third group of people, especially active in Germany, which strove for the return to a non-capitalistic economy in which competition was absent—in other words, a return to the medieval conditions. They demanded the establishment of a *ständische* (i.e. vocational, or as it came to be internationally known, " corporative ") economic system, which however they were never able to visualise very clearly. They regarded the economic freedom of modern times as the root of all evil, and demanded a return to a " tied " economy (organised in groups). This, they believed, would produce a type of man who would be frugal, well-balanced within himself, and of the strictest honesty.

The nineteenth century advocates of these theories were the literati of the Romantic School. The most distinguished of them, undoubtedly, was Adam von Müller. A part of the Catholic clergy in Germany and Austria went along with this movement ; and more recently Othmar Spann, an Austrian professor of national economy, developed a vocational system within the framework of his theory of " economic universalism." At the beginning of the National Socialist movement many party men were avowed adherents of Spann's idea.

In this connection it may be mentioned that in 1919, during the German democratic revolution after the World War collapse, there was an attempt to produce a modernised system of economic groups, inspired by the soviet system of the Bolsheviks. At the second Congress of the Workmen's and Soldiers' Councils held in that year, a proposal was adopted by the votes of delegates of various socialistic tendencies. This plan provided for a horizontal organisation

L

of all the various branches of economic life. The
directing body of each branch of trade or industry consisted of an equal number of elected employers and
workmen. This elected body had the duty to see that
each trade or industry was managed so as to achieve the
highest possible production. The governing body of the
trade groups had wide powers of self-government.

The workmen elected to the governing bodies were to
be taken from among the members of the so-called Production Councils, chosen within each industrial or business
establishment. (These were independent of the so-called
Works Councils, which were to continue as representatives
of the labour unions, with the task of protecting the social
interests of workers.) The Production Councils had to
try to increase production, in conjunction with the employers. They were also to advocate such measures
among the workers as would be of permanent value to the
establishment (the basis of the workers' existence), even if
this meant a temporary sacrifice on the part of the workers.

The plan also projected the establishment of an economic
parliament of the Reich, in which the representations of
all organised branches of industry came together to form
the highest self-governing corporate economic body of the
country. The originators of this economic constitution
(if you will, a synthesis of the socialistic and the traditional
guild system) tried, at the second Congress of Workmen's
and Soldiers' Councils, to get it incorporated into the
republican constitution of the Reich. But the Social
Democratic government then in power believed that the
proposal represented a far-reaching concession to the ideas
of Moscow. Only one part of the proposal, namely the
highest economic parliament, was written into the constitution, under the name of Reich Economic Council
(*Reichswirtschaftsrat*). This council had only advisory
powers, as the highest expert body of German economy ;
but, until the coming to power of the National Socialists,
it played a considerable rôle.

CHAPTER TWO

NAZI ECONOMY AFTER THE TRANSITION PERIOD

From Schacht to Funk, and the Victory of Nazi Politicians over Economics Experts

ALTHOUGH I had failed in my endeavours to create a corporative system (*Ständische Wirtschaftsordnung*), and thus to put German economy on a sound basis, I did not at first give up all hope for a rational economic leadership. The State Council seemed to function quite well at the beginning, and Franz von Papen, who remained vice-chancellor until 1934, made a few quite sensible speeches. I was especially favourably impressed by the great speech he made at Marburg, toward the end of 1933. He seemed to endeavour to strengthen the influence of the conservative elements which he had brought into power along with Hitler.

I congratulated him on his speech, and I had the impression that he himself believed he had accomplished much by delivering it. Many interpreted it at the time as a warning to the National Socialists not to misuse their power.

However, I soon realised that a group of National Socialists, with Goebbels and Ley at their head, were in disagreement with Herr von Papen. Minister of Propaganda Goebbels even prevented the speech from being made known to large sections of the public. Perhaps it was this that made many people think that all this had been prearranged between Papen and Goebbels. This would mean that Papen wanted to lull German business into a sense of security by making his speech, on the assumption that only those present at Marburg would ever get to know it. In this case he would have had to have knowledge of the plan to keep his speech from the broad masses of the people and from the large number of minor business men. However great a scoundrel Herr von Papen may be, I cannot believe that from the very beginning he should have based everything on deceit.

What with the experience I have now acquired, I have come to the conviction that politics and business ought to be pursued by two entirely different sets of people. Indeed, the two things are radically different. It is true that Bismarck demanded that a politician should be honest, thus inferring that a politician *can* be honest. Whether this be possible, I don't know. Yet one thing I do know : that business people are much more likely to tell each other the truth than politicians are. I recollect that, in the course of the conferences of the International Steel Cartel, we always told all the truth to our French, Belgian, and English colleagues. Thus we succeeded in distributing among us the international spheres of influence in a manner satisfactory to all parties.

The National Socialists never had a real economic plan. Some of them were entirely reactionary ; some of them advocated a corporative system ; others represented the viewpoint of the extreme Left. In my opinion, Hitler failed because he thought it very clever to agree with everybody's opinion.

As will be shown in the following chapter, the present nature of National Socialist economy has necessarily led to war. As will be shown later on, it will also lead German economy to complete bankruptcy.

Hitler had an unprecedented opportunity, such as no man will ever again be offered so easily, to create something entirely new. However, besides the fact that he knows absolutely nothing about matters economic, he cannot even fully understand his economic advisers. He is impulsive and always follows his last impressions, but he is not energetic. His constant worry has ever been to keep himself in power. In addition to this, he believes that he alone is a great man, and all others nonentities.

What we witness to-day in German politics, as well as in German economy, is a manifestation of the Prussian spirit. It might be objected that Hitler is not a Prussian, but an Austrian. The only answer to this is that his entourage is entirely Prussian, and Prussian in the worst possible sense. Indeed, his entourage, which is always near him, consists mainly of corporals. It takes a good deal of knowledge of Prussian history to know what the idea of a Prussian corporal really implies. It means the transfer of the barrack-yard into the fields of politics and economics. Whenever new recruits came to a barrack they used to begin their new career by being flogged, by way of enlightenment as to the meaning of military discipline and the respect they owed to those who were doing their second term of military service. This is not necessarily the expression of particular brutality, but rather the continuation of a tradition handed down from the days when the Prussian army consisted not of natives of the country, but of hired soldiers, to whom respect had to be taught right from the start.

Thus the whole population is being oppressed by means of terror, even if they have not been guilty of anything. People must be taught what awaits them if ever they should take any liberties ! This is why no one in Germany dares to criticise anything.

In the early days of the regime, a Supreme Economic Council was created. If at least we had succeeded in keeping it alive, a considerable number of influential industrialists might have stated their opinions without restraint in the council ; and perhaps it would after all have been more difficult to act contrary to their opinion, without further ado. But the Supreme Council held but a single session ; it was never called together again.

The administration of Germany's economy was subsequently distributed among the different national vocational groups (*Reichsstände*). These vocational and economic groups exert a great influence. However, they are under the leadership of men who are either National Socialists, or entirely subservient to National Socialists. At the head of the National Industrialists' Group is Herr Krupp von Bohlen und Halbach. I have already said how well the latter plays the part of a super-Nazi. Among the higher officials of the group of industrialists there also was, for some time, Geheimrat Kastl, who had been one of the leading men of the former National Association of German Industries. Kastl was formerly a Jew. He suffered many vexations on this account, but to-day he is again a much-respected lawyer in Munich. Indeed, everything is possible with the Nazis. They are capable of calling back to-morrow the Jews whom they ousted only yesterday.

Goering himself once told me about the great quarrel he had on account of one of his collaborators, who, it was said, was of Jewish origin. He was none other than the present head of the Air Force, General Milch. Goering told me that he had invited to his house all those who had started the quarrel ; that he had addressed them in an impetuous speech, and that he had declared at the end, " I myself decide who is a Jew, or who is not, and that's all there is to it." But, despite this dictum, the fact remains that Milch has Jewish blood. However, it was simply stated that his mother, who was not Jewish, had conceived him out of wedlock. This is typical of the way in which things are being settled in Germany when no other way out is left. Thanks to a mother's alleged adultery, the world is presented with one more 100 per cent Aryan.

Despite my small fondness for politics, I have attempted on many occasions, at the beginning of the regime, to intervene politically whenever I thought it necessary. However, a single industrialist can really do nothing in Germany. An eminent man once told me he was surprised that nothing had happened to me as yet, although I expressed my opinions so often. Another influential personality, who has made several attempts to protest against the regime (and in dangerous circumstances), told me confidentially that he always carried poison with him. This man did not wish, as he put it, to inflict the National Socialist regime with the guilt of murdering him in his old age. In a word, conditions in Germany have become the same as in Russia. As the GPU rules in Russia, so the Gestapo rules in Germany.

It is a dangerous game, the game that is being played by Himmler, the supreme head of the Gestapo, and next to him by Heydrich, who makes a practice of operating in the dark, although his official power is very great. It has come to the point when even Hitler is afraid of the Gestapo. Those scoundrels know how to turn this to their profit. They constantly tell him that they must protect him, and they protect him so well that he is almost their prisoner. Indeed, Hitler is not at all what he seems to be. He is not a daredevil like Goering ; he constantly fears for his own security. What the Gestapo does in order to " protect him," as they put it, is beyond all imagination.

Hjalmar Schacht, even while as president of the German Reichsbank and minister of economics he was still exerting a relatively great influence, was by no means the man who could put German economy on a safe basis. Indeed, he is not an economist, but a financial technician. Consequently he has not only tolerated the substitution of barter trade for normal export methods, but for propaganda purposes he has announced it to be a great achievement. And yet export is one of Germany's great needs.

My father, August Thyssen, spent his whole life working with the purpose of finding and preserving export markets for his enterprises. And I fully agree with him that the maintenance of a sufficient German export trade would be the only sound basis for the country's well-being. The limitation of the export markets to the south-east of Europe is based on dubious foundations that have little to do with commercial

considerations. The slogan that eighty million people
" need space " is entirely beside the point. It corresponds to the idea of the Roman legionaries when they
wanted to be rewarded for their services with lands
in the conquered territories. A nation of eighty
million people needs export trade to be able to live
on the soil where it is settled. But it needs no new
space, as in the times of the great migrations.

Not even all of the things which Dr. Schacht did in
the financial field were well done. When all is said
and done, he has taken from the German people the
last of their savings. It was he who invented those
false bills of exchange with which armament manufacturers were paid, bills which their banks were
forced to accept. The banks gave those bills to the
Reichsbank when they needed money themselves in
order to pay their clients. The Reichsbank's authority
to discount them represented the only true value of
the bills. What will happen to the depositors of
savings banks after this war no one knows. The only
possible solution I can see is to deal separately with
those whose savings do not exceed 10,000 marks.
For the rest, certainly nothing will be left.

Infinitely worse than Dr. Schacht is his successor as
president of the Reichsbank and minister of economics,
Dr. Funk, a former journalist employed by the
Berliner Börsenzeitung. He is a blind partisan of
National Socialism and pursues an entirely reactionary
economic policy.

On the day Dr. Schacht was virtually dismissed
from his post, a meeting of the Central Administrative
Board of the Reichsbank took place. I was invited by
Dr. Funk to attend. At first I did not desire to go, but
then I thought that the session might in some respects

be entertaining.   My first thought after I had decided to attend the meeting was to say something in praise of Dr. Schacht.   Many newspaper reporters were present, and a series of panegyrics were addressed to Dr. Funk. No one wasted a single word on Schacht.   At last I also thought it was wiser to restrain myself.

The meeting was not followed by the simple *Bierabend* or " beer evening," which was traditional after meetings of the Central Administrative Board of the Reichsbank so long as Dr. Schacht was in office, but by a phenomenal dinner with champagne and all kinds of delicacies.   After dinner was over, Dr. Funk asked me what I thought of his new financial methods. What he had done was to replace the payment in advance by means of Dr. Schacht's false bills with a new method, according to which the arms manufacturers received only official acknowledgments for the receipt of their goods, after the goods were delivered.   These certificates of delivery could be used only with great difficulty.   I told Dr. Funk that all this was merely a plaster which, in my opinion, could not stick for a long time.   Except for this I kept silent and sat down in a distant corner.   Soon, however, numerous gentlemen came over to my table to hear my opinion.   I said nothing and let them talk.

On this occasion I could observe how all the industrialists and bankers present at the meeting had changed sides.   A gentleman who had particularly praised Dr. Funk on this occasion approached me later, in order to have a talk with me.   I discovered a complete lack of character.   Formerly all those who knew anything about business used to say, " As long as Dr. Schacht is there, there is hope."   Now all this was forgotten.

CHAPTER THREE

NAZI QUACK ECONOMY

The Road to National Bankruptcy

HITLER and the Nazi leaders boast that they have freed the German people from misery by rebuilding its economy and by creating work for all. When Hitler came to power, Germany had six to seven million unemployed. There was a terrible economic crisis, and it was necessary to stop a movement that would have led Germany into frightful misery—economic and moral.

But the so-called economic recovery of the Nazi regime is but a blind. In truth, Hitler has created no wealth. He has exhausted all the resources of Germany. He has squandered the taxes and stolen the savings of the people. The entire economic structure of the regime is crumbling to-day under the strain of war. In truth, Hitler resorted to war because he realised, despite his ignorance, that before long his economic methods would lead to inflation and the total ruin of the country.

I was a close observer of all the efforts the Nazis made in the field of economics. Never have I had the impression that the leaders had a plan, nor even that they were animated by a cautious opportunism looking to the rebuilding of German economy. On the contrary, it was obvious that they sought to obtain immediate results for propaganda purposes. Their ideas were sometimes grandiose, but almost always incoherent.

In fact, all the economic ideas of the regime went no further than the building of motor highways, sumptuous architectural projects, and rearmament.

Why did Hitler, as soon as he came to power, make up his mind to build a network of gigantic highways ? There were few automobiles in Germany, and in any case the existing roads were sufficient in almost all parts of the country. I suggested at the time that all German railways should be electrified. This would have created business for the mechanical industries and employed many thousands of skilled workers. Besides, the economic advantage of the enterprise was indisputable.

But Hitler, without ever admitting it, is inspired by Napoleon's example. This turns his mind towards such projects as the replanning and transformation of cities like Berlin, Munich and Hamburg. He desires people to speak of " Adolf Hitler's Highways " as they speak of Napoleon's roads. These highways are certainly important in facilitating rapid long-distance communication. Some of them are splendid roads for tourists. Others even satisfy economic needs. But the network constructed or projected in the course of the pre-war years cannot seriously be justified. Travellers who have driven over the German highways before the war have had an opportunity to notice that they were more than adequate for the volume of automobile traffic. With a few exceptions it would have been less expensive to rebuild the then existing network of roads. This would probably have cost one or two billion marks, instead of the eight billion that have been spent for " Adolf Hitler's Highways."

The first highway built was a tourists' road from Munich to the Austrian frontier. This was the " road of the Führer "—built specially for him. Then the highway from Berlin to Munich was built, in great haste. The engineer in charge of the construction, anxious to court the Führer's favour, was impatient to see him proceed directly from his estate in the Bavarian Alps to Berlin, without leaving the new highway. But far less impatience was shown in the construction of the highway that was to link the industrial cities of the Ruhr, or the arterial road from Hamburg to Berlin. Indeed, even military needs were neglected. For instance, there are no highways west of the Rhine. A road to Aix-la-Chapelle had only just been begun when the war broke out. On the other hand, the military leaders have always been sceptical about the military value of highways. They are broad stripes that run through the landscape in a straight line ; and thus may guide enemy aviation much better than capriciously winding rivers and streams. Moreover they are extremely vulnerable to air raids on account of the innumerable artful constructions along the way. A single bridge, if destroyed, can obstruct the road for hundreds of miles, because the points of communication with the rest of the system are rare and often badly devised.

In the building of highways, as in everything he does, Hitler did not proceed according to a plan. He wanted to create immediately something that would appeal to the public's imagination.

The construction of highways was obviously one of his hobbies. He announced his programme as early as May 1st, 1933, on the occasion of the first National Socialist Labour Day, adding that he would crush all opposition to it. Two months later he forced the government to begin work. Those among the supporters of the party who were penniless and starving immediately began to object in secret. " They build roads for the rich," they said, " it's the rich who own the cars. Workers will never benefit by highways." In fact, the highways have been useful mainly to party leaders, who are all owners of luxurious cars, acquired by the means described in a subsequent chapter.

In order to allay discontent, Hitler conceived of a new idea. Every German shall own his car. He asked industry to devise a popular car model to be built at such a low price that millions could buy it. The *Volkswagen* (People's Car) has been talked of for the past five years and has never been seen on the market. " These cars will be built for the new highways," said the party propagandists ; " an entire family will be able to ride in one of them at 100 kilometres (60 miles) an hour. It is the Führer's Car for the Führer's Roads." The party leaders say that the highways were built for the People's Car. But the People's Car is one of the most bizarre ideas the Nazis ever had. Germany is not the United States. Wages are low. Petrol is expensive. German workers never dreamed of buying a car. They cannot afford the upkeep ; to them it is a luxury. If the Nazis' pretentious dreams had come true, where would millions of gallons of petrol have been taken from?

However, the People's Car has never seen daylight. Dr. Ley had pocketed several million marks' worth of advance subscriptions when the war came—and now there is more important business than manufacturing the People's Car.

Hitler is totally ignorant of economics. He lets himself be taken in by notions which he thinks he understands and which do not make the slightest sense. One day, the great "economist" of the party, Bernard Koehler, grandiloquently pronounced in his presence the slogan that "labour is capital." This signifies absolutely nothing. Yet Hitler has repeated this nonsense, variously paraphrased, in at least twenty speeches. An unfortunate consequence was that the slogan was put into practice and people in Germany began to do just anything, since "labour is capital!"

One day Dr. Schacht, weary of all the futile and costly agitation of the party economists, declared publicly that it was absurd from the economic standpoint to build pyramids in order to occupy the unemployed. Everybody understood what he meant. Through his utterance he attacked the building of highways which cost billions, but which official propaganda proclaimed every day to be the future monument to the imperishable glory of the Führer and the regime. With the same words Dr. Schacht denounced the building mania which possessed all Nazi leaders, from Hitler down to the smallest burgomaster.

His criticism created a sensation. Hitler felt personally attacked, and in his May Day speech he cried : " The men who, several thousands of years ago, imposed upon their people the task of building pyramids knew well what they wanted. By accomplishing that gigantic monument, they wrote four thousand years of history." This was a paraphrase in Nazi style of Bonaparte's address to the soldiers of the Egyptian army : " From the heights of the pyramids forty centuries look down upon you." But Hitler takes himself to be a Pharaoh. His grotesque utterance gives the measure of his understanding in matters economic.

All those redundant formulæ of the type " labour is capital " have contributed to the ruin of German economy. As they were ceaselessly repeated, people who might have been considered to be sensible have ended up by believing them too. During a trip to Brazil, even Ambassador Ritter said to me : " Labour is capital." I was dumbfounded, for he had been for years the head of the economic section of the ministry of foreign affairs. How could he endorse such nonsense ?

The effect of such empty phrases proved disastrous. Everybody began to build, in order to do something. In Düsseldorf three high Nazi officials had each their own project : the one wanted to build a large assembly hall accommodating twenty thousand people ; the other desired a city hall ; the third, a theatre. Of the three projects, the building of a city hall was the most sensible, as it was justified to a certain extent. Hitler decided the matter. He ordered a theatre to be built. Ten million marks in excess of the city budget had to be found. The Nazi have reproached the Socialists of the Weimar Republic with squandering money in building swimming pool and health insurance offices. How modest were the Social Democrats, compared with their successors !

Hitler is constantly afraid of not seeing things in large enough proportions. Pyramids, Napoleonic roads, Roman roads are an obsession with him. He plans his highways for centuries to come. At Nuremberg he builds a congress auditorium to hold several hundred thousand people. He tears down half Berlin to reconstruct it. Money does not count. And unhappy Dr. Schacht had to torture his brain to find a way of financing these unproductive projects. After exhausting himself in protesting he eventually resigned his office. Yet he must bear part of the responsibility. It was he, indeed, who at the beginning of the new regime showed the Nazis how to use credit. No doubt he desired to remain within reasonable limits. But Hitler, seeing that " credit could be created " —according to Dr. Schacht's incautious formula— never wanted to halt his course.

One of Hitler's most incredible projects is the construction of a giant bridge in Hamburg. He has seen photographs of the George Washington Bridge in New York and dreams of having just as imposing a structure in Germany. One day, accompanied by a large staff of Nazi dignitaries, he walked along the banks of the Elbe. Suddenly he stopped and declared, " Here the bridge shall be built ! " The project was submitted to experts. It would have necessitated the building of an immense suspension bridge with foundations about one thousand feet deep, because of the bad terrain. Moreover, the bridge would have obstructed the port. Military experts declared that if it should collapse, under an air bombardment, for instance, the consequences would be disastrous. The

M

cost would have exceeded one billion marks. But the Führer had made up his mind, and, of course, he can never err. If war had not intervened, this absurd structure would have been begun. No one has dared submit the only reasonable solution imposed by necessity. To join the two banks of the Elbe, a tunnel should be dug ; it would be less costly, without involving the disadvantages of a bridge. The Nazis, however, dislike underground construction, probably because there they cannot be seen.

The pet enterprise of the regime was the famous Four-Year Plan. I have always wondered why it was called a " plan." Government regulation of commerce and industry in Germany had led to total state control ; Hitler picked up the Russian idea of the Five-Year Plan. Yet the difference is considerable. The Russians desired to create large-scale industrial production in a country where it was as yet non-existent. Hitler's Four-Year Plan, on the contrary, had no aim except its demagogical effect. All the incoherent enterprises that fall under the head of the so-called Four-Year Plan are as little the fruit of a logical concept and a preconceived plan as the highways, the People's Car, or the pyramids against which Dr. Schacht protested. When Hitler announced the Four-Year Plan at Nuremberg, German industrialists were greatly surprised. He had consulted nobody and no one knew what he meant.

Highways, uniforms, rearmament, large-scale building enterprises, and the leaders' luxury caused vast expenditures. German exports did not suffice to afford the import of the necessary supplies. German exports decreased. They did not bring in sufficient foreign exchange to provide food for the German people and raw materials for industry.

"This shall not embarrass us," Hitler said to himself. "Germany shall produce all she needs. She has scientists, technicians, and inventors. Germany will be explored in its depths. It is a question of will power, intelligence, and energy. The National Socialist regime will overcome all difficulties." And he commissioned Goering with the carrying out of the plan.

Goering knows nothing about economic problems. He is the first to admit it. But he has recipes which he thinks infallible. The first of these is to order. Goering says, "Build a factory that produces a hundred thousand tons of gas per year!" And the factory must be built. Suddenly he declares, "Production must be doubled!" And he thinks that it is enough to will in order to succeed.

His great idea was to make Germany independent of the outside world with regard to iron ore. There are only a few iron mines in Germany, and their ore is of inferior quality. Almost all the ore needed for the metal industries has to be imported from abroad. One day the Nazi experts declared, "There is plenty of iron ore in Germany. But the industrialists do not want to mine it." Indeed, the experts pretended to have discovered considerable deposits at Salzgitter, at the foot of the Harz Mountains, others in the state of Baden and various other places I cannot recall. As a matter of fact, all those deposits were known. The best known of them is the one at Salzgitter. The ore is rather rich, but it contains large quantities of silicon. To be suitable for profitable mining, iron ore must be magnetic ore. It has to be crushed and the iron particles are extracted by means of an electromagnet. But Salzgitter ore is not magnetic. Conditions there are not the same as in Lorraine, where both silicon and calcium iron ores are found, both being mixed in the blast furnaces.

Industrialists, of course, had long known about the Salzgitter ore. It belonged to the Prussian state, and the state had sold it during the previous year. Suddenly Goering became interested in it again, and miracles had to be performed. An American engineer was consulted. He declared that it was a splendid affair and that a large factory had to be built. A party representative, one Pleiger, began to attack industry, which, he said, had not been willing to do anything, To-day he is the director general of the Hermann Goering Works. For this is the name given to the new enterprise.

After consulting the party men, Goering gave the order to build at Salzgitter the largest metal works in the world. The engineer was to carry out the order. His business was building factories. To him it meant a good piece of business. The German metallurgists had not been consulted—no doubt because they knew too much. Now, however, they were invited to take part in the enterprise, so they decided to intervene. They told Goering that they thought that the ore was no good, but they nevertheless agreed to exploit it. If the engineer's statements were correct, they said, they would build blast furnaces and a metal plant at Salzgitter. This would have cost about half a billion marks. The most important industrialists joined to draw up a memorandum which they intended to address to Goering. The latter knew of this intention. At the moment when the memorandum was to be signed, he sent a telegram to two of the firms concerned and let them know that he considered all opposition to his project (and consequently the signing of the memorandum) to be an attempt at sabotage against Germany's iron supply, which was an act of treason. In these conditions it was natural that nobody signed. The factory was built with the participation of the main metallurgical enterprises of Germany : Krupp, Klöckner, the United Steel Works, Mannesmann, etc. There was no way out. Goering had given the order.

This, however, did not prevent the enterprise from turning out a complete failure. The Salzgitter ore cannot be used in its pure state. It must be mixed with Swedish ore according to a formula, which calls for very little native ore and as much Swedish ore as possible.

Uncounted sums of money were spent on the building of the Hermann Goering Works. The best possible equipment was ordered from the United States. Workers' settlements and railroads were constructed ; canals will probably have to be dug. In the meantime, the factory does not work.

Metal industry is above all a matter of transportation. Its raw materials are heavy and unwieldy, and so is the finished product. The ideal site for a metal works is in the neighbourhood of both a coal mine and an iron mine. Before building a new factory my father always used to study the transportation problem with utmost care. The blast furnaces and steel mills of the Ruhr are located in the immediate neighbourhood of the coal mines, and the ore is brought to them either by river or by canal. Similarly, the processing works must be near the places where iron and steel are produced.

In the light of these logical principles, corroborated

by experience, the Salzgitter works are an absurdity.
They are located right in the centre of Germany.
No coal is near them. There is some ore, to be true,
but it cannot be utilised in its pure state. Consequently, all the coal and the ores needed for mixing
have to be brought from distant places, and the pig
iron has to be sent to the industrial regions. It will
never be possible to make such a set-up function
properly.

There you have one of the greatest achievements
of the Four-Year Plan. Under the pretext of making
Germany independent of foreign iron ore, they have
set up a factory which cannot function and which is
forced nevertheless to use imported ore. Such considerations do not stop the Nazis, however. One of
the motives alleged for the construction of the Salzgitter works was to provide Germany with iron in
case of war. Yet the blast furnaces of the Ruhr
have not nearly exhausted their capacity. The Ruhr
furnaces will have to be kept cold in order to keep
Salzgitter producing—and needlessly hauling its coal
and its products to and fro. Workers will also have
to be found and taken away from other occupations.
It is a tissue of nonsense.

One day, Goering declared : " Copper ? Why,
we have plenty of copper in Germany. For years
we have imported it ; consequently, we have considerable stocks."

This is the kind of reasoning that guides the leader
of German economy. It is true, no doubt, that there
are thousands of tons of copper in Germany. But
they are being used. After the war broke out, Goering confiscated all copper utensils that were not
essential. This, however, represents very little. The

copper is in the machines, in the factories, in electric wires, etc., and to recapture it, all the electrical plants of Germany would have to be demolished. This is childish. These people have as primitive notions of technology and economy as the aborigines of Australia. The simple working man is more intelligent in such matters than these " leaders."

Not a single blunder was avoided. At Düsseldorf there lived a swindler who pretended he could make gold. Everybody knew he was a dishonest quack. But he knew the proprietor of the famous hotel at Godesberg where the Führer decided to kill Röhm and where he later received Mr. Neville Chamberlain. Dreesen is the hotel-keeper's name; and Dreesen, who knows all the party dignitaries, told them about the gold maker. So one day Düsseldorf received the visit of Herr Wilhelm Keppler, the personal technical adviser of the Führer; he came with three experts in order to study this extraordinary phenomenon.

An industrialist and mine owner had a chemist who one day submitted to him a report proving that an edible fat which could replace butter could be derived from coal. The industrialist in question is on excellent terms with Goering. The basis of this friendship is worthy of being related. There was in Düsseldorf a kind of painter of a rather bohemian type who used to hunt with a falcon. The industrialist introduced this man to Goering, who decided immediately that this form of hunting, which was practised by the mediæval knights, should be revived. This industrialist, then, went to see Goering and talked to him of the miraculous project of getting butter out of coal. " At last," he said, " we have found the way to fill the largest hole in our food supply." I should insert here that Germany is obliged to import about half of the edible fats she needs. Goering ordered the installation of a large laboratory in order to study the possibilities of making butter with coal. It seems that the laboratory succeeded in extracting a kind of rather solid grease. It is even said that experiments were made on the inmates of the Ploetzensee prison near Berlin. All the prisoners who had eaten their bread with coal butter speedily fell ill with a scurvy-like malady.

Speaking of butter, Goering has just made another discovery worthy of his genius. German farmers use a certain quantity of milk in feeding their livestock. It is indispensable to the young animals.

By skimming the milk, Goering said to himself, additional butter can be produced from the cream. Humans drink skimmed milk, after all. Putting this brilliant idea into practice as soon as it was conceived, Goering ordered all calves to be given skimmed milk. This episode probably had the same *dénouement* for the calves as for the prisoners of Ploetzensee.

The Four-Year Plan provides for the exploitation of all Germany's natural resources. One day the Nazis of Goering's economic staff discovered the Rhine gold. It is true there are some barely perceptible traces of gold in the sand of the river. Upon the Nibelungs'—and Richard Wagner's—testimony it was asserted that this gold was being exploited in the Middle Ages, or by the prehistoric Germans. The Nazi experts proceeded to wash the sand of the Rhine. The result, of course, was nil.

Another story of the same kind, but much more annoying so far as the metal industries are concerned, was the report of a geologist who pretended that the sands of the Baltic Sea contained large quantities of iron. It may be true that there are traces of iron in the sand of the sea. Goering had the question studied with great seriousness and sent us a long memorandum with a request for our opinions. He imagined no doubt that the sea was going to wash Swedish ore to the German shores without its being loaded on board ships.

The Nazis go about trumpeting to the world everything that they think is a discovery. They have made much more ado about the so-called new raw materials invented under the Four-Year Plan. Ingeniously, they have called them *neue Werkstoffe*—new production materials—so as to avoid the word *Ersatz* which has had so bad a sound ever since the last war. Actually they have found several useful substitutes. The use of aluminium and light metals (alloys based on magnesium) has been extended. The use of artificial resins has been broadened. What they have done, on the whole, is to make a virtue of necessity, rather than invent.

All this, however, does not interest heavy industry. The only two products that present a certain interest are artificial rubber and wool. As for rubber, chemists have obtained rather satisfactory results so far as quality is concerned. But the price of production exceeds the price of the natural product to such an extent that it will be a long time before it can be produced on a rational economic basis.

As for cellulose fabrics, the matter is different. The board of German chemical industries have persuaded Goering that to chemists everything is possible. Thus they have produced a fibrous material to which they manage to give the appearance of sheep wool.

This pseudo-wool has, however, two defects. It is not solid, and consequently, no matter how low the price may be, it is too expensive. And, above all, it is not warm. The hair of a sheep is, like all hair, a tube. It seems that it is chiefly the canal in this tube that makes wool a bad conductor of heat. In spite of their dexterity, the chemists of the I.G. Farben concern have not yet been able to poke holes through their fibres of cellulose. Nevertheless, large factories have been built all over Germany for converting tree trunks into wool. The timber has to be imported, but this does not seem to matter. Goering declares that it is less expensive than to import the wool. At the beginning of the regime, I drew attention to the fact that it was unwise to clothe everybody in uniform. It increased to an unjustifiable extent the need for wool. To-day even army uniforms contain a large percentage of artificial wool. During the winter of 1937 it was impossible in my native town of Mühlheim to find woollen underwear for the working population. In order to put the chemists' ideas into practice, the regime has not hesitated to ruin the entire German cloth industry.

In everything incoherence is manifest. The United Steel Works have built a large distillation plant in order to produce artificial gas from coal. The plant was finished and production was to begin. We expected to receive Goering's congratulations. Far from it ! One day we were ordered to transform the entire plant. The factory which had been built to distil coal was to be adapted to the distillation of raw oil. The reason for this is a story in itself. A new oil well had just been discovered, the yield of which was greater than that which previous drillings in Germany had produced. On this ground the men of Berlin imagined that they were going to discover oil-fields comparable to those in Texas ! This is why Goering suddenly desired the transformation of our plant, applying a kind of reasoning that is absolutely typical of him. Once he had said, " There is oil in our country ; we have but to seek and we shall find." And the moment a new well, no matter how mediocre, is found, his imagination immediately pictures quantities of oil gushing from Germany's soil.

The same thing happened with regard to the production of synthetic gasoline. Goering decided that it had to be raised to five million tons. It was said that in this case money was no object ; the government would provide all the needed credits. In fact, all there was to do was build new plants and extend the old ones. No doubt they were right, but to produce one ton of gas requires ten tons of coal. Consequently it would be necessary to raise the output of the coal mines accordingly. But in Berlin they had not thought that far.

Goering is an army man. He imagines that it is enough to give orders for industry to carry them out. If the industrialists declare that it is impossible, they are accused of sabotage. Soon Germany will not be any different from Bolshevik Russia ; the heads of enterprises who do not fulfil the conditions which the " Plan " prescribes will be accused of treason against the German people, and shot.

The United Steel Works owned a small shipyard at Emden. One day Hitler issued orders to transform the yard into a large naval construction plant. We answered that we lacked the funds. Immediately we were given twenty-four million marks. This was two years before the war.   Hitler had suddenly decided to build a large navy.

Taken as a whole, these Nazi achievements are a farrago of economic absurdities.   For seven years I had to struggle with all these ignorant and incapable men.   It is a waste of time to discuss their stupid projects or refute their specious arguments.   In fact, the Nazi regime has ruined German industry.   All the above-mentioned experiments with artificial products will become useless as soon as international trade is restored.   Then Germany will have on her hands immense plants which have swallowed billions of marks and there will be nothing to do but turn them over to the wreckers.   Industries which no longer have enough money to follow technical progress and to keep their equipment up-to-date are in an unfavourable position compared with foreign competition, especially in America.

I have not attempted to describe the theory of the Nazi economic system.   It would be truer to say that the Nazis have no economic system.   They have resorted—in this field, as in most other fields—to all the expedients that happened to come into their heads, with the idea of building up in record time the formidable armaments with which they have attacked the world in order to escape bankruptcy. They have deliberately sacrificed peace-time economy to war production.   The great problem for German industry after the war, will be to re-adapt itself to normal production so as to be able to export and to feed the workers.   If this cannot be done, there will not be six or seven million unemployed, as there were when Nazism came to power, but fifteen million.

CHAPTER FOUR

ADOLF HITLER HAS FAILED

The All-Powerful Gestapo—The Cases of
General Fritsch and General Brauchitsch

WITH Adolf Hitler everything is propaganda. National Socialist Germany has evolved entirely new methods of propaganda, and has used them with great effect and with a profound knowledge of mass psychology. Yet Hitler despises the common people. He has no sympathy for the working man, and is entirely devoid of any social sense. What he does, he does not for the people but for publicity. His " social " policy, therefore, is fundamentally false.

Hitler even started this war for the sake of propaganda. I and many others have taken great pains to keep Germany at peace. But to-day nobody, not even the generals, dare dissent. The Nazi terror imposes a fatal silence on all.

Hitler believed, at first, that neither England nor France would take any action regarding the invasion of Poland. It is true that, despite the consternation caused by Hitler's shocking breach of faith after Munich, some people in England still believed that peace could be maintained. They placed particular trust, it seems, in Heinrich Himmler, head of the Gestapo, because he was a member of the Oxford Group and, by

implication, a pacifist. Even so, Hitler would probabl
not have dared attack if Winston Churchill, then a
ordinary member of Parliament, had not publicl
revealed the incompleteness of British armaments i
the air. It is on such motives as this that Germany
decisions are based.

It is, in any case, difficult for any foreigner t
understand Adolf Hitler's character. Sometimes, ir
deed, his intelligence is astonishing. This peasant
son (for such, at least he pretends to be) often exhibi
miraculous political intuition, devoid of all mora
sense, but extraordinarily precise. Even in a ver
complex situation he discerns what is possible, an
what is not. It is hard to believe that the scion of a
Austrian peasant family should be endowed with so muc
intelligence. One is less puzzled, perhaps, when on
discovers an important gap in Hitler's ancestral line.

According to the published records, Hitler's grand
mother had an illegitimate son, and this son wa
to become the father of Germany's present leade
But an inquiry once ordered by the late Austria
chancellor, Engelbert Dollfuss, yielded some interes
ing results, owing to the fact that the dossiers of th
police department of the Austro-Hungarian monarch
were remarkably complete. According to the
records, the Führer's grandmother became pregnan
during her employment as a servant in a Vienne
family. For this reason she was sent back to h
home in the country. And the family in which th
unfortunate country girl (afterwards Frau Schicke
gruber) was serving, was none other than that
Baron Rothschild. This circumstance throws a ne
light on the story. The Rothschilds, who in th
course of a century had risen from nothing to th

position of one of Europe's great families, certainly did not lack a prescient intelligence—at least not in business! And it is this very type of intelligence that Hitler has been shown to possess in politics. Moreover, this presumed Jewish ancestry of Hitler might also give us a psycho-analytical explanation of his anti-Semitism. By persecuting the Jews, the psycho-analysts would say, Hitler is trying to cleanse himself of his Jewish " taint."

However this may be, Dollfuss prepared a document in which all these facts were established. After his assassination his successor, Dr. Schuschnigg, took possession of the document. Through his spies Hitler was informed of this compromising inquiry. When he asked the Austrian chancellor to come to Berchtesgaden, in February, 1938, he intended to get possession of the document. In order to get hold of it, he began by ordering the arrest of Countess Fugger, Chancellor Schuschnigg's friend, who later—after he was taken prisoner by the Gestapo—became his wife. The compromising document was then given to Baron von Ketteler, the secretary of the Führer's ambassador in Vienna, Herr von Papen. It is quite possible that Papen took care to have the incriminating papers photographed before having them carried to Berlin by Ketteler. It is clear that in these circumstances the unfortunate Schuschnigg, faced by his terrible adversary at Berchtesgaden, was deprived of his one weapon against him— the threat to publish the Dollfuss document which would have revealed Hitler's true origin to the world.

Incidentally, a copy of the document in question is said to be now in the hands of the British Secret Service. At any rate, it may be presumed that the assassination of Chancellor Dollfuss was connected with his inquiry into Hitler's genealogy.

Such details, which would fit admirably into a mystery story, explain many of the Nazis' foreign policy moves. Hitler's domestic policy, however, can be largely interpreted in the light of his relations to the SA. Because he did not succeed in disbanding, at the right moment, this Brown militia, which clamoured for the common reward of proper mercenaries (such as the legionaries of ancient Rome), Hitler was never able to achieve a well-ordered body politic. The Storm Troopers always maintained that it was their great merit to have demonstrated with Hitler in front of the Feldherrnhalle at Munich. This they considered a great deed of heroism. The situation eventually culminated in the June massacres of 1934. In these " purges " Hitler was obliged to order the murder of Röhm, the organiser of the SA, because he feared a conflict with the army to be imminent. After Röhm's death the leadership of the SA was taken over by one Herr Lutze, a grossly stupid person, certainly no " leader " for these gangs, over whom he had no control.

Strangely enough, the army took no further action once it had got rid of its chief enemy, Röhm. The generals considered his elimination to be sufficient, and eventually became the faithful servants of the National Socialists. Only old General von Mackensen tried at first to protest. Now, however, his son is married to the daughter of the former German minister of foreign affairs, the present " protector " of Bohemia-Moravia, Baron von Neurath. Old General von Mackensen has been presented with an estate by the Reich. That the Mackensen family should thus accept gifts from Hitler as though they came from the emperor, is more than strange. Mackensen, by the way, persisted in his opinion that he received the present as a reward for his services in the first World War.

Certain high officers have probably also been bought. The following story, for instance, is told about General von Brauchitsch. The general, who was over fifty years of age, had fallen in love with a young lady and wished to marry her. For this purpose he had to be divorced, but his first wife demanded an extremely high settlement for her consent. The general did not possess the means of satisfying her demands, for —in contrast to the party —corruption in the army is still unknown. The Brauchitsch story was reported to Adolf Hitler, who is always eager to be informed of all kinds of personal affairs. It was he who gave General von Brauchitsch the needed sum. This episode is quite typical of Hitler's character. He misses no opportunity of buying important people, or their conscience.

General von Fritsch's affair is also a good sample of the peculiar methods used by the Hitler regime. Fritsch was known to be one of the most efficient officers in the German army, and was backed by a great number of high officers. Fritsch was to be " liquidated." To achieve this, it is said, the head of the Gestapo personally reproached him with practising homo-sexuality. Fritsch, who denied this from the very start, was ordered to call at the chancellery of the Reich, where he was to be unmasked in the presence of the Supreme Leader. There he was confronted with a young man who was supposed to be the chief witness for the prosecution. This young man had actually had relations with a gentleman called Fritsch, but he had to admit that it was not the general.

Nevertheless the Gestapo persisted for a long time

N

in asserting that the man in question was really General von Fritsch. To rehabilitate him, a court-martial was summoned under Goering's chairmanship. Here Goering had an opportunity to win over the entire army, simply by a few reasonable words. He did not say them, however, and ever since then his relations with the army have been strained.

It seems certain that General von Fritsch has subsequently committed suicide. I can at least say that whatever the actual circumstances of his death may have been, he was anxious to die. This had nothing to do, however, with the above-mentioned affair, after which he was completely rehabilitated. It was because, to his utter grief, he eventually had to witness the entire army's submission to Hitler. He had never been a sincere follower of Hitler, like, for instance, General von Reichenau. Fritsch always advocated an alliance with Russia, though not with a Communist Russia. Attempts were made to establish relations between Fritsch and the Russian generalissimo, Tuchachevsky. The two had one point in common : each desired to overthrow the dictator in his own country.

Fritsch, moreover, was one of those generals who opposed an attack on Belgium and Holland, and it is he who must definitely be credited with preventing Germany from occupying these countries before the actual outbreak of war. Incidentally, even the National Socialist General von Reichenau opposed this plan. Fritsch was in despair when the attack on Poland began. He had always opposed it.

Hitler owes it to Himmler that a final solution of the SA question was reached. Himmler had created the black-clad SS organisations, and with their help he ruthlessly carried out the execution of thousands of SA men in June, 1934. Now Himmler is the most powerful man in National Socialist Germany. Indeed, he holds much more power than Goering himself. He is everywhere and dominates everything.

Himmler has his own personal circle of industrialists. Director General Vögler, among others, belongs to this circle. Everybody in Germany is literally spying to find out who holds the greatest power at the moment, so as to become as close an ally of the powerful one as possible.

Himmler has strongly developed inclinations for Germanic research. He sponsored the search for the ashes of the ancient Saxon King, Henry I (the " Fowler "). These remains were interred at a great ceremony to which crowds of people were invited, among them also some leaders of industry. One of those present gave me the following account of it.

At night, by the light of torches and flames, a strange procession moved in the direction of the cathedral of Quedlinburg. Heinrich Himmler marched at the head, followed by the general staff of the SS, wearing their " Death Helmets," and industrialists in long coats. The whole thing seemed to be an imitation of the ceremonies performed by the Catholic Church, when a sacred relic has been discovered. They descended into the crypt, where officers of the SS stood guard before an open coffin. The participants in the procession stood at a respectful distance. Himmler alone proceeded to the coffin of the royal protagonist of his race. The chief of the parading SS troops, who had supervised the excavations, made a report. " I herewith present to you," he said, " within this coffin, the mortal remains of Henry the Fowler."

Heinrich Himmler examined the bones and declared them to be authentic. In National Socialist Germany the decision of the chief of the Gestapo is naturally infallible, even in such matters as this. So the coffin was shut, sealed, and solemnly buried in the crypt.

It is perhaps not unimportant to remind the reader that Herr Himmler and his aide, Herr Heydrich, who has already been described, are more than anyone else responsible for the crimes committed in Germany's concentration camps. It is sad, indeed, that so many great industrialists court the favour of the strongest, even when he is an executioner.

Let me mention incidentally that Alfred Rosenberg is less interested in the earthly remains of mediæval Saxon kings than in the remains of Scandinavians in Germany. Herr Rosenberg, the author of the book entitled *The Myth of the Twentieth Century*, is the representative of National Socialist Germany's education and culture. He is not really a German ; he was educated at Russian universities and belonged to Latvian student societies. However, he is one of the super-Aryans of the National Socialist Reich.

Shortly before the outbreak of the war I was invited to Pomerania. There I heard to my surprise that excavations were in progress in the neighbourhood. In fact, the excavations had just met with success. Bones of Scandinavians were found. This " proved " Rosenberg's old theory that the Prussian province of Pomerania has always been purely Aryan. I expressed my astonishment, for so far as I knew Pomerania was settled by Slavs. But this well-known fact signifies nothing to-day, for Rosenberg wills it differently. All these excavations are, of course, childish ; yet in Germany there is method even in the most absurd childishness.

All this might perhaps be overlooked if politics were practised as methodically. But whoever thinks that this is being done has an entirely wrong conception of the country. There is no such thing as an administration with its centre in Berlin. As regards internal order, Hitler has achieved exactly nothing. He thought it was very smart to build up a governmental system in which all the powers cancel each other out. Alongside the mayor of a city there always sits a party functionary known as a *Kreisleiter* (district leader). And so it is with every important post. If the two men who have been put side by side agree with each other, the situation is tolerable ; if not, there is perpetual strife, which of course is harmful to the entire government structure. These conditions are entirely unknown to the public ; yet they are pernicious.

Indeed, this mutual cancelling out of forces is noticeable in all fields. Theoretically, for instance, the owner of a factory is also its manager ; yet a representative of the Labour Front is put alongside of him, and unless he is bribed he constantly interferes.

The first National Socialist minister of economy, Dr. Schmidt, who had previously been one of the most esteemed insurance directors, and who later on was dismissed by the National Socialists, has given me several particulars on the subject. According to him, it is sometimes the minister of economy who governs, and sometimes someone else. The central power no longer functions at all. For two years the German cabinet has not met. No directions are given anywhere. The only institution that exists to-day in Germany, in the place of order, is a colossal system of corruption. Examples of the technique and the new methods of this unparalleled corruption, as I came to know them through personal experience, will be given in the following chapter.

CHAPTER FIVE

NAZI ORGANISED GRAFT

The Exploitation of the State

WHEN the National Socialist party came to power in 1933, its leaders were poor. Hitler lived an ascetic life in his modest house at Berchtesgaden. He used almost all the proceeds of his literary labours to finance his political activity. The party was burdened with debts. Its cash had been exhausted by the financing of the electoral campaign of 1932.

To-day, however, " the Party governs the State." It no longer has debts. Everywhere, palaces are being built in its name. Even its small-time leaders have become millionaires. Goering owns about half a dozen castles in Germany and a villa in Switzerland. In 1933 he had nothing but debts. Goebbels has a sumptuous home, which formerly belonged to a Jewish banker, on the island of Schwanenwerder near Berlin. Himmler owns a villa in Berlin and has bought a large estate in Bavaria. Ribbentrop is the only one who was not poor, since he had married the daughter of the rich German champagne manufacturer Henckel. Nevertheless he has become a thief. After the assassination of my nephew, von Remnitz, in the concentration camp of Dachau, he took over his castle at Fuschl near Salzburg; and he even had the impudence to invite Count Ciano, the Italian minister of foreign affairs, to his stolen home.

In the lower party ranks, the picture is the same. The Gauleiters and the delegates of the Labour Front have their seats on the boards of directors of the great industrial corporations. Albert Förster, the young Gauleiter of Danzig, arrived in that ancient city without a penny in his pockets. To-day, he is a landowner of great wealth.

Where are the times when National Socialism fought against the " rottenness of the Weimar system " ? The party then demanded a thousand-mark limit to the salaries of state officials. In all mass meetings Goebbels exposed the " corruption " of the political *Bonzen* (moguls) holding government posts. A former Social Democratic minister, attacked by Goebbels and accused of having grown rich at the expense of the state, was obliged to explain that the modest house in which he lived near Berlin had been built by a low-priced building and loan society, to which he continued to pay annuities.

In those days of the distant past the National Socialists presented themselves to the public as the champions of virtue and disinterestedness. As soon as they held the power, they raised graft to the status of a state institution.

Ever since 1933 there has been no regular public accounting in Germany. The budgets of the Reich, of the individual states, of the municipalities, of the party, and of party organisations are secret and uncontrollable. How Germany's public finances are being handled I shall explain later on.

Aside from public finance, there is a multitude of special funds that are fed by the public without its knowledge. Those funds are at the disposal of some party leader who can draw from them without accounting for his drafts. The methods used are of various kinds. In the end, however, it is the German people who always pay for the luxuries of all their satraps, great and small.

To everyone his due. Goering, field marshal and prime minister of Prussia, incarnates the corruption of the regime. He practises graft on a scale commensurate with government operations rather than private or business deals. Goering is the sovereign of Prussia ; he administers its state domains (the former crown properties). The Prussian state grants him free disposal over its lands for his own personal use. He distributes those lands as compensations for services rendered to him. Old President von Hindenburg did not disdain to accept a castle and several thousand hectares of lands and forests from the hands of Goering, whom he had just made a general. This looked like a gift of gratitude. But the old field marshal, and, above all his son, Oscar, land-greedy like all Junkers, considered this quite normal, as though Goering had been king of Prussia. Field Marshal von Mackensen, who was then over eighty, was gratified with a more modest domain. This also came from Goering as a gift in the name of the state of Prussia. Yet Mackensen far from approved of all the acts of the present rulers of Germany, toward whom his attitude was definitely cool—especially after the religious persecutions which have taken place.

But Goering is generous especially to himself. He accumulates various public salaries ; he receives a field marshal's pay, a salary as president of the

Reichstag, another as minister for air, and another as prime minister of Prussia. I mention only in passing his titles of Great Master of the Forests and Chief Huntsman of the Reich and of Prussia : in connection with these, too, Goering is not the man to refuse a monthly salary. The revenues he derives from his public functions certainly exceed two million marks a year, paid out of the budgets of the Reich and the state of Prussia. Where is the thousand-mark limit to which the Nazis once promised to reduce the monthly salaries of all state officials and public administrators?

But Goering is not content with merely depleting the budget by his salaries. As prime minister he is virtually proprietor of the Prussian state. Hitler boasts of having unified Germany and suppressed the old federated states. But so far as Goering is concerned, the Prussian state certainly does continue to exist. It is the domain which he exploits, and never has any king of Prussia lived on his subjects as magnificently as the field marshal ! Whatever belongs to Prussia belongs to him. He made himself a present —for his private use—of several thousand hectares of wooded lands in the beautiful forest of Schorfheide north of Berlin. This forms a superb natural park, where Goering breeds elks and aurochs. I shall not speak of the hunting personnel, which is extravagant. The gamekeepers of course are state officials ; for Goering, differing from the kings of Prussia, maintains no royal household out of his own pocket. In these magnificent surroundings he has built his mansion of Karin Hall. Sans Souci, in comparison, is but a hut, although Frederick the Great spent the whole of his reign embellishing it.

Goering owns another palace in Berlin. After the

Reichstag fire he left the house of the president of the
Reichstag where he had lived until then. No doubt
the atmosphere no longer agreed with him.[1] A new
residence has been built for him in the gardens of the
old Prussian House of Lords, next to the new Air
Ministry. A whole section of Berlin at the very
centre of the city forms a regular " Goering City,"
with his private palace, the *Herrenhaus*, the House of
Aviators, and the impressive building of the Air
Ministry, completed in 1935.

Being the second most important man in Germany,
Goering felt he owed it to himself to own, like the Führer,
a villa in the Bavarian Alps. The prime minister of
Bavaria, knowing his desire, offered him land at Obersalzberg, facing the Führer's property. Goering's public revenues, however important, would not suffice to
finance all these luxuries. Several years after his coming
to power he continued to have debts, and the personal
intervention of Hitler was necessary to make him pay up.

Goering also receives bribes. He was made commissioner of the Four-Year Plan and the economic
dictator of Germany. The industrialists are anxious
to remain on good terms with him. They offer him
gifts on such occasions as his marriage or his birthday.
The latter, inevitably, returns every year ; and this
is the date for which the generosity of donors is
organised long in advance. Several months before
the day the head of such-and-such an industrial
organisation receives suggestions for a gift in cash or
in kind. An emissary of Goering's comes to inform
him discreetly that a certain picture, a statue, or an
ancient tapestry would please the field marshal. The

[1] *Author's Note* : It was established at the Reichstag fire trial
that a subterranean passage connected this building with the Reichstag, through which incendiary materials could have been transported.

location of the object in question and the address of the antiquary is given on this occasion. Sometimes the antiquary himself comes to see the chosen victim. This victim cannot evade the honour done him. The antiquary and Goering always manage to arrange a good bargain.

The prime minister of Prussia owns several collections of paintings. Some of the pictures come from the various Prussian state museums. One day a picture was taken from the Cologne Museum. When its director asked for explanations, it was declared that the picture was to be exchanged in Paris for a tapestry. The tapestry should at least have been sent to the museum ; but the reply to the director's questions was, " Don't worry, it is at Goering's."

I, too, have the satisfaction of also having contributed in a modest way to the enhancement of the field marshal's picture gallery ; for he has had taken away the paintings that belonged to me at my home at Mühlheim, and those belonging to my children in Bavaria.

But Goering, amidst this artistic luxury, does not forget that the Führer is the father of his wealth. When visitors come to see him at his Berlin residence he shows them, with great feeling, a small water colour representing a ruined village in the north of France. This is a personal gift from the Führer, who painted it during the first World War. Goering affects to hold it above a Flemish primitive or an Italian master.

He also displays other picturesque traits of character. He likes jewels. He used to have an agent, the well-known Jewish jeweller Friedlaender in Berlin. It was even said that he owed him a large sum of money. After Jews had been expelled from German business, Goering became the proprietor of the Friedlaender jewellery firm.

Goering does not stick to any particular method or

satisfying his luxurious tastes—or, rather, he uses all methods. He disposes of the Prussian state revenues, he accepts bribes from industry, he takes advantage of confiscations—all is grist to his mill.

Next to him, Hitler is a model of virtue. When he became chancellor of the Reich he renounced the usual salary with a noble gesture. Never had his predecessors, Stresemann or Dr. Brüning, done as much ! I do not know whether this gesture has been followed through. Nevertheless, Hitler is the richest man in Germany. It is true that he has not grown rich on public revenues. His whole fortune is due to his pen. Indeed, Hitler is a man of letters. He is, if not the most read, at least the most purchased, of all men of letters in the world. *Mein Kampf* has reached a sale of seven or eight million copies. By a decision of the Reich ministry of the interior this book is distributed at the cost of the municipalities to all newly-wed couples. And marriages have increased a great deal in Germany since Hitler's rule, although the Führer himself has remained a bachelor.

Hitler holds most of the stock in the party publishing house—Franz Eher, of Munich, Berlin, and Vienna. Franz Eher publishes the *Völkischer Beobachter* and all the party periodicals. These official party papers are widely circulated. For all officials and notables, and for all those who depend more or less on public authority, a subscription is morally obligatory ; it is a proof of loyalty toward the regime. Party officials solicit subscriptions from door to door, through the country and in the towns. It is difficult to refuse. The *Völkischer Beobachter*, the most widely read Nazi daily, has succeeded in monopolising all the advertisements that once appeared in the organs of business and industry. All this is very profitable. Herr Hitler, man of letters, publisher, owner of several papers, earns several million marks yearly in his own right, as has just been shown. He can, therefore, renounce the salary due to him as chancellor. Besides, he also receives the emoluments of the president of the Reich.

It is true that his needs are modest. He does not care for good food, he neither smokes nor drinks, and he has no mistress. Brüning, the ascetic, at least smoked cigars. But Hitler, like Goering, has a weakness for paintings. In truth, as he likes to say, if he had not entered politics he would have devoted his life to painting. Sometimes he buys pictures by the Old Masters with his own money, but above all he accepts gifts. Cities and states have offered him several museum pieces. Numerous also are those private citizens who wish to prove their gratitude or their admiration to the Führer. But Hitler does not go himself to the art dealers, as Goering does. He uses his photographer, Hoffmann, as an intermediary. The latter is the only official photographer authorised by Hitler and his regime. This monopoly brings him a fortune. But he does not consider it beneath his dignity to earn commissions on works of art. His method is about the same as people who serve Goering, with the difference that it costs the victim even more. An art dealer of reputation will go to one of his best customers and address him somewhat as follows : " I now have a certain picture for sale. I know that our beloved Führer would like it very much. Wouldn't you like to make him a gift of it ? " Everybody knows what this means, and the suggestion is complied with.

But it also happens that Hitler presents a painting to someone to whom he wishes to do a favour. One day he sent to Dr. Hjalmar Schacht a painting by the classic German genre painter Spitzweg, in a superb frame. Schacht noticed immediately that it was a vulgar copy of a well-known original. Thinking that the Führer had been deceived, he sent the painting back to him saying it was a copy. Infuriated, Hitler declared, " This copy is an original ! " After all, why not, since the axiom of the regime is " the Führer is always right " ? Several months later visitors still could see in Schacht's drawing-room an empty frame with a small note in the owner's hand : " This frame contained a copy from Spitzweg presented by the Führer."

Poor Schacht ! He used to control the finances of the regime, but never was able to obtain a correct account from its masters. I do not think that one can find in any modern state procedures similar to those current in Germany for financing irregular expenses. The party has its private army. I do not refer to the Storm Troopers—the S.A.—for since the purging of Röhm they have been reduced to the second rank. The local sections live at the expense of the central party funds, or on the proceeds of their lootings, especially after the confiscation of Jewish property. But the SS, Himmler's Black militia, who serve as a Prætorian Guard for Hitler and the grandees of the regime, have their own means of existence. In this particular case graft plays an important political rôle. It is Walter Darré, minister of agriculture, who finances Himmler and his SS. In return, Himmler and the Gestapo support Darré against his enemies. This accounts for the fact that he still retains his position, despite his insignificance.

One may well ask, whence come these funds? The answer is simple. In the early years of the regime Darré established a so-called domestic price control, in order to protect German agriculture. The aim of this measure is, according to Darré, to encourage farmers to grow all that the German people need. This undertaking is absurd, but it plays an important part in Nazi phraseology. It plunged Germany into a food crisis long before the present war and reduced it to the use of ration cards. In peacetime, and even now in wartime, despite very severe restrictions, Germany is obliged to import part of the produce necessary for its maintenance. In the course of the past few years these imports have amounted to about a billion and a half marks per annum. Purchases abroad are made for the account of the *Reichsnährstand*, the National Food Corporation, directed by Darré in his quality of Reich minister and chief of the farmers' organisation, which is dependent on the party. The merchandise bought at the exchange current abroad is resold in the German market at a rate fixed by Herr Darré. The difference is appreciable ; it can reach several hundreds of millions of marks, according to the year. An estimate of half a billion marks annually would not be too high. The Reichsnährstand in consequence is very rich. With the sums thus acquired it finances its own " Politico-Agrarian " apparatus, as they call it. This organisation has a representative in every region, every district, every village ; and each representative is paid according to his grade. Herr Walter Darré has acquired and renovated a medieval imperial castle at Goslar, an ancient and picturesque town in the centre of Germany. It is there that he has installed his offices, far from Berlin and the central administration. In his choice of surroundings he shows romantic leanings, but this romanticism also serves to mask corruption.

He runs experimental farms for the raising of silk-worms, hemp, flax, mulberries, soya beans, and for various other useless and bizarre projects. He subsidises Alfred Rosenberg, the originator of the neo-pagan Aryan cult, and his historical or pre-historical researches. The sums are taken from the household budgets of every German worker, since they are the product of the arbitrary level of German food prices. This is the way in which the Aryan hobby-horses of the regime are being fed. As she buys her scant portion of rationed food, every German housewife can look with satisfaction upon her modest contribution toward the exhumation of Viking bones from the sands of Pomerania, or upon the support she gives to the archæological pseudo-science with which the Nazis fill our ears.

All this does not go far enough. The man who appropriates most of the budget of the Reichsnähr-stand, and consequently the tribute levied on the budget of every German worker, is Heinrich Himmler, who needs it for his Gestapo and his army of prætorians, spies, and torturers. The difference between domestic prices and foreign prices might have been converted into a compensation fund and thus served to lower the price level of certain necessities of life. But nothing of the kind has been done. The German people pay for all edibles a price far above the world price, not in order to favour the development of agriculture, but to support the spies set to watch them, and the torturers of their kind.

These gentry still have another accessory source of

income. A certain number of well-to-do personalities are solicited to pay a regular contribution to the SS. In return they receive a diploma and a pin bearing the two initials of the Black militia. They are called " Protectors of the SS." This honour costs dear, but it serves as a " recommendation " to the Gestapo. Industrialists, merchants, and officials compete for it, especially if they are not members of the party. Thus they believe themselves to be protected by Himmler. This is reminiscent of the tribute which merchants and burghers of the Middle Ages used to pay to the robber barons in order to protect their goods and lives.

How does Himmler dispose of all these funds ? He pays his men, builds barracks and social centres for his troops, villas or country homes for himself and other chiefs of the Gestapo, and purchases arms independently of the ministry of war. Himmler, like Darré, likes to give sumptuous feasts. He pays his spies in Germany and abroad. Who knows ?—perhaps even the concentration camps that depend on the chief of the Gestapo may be supported by the modest budget of the workers, thanks to the arbitrary level of prices of food.

I have already mentioned one particular customer of Darré—Alfred Rosenberg. This pseudo-philosopher of Russian origin directs an organisation named " Foreign Policy Bureau of the National Socialist Party." It includes an entire staff of conspirators who spread their ramifications even abroad. It is Alfred Rosenberg who subsidises the White Russians residing in Germany. He supports a militia composed of young Russians who are resolved to do anything to bring about the overthrow of Stalin. I do not

O

know whether the pact with the Russian dictator has put an end to that underground activity.[1]

So far as he himself is concerned, Rosenberg passes for being disinterested. It is said that he sacrifices his personal income to the cause. When Hitler presented him with the German Grand Prize for philosophy (which has replaced the Nobel Prize so far as Germany is concerned), he was said to be very poor. However, his anti-Christian books sell well. School libraries, even in the Catholic Rhineland, are obliged to buy them !

Baldur von Schirach and his " Hitler Youth " are also subsidised out of the budget of the housewives through the food ministry. Thus Baldur von Schirach defrays the expenses of his staff, pays for his journeys abroad, and keeps his whole army of young boys and young girls. Darré, Himmler, and Baldur von Schirach form the radical group of the National Socialist party ; its influence is considerable. Their alliance rests on their complicity in graft. This is one of the consequences of the curious methods of financing that exist in Germany to-day.

After those of Darré, the most considerable " black " funds are probably those of Dr. Ley, the stammering drunkard who is the chief of the German Labour Front. He controls the four to five hundred million marks paid in every year by the German workers as dues to the Labour Front.

I do not say that he puts all this money into his own pocket. But the figure has certainly turned his head. He is in the situation of a man who has won a million in the sweepstakes. He is in quest of oppor-

---

[1] *Publisher's Note* : This was, of course, written before the outbreak of the Nazi-Soviet war.

tunities to spend his money. He ordered the construction of an entire fleet. One of the boats bore his name and has been sunk, it seems, while transporting troops to Norway. With these boats he used to organise trips to Madeira and the Scandinavian fjords. He had an automobile factory built for the production of the People's Car. On this occasion he invented a brand new form of knavery. The future buyers of the People's Car were invited to buy it in advance, by making pre-delivery instalments. This is the reverse of the credit instalment system. The system shows genius. Ley pocketed about a hundred million marks when the war came ; because the People's Car factory now had to produce tanks and motor-cycles for the army.

It is Ley who has invented the holiday organisation bearing the strange name of *Kraft durch Freude* (Strength through Joy). This organisation owns large and new tourist boats which Ley uses for " workers' cruises." In fact, it is the Nazi moguls, large and small, who were the first ones to profit. Strength through Joy publishes several illustrated reviews of incredible lavishness and utter uselessness. It has rented beaches along the Baltic Sea. At the famous resort of Rügen Dr. Ley has had constructed an enormous hotel, accommodating twenty-five thousand people. One might wonder how people can rest in such a crush. But Ley does not take them to Rügen for their rest. The National Socialist purpose in organising the Strength through Joy was not leisure for the worker. Leisure would be dangerous to the Nazi regime. People would have time to think, and this must be avoided by keeping them busy without interruption. To prevent them from thinking, they are provided with physical pastimes. They are never allowed to be their own masters. Such is, in Ley's own words, the idea that inspired the construction of the hotel on the island of Rügen.

Ley is also responsible for the building of an immense palace for the Labour Front, in the west of Berlin. The building is larger than any other ministry, even Goering's Ministry of the Air, which is of grandiose proportions. Thousands of officials " work " there. It also comprises sumptuous reception halls. One day I was invited to one of Ley's receptions. It was magnificent. In the lobby a fat man was parading up and down in a beautiful uniform and with numerous decorations. He was the hall-porter of the palace. Some workers who were invited to the reception took him for Goering and greeted him most respectfully.

In order not to lag behind Himmler (to whom he certainly also gives money) Ley has created his own workers' militia, called the *Werkscharen*, or Factory Legions. They are composed of tall young men from eighteen to twenty, clad in a blue uniform. Ley is very proud of them. Thus he owns, like every other Nazi grandee, his own little private army.

Out of the hundred of millions that go through his hands, Ley keeps a small share for his personal needs. He has had built for himself a handsome villa in an aristocratic section of Berlin. An antiquary who is a friend of mine told me that he had one day been called to Ley's house. He had to wait for about half an hour in the waiting-room where the S.S. men on watch were comfortably resting in large armchairs, their revolvers sticking in their belts. At last he was ushered into Frau Ley's apartment. She once was a salesgirl in a large Cologne store. She had decided to buy a " tapestry," no doubt because the possession of tapestry to her was the sure hallmark of a certain social rank.

" I have asked you to come," she said to the antiquary, " because I should like to have a tapestry."

" I am at your disposal, madam. Have you something particular in mind ? "

" No," said Frau Ley, " except that I want to have a genuine one."

At that moment Dr. Ley came in and solved the problem : " That's very easy—we'll take the most expensive one ! "

Frau Himmler, the wife of the Gestapo chief, is on about the same cultural level.

Frau von Mackensen, daughter of Baron von Neurath (now " protector " of Bohemia) and wife of the German ambassador to Rome, thought one day that it would be a good thing to pay a call on the wife of the most powerful person in Germany. An ambassador may deem it useful to take certain precautions. Frau von Mackensen arrived and made her curtsey to Frau Himmler almost as though she were the queen of Italy. But Frau Himmler, without giving herself the time to return the compliment, rushed to her guest in order to feel the material of her dress, exclaiming, " What ! You still have genuine silk ? " The ladies of the new gentlemen who are ruling Germany appreciate " genuine " values.

Next to Goering, Himmler, Darré, and Ley, Dr. Goebbels appears rather like a pauper. He has no private army, and his " black " funds amount to scarcely more than two hundred million marks a year. Darré's and Ley's both exceed half a billion. Goebbels' two hundred million are the monthly licence fees from the radio listeners. From these sums Goebbels has to defray the programme costs. Nevertheless, a nice sum is left over for his personal use. For his private needs he has, besides, the products of his pen—an appreciable sum—for under the Nazi regime the prose of the official authors finds many compulsory buyers. Besides this, Goebbels owns shares in a film corporation. His luxury, however, is of a more modest character than Goering's or Himmler's. Goebbels has not the physique of a castle knight. He is content with a sumptuous but discreetly hidden villa at Schwanenwerder on the River Havel (near Berlin). Instead of buying lands in Germany he cautiously converts his savings into international values, deposited in foreign banks.

It is interesting to note that the Berlin population tolerates with a certain amount of indulgence the extravagances of Goering, but does not forgive Dr. Goebbels anything. One day the latter had a film shown in Berlin picture-houses ; it represented his family in his beautiful home at Schwanenwerder. The audience hissed energetically in the dark. The picture was immediately withdrawn.

Such are the people who to-day govern Germany. It is astonishing how they can afford the impudence of proclaiming themselves Socialists and of insulting, from amidst their corruption, the " western plutocracies," to use their phrase. The vast majority of the German people know nothing of these refined methods of growing rich at the expense of the common weal and the sweat of the working masses. Some day, when they learn how they were deceived and scorned by their leaders, their fury will be terrible.

CHAPTER SIX

THE ANTI-JEWISH CAMPAIGN AND THE CONCENTRATION CAMPS

FROM the moment they seized power, the Nazi leaders professed the greatest contempt for the individual. A large number of German conservatives, ignorant of the facts and appalled by the burning of the Reichstag, assented to the incarceration of the political enemies of the regime without a trial. They may have regarded this measure as purely provisional and justified by the danger of civil war, and assumed that the National Socialists would soon reinstate legal procedure. They were mistaken. The concentration camps, better called torture camps, are, to this day, a state institution. Despite all my inquiries, I have never learned in what circumstances my nephew, von Remnitz, died at Dachau.

One of the outstanding cases which I found particularly shocking was the imprisonment of the Protestant pastor, Martin Niemöller, in the concentration camp of Oranienburg. Martin Niemöller had been a naval officer. During the war of 1914–1918 he commanded a submarine. After the war he became a pastor. When the National Socialists attempted to lay hands on the Protestant Church and to compel it to bow to the anti-Christian spirit of the regime, Niemöller led the resistance in the religious field. For a long time that tall and imposing figure with its pale, ascetic countenance stood erect in the pulpit of his church in Dahlem near Berlin. He courageously defended the law of the Gospel against the Nazis' outrageous schemes. He was the champion of freedom of conscience against the oppressor. The little church was too small to hold the numbers of people who crowded to hear him, in spite of the watchfulness of the Gestapo. Among the followers of the fearless priest was the finance minister of the Reich, Count Lutz von Schwerin-Krosigk. Goering's sister, Frau Rigle, had had her son confirmed by Niemöller. He had long been protected by Goering and the army, for Frau Rigle had undertaken to intercede for him with her brother. But there came a day when Goering forbade her to mention his name.

Hitler felt that the tongue of this free and fearless man was a danger to his regime. It was he who gave the order for Niemöller's arrest. The pastor was summoned before the Berlin court on the charge of breaking some old law of Bismarck's concerning preaching. He was acquitted by the court. He ought to have been released at once. But, despite his popularity, despite the vindication of his honesty and his innocence by the court, Hitler did not hesitate to commit a fresh inquiry. On leaving the court Niemöller was taken by the Gestapo and interned in the concentration camp of Oranienburg. Later, old Marshal von Mackensen made a touching attempt to obtain his release. Hitler refused.

Deprived of their home, Frau Niemöller and the pastor's eight children were in a very difficult situation. A friend of the family came to their aid. As he was not well off himself, he approached some Westphalian industrialists—Niemöller was a native of Elberfeld— and asked them to help. They all agreed with alacrity —except Albert Vögler, who promised his assistance, but revoked it at the last moment for fear of displeasing the regime.

Catholic that I am, and brought up in that tradition, I bow before that noble Protestant, Martin Niemöller. As an officer, he displayed courage during the war. But more than that, he has set the Germans an example of a rarer virtue : in refusing to be silenced by the Gestapo, Pastor Martin Niemöller has shown the Germans what is meant by civic courage—that virtue which Bismarck used to say was unknown in the country.

The persecution of the Jews reached its height in the autumn of 1938 and aroused universal protest. Up to 1933 I had not attached much importance to the anti-Semitic brawls of the National Socialist party. The inhabitants of the Catholic provinces of the Rhine are not anti-Semitic. There may be regions in Germany where the slow-wittedness of the popula tion has enabled the Jews to play an exaggerated rôle. This has never been the case in the Rhineland. We have always considered the Jew Heinrich Heine as one of our national poets. The Nazis may destroy Heine's statue in his native city of Düsseldorf, but they will never be able to prevent people from singing " Die Lorelei " on the boats that sail down the Rhine.

Some months after coming to power the National Socialist party organised riotous anti-Jewish demonstrations throughout Germany. To please their following of small shopkeepers suffering from the depression, and to give their Storm Troopers, who love street fights, something to do, the Nazi leaders ordered coarse and insulting epithets to be painted on the Jews' shop windows. This new departure was not taken seriously in the great Rhenish cities. In all of our towns with a large working population, the department stores remained open. The people could not have done without them. Later on, when the Jews were ousted from trade, the Jewish stores were not suppressed as announced in the Nazi programme. The Jews were merely robbed of their holdings. As for the small retailers, who stupidly believed that the slump of their business was due to Jewish competition, they were subsequently ruined by the disastrous armament policy and sent to work on the fortifications on the western frontier.

No one knows better than I, an industrialist, what services were rendered by Jews to German national economy after the war. The Nazis accuse the Jewish bankers of being responsible for Germany's indebtedness. According to them, the Jews had conspired " to make Germany the prey of international finance." A sinister stupidity. The Jewish bankers saved German economy after the war. It was thanks to these Jews that medium and small enterprises were able to obtain from the American banks the necessary credits for their re-equipment.

Some of the large firms succeeded in floating loans in America on their own account. But most of the others, unknown to the leaders, could only get money through the Jewish banks. In guaranteeing loans contracted abroad, the latter took certain risks. But in doing so, the Jewish bankers bore witness to their

confidence in the future of German business. The
Simon Hirschland Bank at Essen, for instance, obtained
credits to the amount of at least fifty millions for the
small and medium establishments of our region. Its
capital did not exceed eight million marks. The
great German banks did not dare to take the risk of
such credits. Moreover, about 1930, at the moment
of the economic crisis the lack of foreign exchange
caused difficulties in payments. Here again the
Jewish banks intervened ; they were able to obtain
moratoriums or renewals from the foreign creditors.
The Nazis themselves have been obliged to recognise
the services rendered by this small Jewish bank in
Essen. It was this bank which negotiated the important American Krupp loan in collaboration with
another Jewish bank, Goldman Sachs & Co., of New
York. For a long time no one dared to lay hands
on the Simon Hirschland bank, notwithstanding the
pressure of the extremist elements of the party. It
was the last Jewish bank in Germany under the Nazi
regime. Owing to the foreign credits, it was impossible
to suppress it.

German economic and financial circles had con-
sistently frowned upon the development of the anti-
Semitic tendencies of National Socialism. Dr. Schacht,
in a speech at the opening of the Königsberg Fair in
1935, did not hesitate to protest against an agitation
which he regarded as a serious danger to German
economy. I, myself, on returning from America in
1935, had an opportunity of bringing up the question with Goering. Even at that time, the general,
who was minister-president of Prussia, had assumed
the air of a sovereign. One day, he invited me to
a deer-stalking party in the Schorfheide. I accepted

in the hope that I should find an opportunity of talking over certain matters of importance.

I do not know whether the keeper, who had been ordered by Goering to prepare my kill, informed his master of the difficulties he experienced. I am not a good shot. It was a rainy day, I had brought no sighting apparatus, and I missed three deer. Finally, I brought off my kill. It was high time, for the keeper was in despair. The poor fellow had been formally instructed to see that I killed my deer. This was my first, and undoubtedly my last.

Goering and I then dined together at a rustic hunting lodge which harmonised with its surroundings. It was only later that Goering built his famous palace, Karin Hall, in the depth of the forest. I have never been there, But I have been told that a Frenchman, who was a guest there of Goering's, and who afterwards visited a former imperial hunting lodge in Prussia, could not help remarking, " I never realised before how simple the kings of Prussia were."

After dinner I had a long conversation with Goering on the religious and Jewish questions. Goering's interest in religious matters is confined to their political angle. It was this principle which had actuated him the summer before, when he had issued his proclamation against political Catholicism in the Rhine provinces. Suspicious of the hostility of the Catholic population to their methods of government, the Nazis interpreted these tendencies as a rebirth of the old Centre party. I tried to explain to Goering what Catholicism really meant. I got the impression that his knowledge of religious problems was virtually non-existent. He told me that in the Bavarian churches he had seen votive offerings in the form of arms or legs in token of gratitude for recovered health. " It is all superstition and stupidity," he said. He was incapable of understanding the gratitude and the profound faith of the Catholic people who render thanks to God by means of these naïve tokens. He would undoubtedly prefer to replace the religion of the masses by a blind belief in Hitler and in the genius of the Führer. To the Nazis this is not a superstition !

I also spoke to Goering about the Jewish question. During my travels in America, I was able to estimate how much harm Germany's treatment of the Jews had done in American public opinion. I explained this to Goering. He fully realised that it was necessary to cultivate good relations with America. " But," he said, " what are we to do ? Should the *Stürmer* be suppressed ? "

The *Stürmer* is a pornographic sheet, published by the leader of the anti-Semites, Julius Streicher of Nuremberg. He had just started to post it up in streets and squares, notwithstanding protests of parents and of the Catholic clergy against such an exhibition of indecency before children. Since the war, it seems that Streicher has finally been certified as a lunatic and confined. If it had only been done before !

I suggested that Goering might send a German official mission to the United States in order to re-assure the American public. The person appointed, I said, should be able to tell President Roosevelt that excesses had doubtless been perpetrated, but that no principle was involved and order would be re-established. Goering himself is not anti-Semitic. He fully realised the harm that Streicher's agitation had done us in America.

"Whom shall we send?" he said. "Herr Schmidt?" Schmidt was the minister of economy, an insurance director, and totally unknown in America. The poor fellow may have known a great deal about insurance. But economic questions were too much for him. It was he who suggested creating that Supreme Chamber of German Economics which met only once. I proposed that Dr. Schacht be entrusted with this mission, But there the matter rested. Goering is not omnipotent, and the Nazis in Hitler's immediate entourage are so limited and presumptuous as to despise America, of which they know nothing.

I was to have attended the famous Nuremberg meeting of the Reichstag which voted the anti-Semitic laws. But when I arrived, I was informed that the Nazis intended to change the German flag, so I took the next train back. Other members of the Reichstag and even of the government, Schacht in particular, were also opposed to these infamous bills, but steps were taken to conceal the fact of their opposition.

It was in November, 1938, that the Nazis, on the pretext of the murder of vom Rath, a secretary of the embassy in Paris, by a young Polish Jew, organised the systematic persecution of the German Jews. The exact circumstances of the murder have never been established. The curious thing about it is that, during a whole year, the National Socialist government made no attempt to hasten the action of the French courts with regard to the murderer. This was unusual. On the occasion of the murder of Gustloff, a Nazi chief, killed by a Jewish student at Davos, the Nazi press had vituperated against the delays and lenience of the Swiss courts. As a matter of fact, the question of justice in this case meant very little to them. What they wanted was a pretext to create disorder and to despoil the Jews of their property. The collective fine then decreed by the Nazi Government was virtually tantamount to confiscation. But this was not the worst. The most scandalous scenes took place in all German cities. The official organisations of the party in power were transformed, under the eyes of a complacent police, into bands of incendiaries. Among them could be found even high magistrates of the Reich, generally in charge of the repression, not the perpetration, of crime. To curry favour with the party, they had joined the ranks of the Storm Troops and the SS guards.

In Berlin, Nuremberg, Düsseldorf, Munich, and Augsburg, in almost all German towns, swastika-flagged columns of militia plundered the Jewish dwellings, smashing the furniture, slashing the pictures, and stealing everything they could carry away. At night and even in broad daylight, they drenched the synagogues with gasoline and set them ablaze. The firemen received instructions not to extinguish the fires, but to confine themselves to saving the neighbouring buildings.

At that time I was travelling in Bavaria. When I heard what was happening throughout the country, I decided that such horrors could not have occurred in our Rhine provinces. On returning to Düsseldorf the next day I learned that the impossible had happened.

The highest official of the local National Socialist group, a man named Florian, the Gauleiter (in the language of the party, this is equivalent to prefect rank), had himself organised the riots. Not content with attacking the Jews, he had planned the murder of the highest official of the local Prussian adminis- tration, the Regierungspräsident S——. I knew the man personally. He was an excellent administrator and had, perhaps for this reason, incurred the hostility of Florian. He was well acquainted with Goering, who had been under obligation to him in the past and who had appointed him to his important post in Düsseldorf.

Florian, who was an official of the party but not of the state, had organised this odious personal attack during the anti-Jewish disturbances, on the pretext that the president's wife had had a Jewish grand- mother. Many men with wives of Jewish origin have divorced them in order to propitiate the party. In such cases, the courts invariably grant the divorce on the ground that the person concerned was married before the " Nuremberg Laws " were enacted, and was unaware of the importance of the ethnical ques- tion. This example was not followed by Presi- dent S——, who happened to be an honourable man. He had informed Goering of his wife's origin and Goering, in agreement with Hitler, had appointed him just the same.

On November 9th, motor-cars, equipped with loud- speakers from the propaganda department, were sent by Florian throughout Düsseldorf to summon the people to demonstrate against the Jews and their sympathisers. All Nazis knew that this was directed against the Regierungspräsident. Extremist element of the party, recruited from the scum of the popula- tion, set themselves to destroy and plunder the dwelling and the shops of the Jews, injuring and torturing all those upon whom they could lay hands. But for the ignoble purpose he had in view, Florian felt that he could not rely on the Düsseldorf Storm Troops. He therefore called in an Elberfeld detachment. These troops, armed with iron bars, were launched against the local government building, which was damaged and plundered. The president narrowly escaped being killed in his own office and got away only by a miracle.

As in other German cities, there were scenes of disorder and pillage throughout the town. Jewish magnates, intellectuals, physicians, and tradesmen were arrested. Many were odiously maltreated, even the old men. The aged legal adviser of the coal syndicate, Heinemann—who was seventy-five years old and universally respected—committed suicide with his wife. He had a small collection of pictures which he had bequeathed to the city of Essen. The Nazis completely destroyed it. Florian had organised these atrocities with particular savagery on the pretext that vom Rath, the young diplomat murdered in Paris, was a native of Düsseldorf.

Such was the news I received on my return. I was horrified. As a councillor of state I was entitled to approach Minister-President Goering in person. I immediately wrote him an explosive letter, saying that it was intolerable that a high official of the party should organise disturbances, and be able to attack, in this odious manner, the Jews and even a government official who was the highest local administrative authority of the Prussian State. I reminded Goering that he himself had appointed the Regierungspräsident and that S—— had never concealed the

P

fact of his wife's ancestry. I firmly declared to the
minister-president of Prussia that the excesses organised by the Nazi Gauleiter at Düsseldorf were the
ruin of all authority and an encouragement to anarchy
and to the vilest instincts of the population. In these
conditions, I said, it was impossible for me to remain
councillor of state. I could not retain this office and
thus, in my native country, seem to approve acts
which I formally condemned. I asked Goering to
accept my resignation.

It should be added that the people of Düsseldorf,
as of many other towns, disapproved of the excesses
organised by the Nazis against the Jews. Some days
later I was dining with Schacht in Berlin. A minister,
who shall be anonymous, for he is still in office,
congratulated me upon my attitude. " At last," he
said, " someone has dared to protest against these
atrocities." He added that I should demand the
punishment of Florian and the release of all the Jews,
who had been arrested. I took further steps with
Goering. Some days later the marshal sent me a
messenger. He reproached me bitterly for resigning,
saying that this caused him personal distress. If I
wanted to protest, why did I not resign from the
Reichstag ? I replied that my intervention was based
on the fact that I was a state councillor and that the
business concerned the Prussian administration. I
repeated my request for Florian's punishment. Goering's emissary replied, " No one can do anything
against a Gauleiter, not even Goering himself."
Florian is a friend of Rudolf Hess, and Hess does
not like Goering, whom he considers a rival.

In order to conclude this affair, I informed the
finance minister of Prussia that I no longer regarded

myself as councillor of state. I requested him therefore to cease paying my salary. This letter, undoubtedly through Goering's instructions, was treated as non-existent, and my councillor's fees continued to be paid into the Thyssen Bank where I had them transferred to a special account and placed at the disposal of the minister-president of Prussia.

In a letter I sent to Goering after the declaration of war, I reminded him of my protest against the excesses committed against the Jews.

Since 1935, I have had no further contact with the National Socialist leaders. I ceased to display the swastika flag and in fact broke off practically all relations with the party. But I took no steps to make my opposition public. The excesses of the autumn of 1938 caused me to abandon this reserve. My resignation from the council of state was proof not only of my displeasure but also of my intention to denounce any semblance of solidarity with a regime tolerating such outrages. But my protest was passed over in silence, just as would have been the case with my protest against the war a year later, if I had returned to Germany.

I have learned since that Hamburg was the only city in Germany where the National Socialist Gauleiter Kauffmann, of Rhenish origin, did not tolerate molestation of the Jews. In the great city which Kauffman administered in his double capacity of Gauleiter of the party and Reich governor, neither arson nor pillage was permitted. Near us, in Mühlheim, a grotesque incident occurred. The Jewish community, feeling the approach of the storm, had sold the synagogue to the town some weeks before the disturbances. The Nazis set fire to the building regardless of the fact that it was municipal property.

It is, above all, in its anti-Jewish campaign, that the party has officially given free rein to the base instincts which lie at the root of its so-called philosophy. The National Socialist government had the miserable privilege of encouraging and even ordering acts which are considered to be crimes by the whole civilised world. Foreigners who were in Germany at the time were appalled at these scenes of sadism and savagery ; they saw the official incendiaries of the synagogues at work. In the capital of the Reich, in the centre of the town and in full view of the embassies, the Storm Troops and the younger Hitlerites, commanded by their chiefs, gutted and plundered dwellings and shops. In tolerating—indeed, actually organising— theft, arson, pillage, and even murder in the concentration camps, the National Socialist regime, especially in that autumn of 1938, revealed itself to the whole world as a government of gangsters.

CHAPTER SEVEN

THE CATHOLIC QUESTION

THE persecution of the Jews and the attack on the liberty of conscience of the German Protestants are morally very significant acts. They discredit the ruling Nazi clique in the eyes of the world. But by these inhuman methods Hitler has been able, little by little, to eliminate the Jews from German life, without serious political consequences within the country. The Jewish minority in Germany was too small and too scattered. The anti-Semitic excesses, from the point of view of general policy, may be regarded as a series of individual crimes for which the perpetrators will one day have to account, while those who have robbed the Jews of their property will have to be forced to disgorge. But the economic consequences of the anti-Jewish action may well be more lasting and serious. It is difficult to appraise them to-day.

The persecution of the Protestants is less spectacular but it has a deeper significance. The Nazi leaders were not concerned with establishing a kind of order among the numerous Protestant sects and churches existing in Germany. It was neither on religious grounds nor for legitimate reasons of state that they

tried to unify Protestantism by appointing a head of
the church with the unusual title of *Reichsbischof*—
Bishop of the Reich. (He was, by the way, a pathetic
little man, this Ludwig Müller. He had been an
employee of Hugo Stinnes at Mühlheim, and then
became a pastor—no one knows why.)   No, the
Nazis' aim was quite a different one. They wished
to make German Protestantism a kind of state religion, after stripping it of all Christian principles. To
delude the simple-minded, they called it " German
Christianity."   I once asked an honest peasant from
East Prussia what his religion was. " I am a German
Christian," he said, " for I am a German." He was
convinced that that was something superior.

As a matter of fact, National Socialism is not a
political system. Rather, it is intended to be a
philosophy and a system of morals—a *Weltanschauung*,
as the Nazis pretentiously call it.

This philosophy is summed up in the phrase *Blut
und Boden* (blood and soil). Most people do not
realise the perniciousness of the doctrine which is
hidden behind those two words. Its comic abbrevia-
tion " Blubo " (pronounced Bloobo) has sometimes
even been made the butt of ridicule. What is this
doctrine ? It teaches that blood and soil have produced man. He is linked to nature by every fibre
of his being. The blood which flows in his veins
endows him with a mysterious force—the life of the
ancestors of whom he is the reincarnation during his
existence. He has a profound affinity with the soil
on which he is born and from which he draws his
sustenance. He represents a tiny fraction of world
energy. His guiding purpose must be to exert this
force to his utmost.

A philosopher friend of mine regards these lucubrations as a philosophy of brute beasts. The Nazis degrade man to the level of an animal ; the breeding process must be watched ; he must be domesticated, fed and broken in by a well-calculated plan to produce a prescribed " performance." It is the method of the stud or the training stable. The Nazis set themselves to produce Nietzsche's superman by a system of animal breeding.* The strict rules imposed for marriage, or rather for mating, in Himmler's SS (Body Guards) all point this way. It is unfortunate that Hitler himself cannot participate in this. One might have been able to produce, in this one case, the coveted result ! This conception of man leaves no room for individual morals concerning the responsibility of each human being to his own conscience and, above all, concerning a religion which recognises the supernatural.

Such are the principles according to which Hitler governs the German people. Unfortunately, he has succeeded in inculcating them in a large part of the younger generation. The youthful followers of this brute philosophy are capable of courage, obedience, and devotion to the service of the composite personification of the race, of which they regard themselves a mere fragment. For them, the race is represented by Germany. Its most powerful expression is to be found in the person of the Führer, whom they venerate almost as a deity. But the materialistic—so to speak animalistic—youth has no knowledge of God in the spiritual sense of the word. The " German God " of the Nazis is Nature, the mysterious source from which they spring. Their act of faith consists of

* See Historical Notes at end of chapter, page 249.

developing to the utmost the natural forces gathered up in each individual.

Some fanatics, still more insane—or perhaps more innocent—than the rest, have endeavoured to add a little fantasy to these doctrines by connecting them up with the legends of ancient Germanic mythology. These fervent disciples of the German God revel in reminiscences of Wotan, Baldur, Thor, and Freya. The names of their children are drawn from the Scandinavian Edda,* in order to avoid those of the calendar saints and above all those of the Old Testament. Goering himself has followed this example. This is one of the grotesque sides of this sad tale.

But there are other and gloomier aspects. One day I was invited to visit one of the schools where the National Socialists propose to educate the party's future elite. These schools are called *Ordensburgen*—castles of order. In the confusion of ideas which characterises the National Socialist regime this aims to simulate a concept of the Catholic Knights of the Teutonic Order,* who left west Germany to convert and conquer the savage Slav tribes of the Baltic region once called Prussia. That is because Alfred Rosenberg has got it into his head to revive the Teutonic Order !

The school is installed in the picturesque ruins of an old castle fortress in the Eifel district. This has been repaired, enlarged, and luxuriously modernised. The boys, known as *Junkers*, are educated as if they were budding knights. Here, then, is a party calling itself a German *labour* party which sets out to revive the feudal system ! The Junkers are trained in sport and the use of arms. They learn to dance ; they

* See Historical Notes at end of chapter, page 249.

do dangerous stunts, and they hunt. I do not know whether they have much time for real lessons, but to my knowledge this is the only school in the world without a library !

The director, or rather the führer, of this Ordensburg is a former engineer. One day he outlined to us his ideas on education. For him, man is nothing but a machine ; the goal of education is to help the pupil to fulfil his function as a human machine. Training is substituted for intellect. I was stupefied. One of the accusations levelled against modern industry is that, by inaugurating the moving belt system, it has transformed men into machines. The industrialists have been the first to do everything possible to minimise the disadvantages of a process which is indispensable to modern production. And here we find a National Socialist pedagogue who has been entrusted with the training of a so-called *élite*, proposing to develop, not individuals with intelligence and a sense of responsibility, but machines.

The followers of Karl Marx have never preached any such materialism. The Nazis have set out to destroy the soul. A dictatorship has no use for personality. A nation of robots is easier to govern.

This is the underlying principle of the so-called philosophy of blood and soil. It is easy to see how useful a political instrument this could be in the hands of unscrupulous leaders who are filled with contempt for the people they govern, especially the common people and the workers.

Such a doctrine is completely incompatible with the principles of Christianity. In order to inculcate it in the masses, the Nazis thought that they might make use of the Protestant Church—after emptying it of Christianity. During the course of its history in Germany, Protestantism as a state religion has often proved to be complacent toward the German princes, and it has always fostered loyal subjects of the ruling house. But no prince has ever demanded of his Church, domesticated as it may have been, that it renounce the essential principles of Christianity. Hitler, however, tried to do just that. His undertaking was frustrated by the heroic resistance of pastors like Martin Niemöller and of their congregations.

Nevertheless, the National Socialists succeeded in persuading many to recant, especially in Protestant regions where religious indifference is often the rule. In Germany adherence to a religious sect is the normal thing. In order to renounce such adherence, formal steps must be taken through the civil authorities. The Nazis have simplified the process. Practically all the young people forming part of the SS have abjured Christianity. The same applies to chiefs of the young Hitlerite detachments. Many are followers of the new German paganism and hold rituals in honour of Wotan, the Sun, or Nature, the mother of all life, if they do not formally worship Hitler.

The doctrine of blood and soil is used as an argument against the use of intelligence. At the beginning of the regime one of my friends had written a book on the Jewish question and had sent it to the more important officials of the party. Florian, the Gauleiter of Düsseldorf, forbade the circulation of a work which was intended as an objective discussion of this important problem. The grounds for the suppression are not devoid of interest. The Gauleiter cut short all discussion with the words, " This book is useless, for our citizens, conscious of their blood and of their soil, could never make a mistake."

This argument is obviously final. But it can be valid only for brute beasts like Florian, who is totally uneducated and, at best, able to take a hand at cards.

The attacks of National Socialism on the Catholic Church have a wider scope and are totally different in character from the attempt to enslave Protestantism. Hitler, a born Catholic, was an admirer of the political sagacity of the Catholic Church, if we are to believe *Mein Kampf*. At the beginning of the regime he endeavoured to reach an agreement with the Church. He concluded a concordat with the Vatican.* In this Vice-Chancellor von Papen was the moving spirit. The concordat was the first treaty concluded by the new regime. Like the others, it was violated. But Hitler saw in it a considerable political advantage. The new and revolutionary National Socialist government was accepted as a partner by one of the most respected moral authorities of the world. It was capable of concluding a treaty.

From the standpoint of domestic politics, the concordat was a definite feather in the cap of the new regime. The Church relaxed the rigour of its hostility to the new party in power, without altogether retracting the German bishops' condemnation of certain Nazi doctrines. For about a year it seemed as though the regime was inclined to keep to its engagements faithfully. Hitler publicly declared that the anti-Christian works of Alfred Rosenberg were purely personal creations and did not officially commit the National Socialist party. In spite of this, the ideas of the Nazi pseudo-philosopher continued to serve as

* See Historical Notes at end of chapter, page 249.

a basis of instruction for the Hitler Youth and the other party organisations. Hitler, as usual, played a double game.

The crisis occurred in the summer of 1935. In my native Rhineland the anti-religious attitude of the Hitler Youth organisations and of their chief, Baldur von Schirach, had aroused sharp discontent among Catholic parents. The clergy had warned against the new spirit which the regime was trying to spread among the youth of the country. Furthermore, a general political discontent had begun to make itself felt. The Nazis saw with anxiety that former Social Democrats, who had ceased to go to church during the republican era, had now returned to the fold. Incidents had taken place in the villages of the Westerwald, near Coblenz, in which young Catholic peasants had beaten the pagans of Hitler Youth who were celebrating the solstice. Tension threatened to become serious. In the whole of the Rhine provinces, completely Catholic, the atmosphere was stormy.

The Nazis, who have no understanding of religious zeal, saw in this restlessness of the Catholic population a display of political hostility. They said that the Catholic Centre party, although it had been officially dissolved, was renewing intrigues against the National Socialists through an underground movement. Goering launched his proclamation against political Christianity. It was not religion that was under discussion, he disclosed. National Socialism is based on positive Christianity. He was a respecter of all faiths. But the enemies of the State were making use of religion in order to conceal their shady designs. At the same time the Gestapo was instructed to proceed rigorously against the young Catholics. This caused a great deal of unrest, but there were no important immediate results. The Catholics maintained their passive resistance.

The Nazi leaders then resorted to an infamous procedure. In order to disgrace the Catholic clergy in the eyes of their congregations, they took as a pretext certain personal weaknesses known to exist in a local community of lay brothers, to instigate a series of scandal trials. The party press began to publish degrading accounts of moral turpitude to be tried in secret. Throughout the Rhineland the party organised lectures in which the speakers recounted the most scandalous details. At Düsseldorf a Reich attorney paraded details of immorality cases and presented them in such a way as to incriminate the clergy and the Church, whether they were true or false. The Nazi Gauleiter, who was well aware of my Catholic convictions, refrained from inviting me. The trials lasted for several months. The Nazis had the effrontery to summon into court Monsignor Bornewasser, the old bishop of Treves, and Monsignor Sebastian, the bishop of Speyer, almost eighty years of age. Bürckel, the sinister Gauleiter of the Palatinate, publicly insulted the venerable bishop, whose patriotic loyalty was above suspicion. A Nazi court dared accuse the Bishop of Treves of perjury. The latter complained to Chancellor Hitler and published his appeal in a letter to the Catholic population. But Hitler approved the whole action.

Meanwhile the increasing indignation of the Catholic population of the Rhineland caused the Nazi leaders to worry. Protests were heard against all the ignominy and bad faith. In pursuing their odious campaign of calumny, the Nazis risked provoking a revolt. They interrupted the trials, but did not cease their attacks against the Church. The Gestapo continued their intrigues. Priests denounced by secret agents were arrested and imprisoned. A young vicar in Essen, whose mission was among the working class, was accused of having fomented a Communist plot and was condemned to ten years' imprisonment. At that very time Hitler was secretly negotiating with Stalin!

Also at this time the Nazis were trying to turn apostate Catholic priests against their own Church. A professor of the Pasing clerical college lent himself to this treason. He was suspended and excommunicated by the Cardinal Archbishop of Munich. For one month his doings were reported in public meetings and the press of the party reported his attacks against the Church, but without success.

While a series of scandal trials was in progress the Nazis attacked the Church in another field. The religious orders, they affirmed, had systematically violated the laws prohibiting the export of foreign exchange. For months the press continued to abound in stories of monks and nuns concealing wads of banknotes in their robes being arrested at the frontier by the vigilant customs officials. The Bishop of Meissen, Monsignor Legge, was implicated in one of these actions, which could, of course, have been brought against any German citizen who had relations with foreign countries. The monsignor escaped imprisonment only with great difficulty.

After attempting to defame the clergy by these detestable means, the Nazis undertook to alienate the children from their influence. In all the Catholic regions of Germany they organised a so-called plebiscite of Catholic parents in favour of secular schools. In the agricultural villages the Nazis profited by the absence of the men working in the fields to collect lists of signatures during the day. The absence of a name was taken as signifying approval. The German bishops courageously protested against these fraudulent methods. The Bishop of Treves denounced them from the pulpit. The Nazis had to retreat. They did not dare to make use of this faked plebiscite. Even in villages where, according to the Nazis, the votes had been 100 per cent in favour of the secular schools, they dared not suppress the Catholic schools.

Nevertheless, the party continued by underground methods, particularly in the towns, to agitate for education without religion. Catholic officials were subjected to constant pressure to withdraw their children from the Catholic school and send them to the secular school. In the colleges, Nazi professors derided the dogma and morals of Christianity. Classes in religion have been made optional, and pupils desiring to do so can take an hour of sport or gymnastics instead. Sermons are supervised by the Gestapo, and preachers are arrested. The Catholic press is suppressed. The weekly religious periodicals and parish bulletins are not allowed to be published. The aim is to stifle all expression of Catholic thought.

But in attacking the Catholic religion the National Socialists have met more than their match. The bishops, the clergy, and the population resist with a silent but tenacious courage. Despite all its efforts, the National Socialist regime has been unable to dethrone Catholicism in Germany. On the contrary, it can even be said that persecution has strengthened it.

Monsignor von Galen, Bishop of Münster, in Westphalia, one day made a profound observation on the
meaning of the fight between the pagan myth of
blood and soil and the traditional religion of Catholic
Westphalia. " People speak," said the bishop, " of
blood and soil. If these words had any significance
whatever, I, more than anyone, should have the
right to invoke this doctrine, for my ancestors have
been established in this country for over five hundred
years. Here, in this Rhenish land, we are on our
own soil and have no need of the false prophets who
come from abroad."

The bishop was alluding to the standard-bearer of
the anti-Christian forces, Alfred Rosenberg. Rosenberg is a Russian intellectual. He has not a drop of
German blood in his veins. His father was a teacher
in a Russian college under the Czarist regime. In
those Russian intellectual circles the " rationalism "
of the eighteenth century and the idea of Rousseau
still had some adherents before the last war. As a
student, Rosenberg had become imbued with this
" rationalism." It is, moreover, curious to note that
at Riga he belonged to a Latvian and not a German
students' association. It is said that during the war
of 1914 his brother was in the French secret service.
And this is the man whom the Nazis wish to impose
upon us as the great German philosopher of modern
times.

He has written a book against Christianity, entitled
The Myth of the Twentieth Century. It is the laboured
product of a Voltaire without brains. Goering
asked me one day what I thought of it. " To me," he
added, " it is completely idiotic." I did not contradict
him.

In this work, Rosenberg serves up once again all the old nonsense which the anticlericals of all the ages have written against the Catholic Church. He flavours this repast with a philosophy inspired by Rousseau and a naïve sort of romantic materialism. For him, man is naturally good ; the Christian dogma of original sin and redemption is an insult to his inherent nobility. Under the Nazi regime the concentration camps are doubtless the expression of the natural goodness of mankind.

This Russian prophet, who has never succeeded in acclimatising himself in Germany, was one day moved to set forth his outlandish ideas at Münster, the diocese of Monsignor von Galen. The bishop preached a thundering sermon against him and forbade all Catholics to attend his lecture. Rosenberg, who had hired the largest hall in the town, was obliged to speak before a few rows of uniforms and many empty benches. The Nazis were furious. The minister of the interior, Frick, remonstrated personally with the Bishop of Münster. But they did not dare to arrest him. The Westphalian peasant is said to be a hard nut to crack. The rustics were perfectly capable of coming to the defence of their bishop with pitchforks and truncheons.

At Christmas in 1939, Monsignor von Galen issued a mandate in the words of the Scriptures : " If the blind lead the blind, shall they not both fall into the ditch ? " By quoting from the Gospel at that critical moment, Monsignor von Galen replied with the whole weight of his authority to the pagan axiom of the Nazis : " The Führer is never wrong." And the bishop admonished his flock not to forget the authentic source of truth.

Q

At the present time the Catholic Church is the sole organised form of resistance to the spirit of National Socialism. It is the only adversary with whom the Nazis are obliged to reckon. The generals, for instance, lack the courage of the bishops. One day, in Düsseldorf, I met the general commanding the Münster army corps. In the course of our conversation I asked him, " What do you think of our bishop ? "

" I have never seen him," the general replied. " How can you think I could visit him under present circumstances ? " This speaks volumes about the situation.

For my own part, I have never concealed my hostility to the religious policy of the Nazis. Since my departure from Germany, they have spread the rumour that my whole behaviour was dictated by the Catholic Church. This, of course, is absurd, but it leaves me indifferent. Still, I do not wish to hide the fact that the revolt of my conscience as a Catholic has largely contributed to my hostility to National Socialism. I have made no secret of it.

In my parish at Mühlheim there was an old priest who was a perfect model of devotion. He gave all he had to the poor. He took his meals with the humblest at the people's canteen we had opened in our factories for the families of the unemployed. I had the greatest admiration for this man. I asked him one day, " Is there anything I can do for you ? " He replied, " My greatest desire is to have a beautiful baptismal chapel in my church." After his death, some months later, I gratified his wish. And I ordered a beautiful carved stone for the fonts from the Benedictines of the famous Abbey of Maria Laach. These monks have revived religious art in Germany ;

they have rediscovered the old secrets of the medieval ecclesiastical sculpture. The carving of the stone took two years. But it turned out a work of art. The chapel was consecrated in 1937 and my grandson was the first to be baptised there.

In a normal country, there would have been nothing out of the common in a Catholic building a chapel. But in Nazi Germany, this was considered a demonstration against the regime. The inhabitants of Mühlheim knew that I was the founder. They made no mistake about it. And the church was always full.

On the occasion of the death of Pope Pius XI, I sent the Cardinal Archbishop of Cologne a public telegram of condolence in which I assured him of my unshakable devotion and that of my family to the Catholic faith. Here again, this would have been nothing unusual in a normal country. But shortly after, Himmler's sinister lieutenant, Heydrich, was sent to Essen to make a personal investigation on my account, especially concerning my attitude in matters of religion. It is perhaps owing to the intervention of the Gauleiter, Terboven, that nothing happened to me at that time. But the fact that one of the foremost industrialists of the region had openly manifested his religious convictions had displeased the Nazis.

They are used to greater compliance. I will give an instance. Albert Vögler, who succeeded me as the head of the United Steel Works after my departure from Germany, has a brother, Eugen Vögler. He is the general manager of the Hochtief Building Company at Essen. This enterprise, one of the most important in Germany, is mainly owned by the Vögler brothers.

The National Socialist regime builds, and the
Hochtief Company is one of its principal builders.
It has worked on the new motor highways ; it has
built the new Chancellery of the Reich, which cost
over twenty million marks. It erected in Nuremberg
those immense constructions of concrete and stone
which, for one week of every year, house the Nazi
Party Congress. But Eugen Vögler has also been
called upon to undertake orders of a more private
character. He has built the great power generator
which furnishes the electric current for Hitler's
residence at Obersalzberg and the neighbouring
offices, the theatre, the villas and hotels. The
Führer's greatest compliment to the Hochtief Company was to order it to build his " eyrie," his Parsifal's
castle on the rocks of Obersalzberg. I myself have
never visited this Wagnerian sanctuary of the Holy
Grail, but no one has better described it than the French
ambassador François-Poncet in a letter reproduced
in the *French Yellow Book*, part of which I quote :

" From a distance, the place looks like a kind of observa-
tory or small hermitage perched up at a height of 6,000
feet on the highest point of a ridge of rock. The approach
is by a winding road about nine miles long, boldly cut
out of the rock ; the boldness of its construction does as
much credit to the ability of the engineer Todt as to the
unremitting toil of the workmen who in three years completed this gigantic task. The road comes to an end in
front of a long underground passage leading into the
mountain, and closed by a heavy double door of bronze.
At the far end of the underground passage a wide lift,
panelled with sheets of copper, awaits the visitor. Through
a vertical shaft of 330 feet cut right through the rock, it
rises up to the level of the Chancellor's dwelling-place.
Here is reached the astonishing climax. The visitor finds

himself in a strong and massive building containing a gallery with Roman pillars, an immense circular hall with windows all round and a vast open fireplace where enormous logs are burning, a table surrounded by about thirty chairs, and opening out at the sides, several sitting-rooms, pleasantly furnished with comfortable arm-chairs. On every side, through the bay-windows, one can look as from a plane high in the air, on to an immense panorama of mountains. At the far end of a vast amphitheatre one can make out Salzburg and the surrounding villages, dominated, as far as the eye can reach, by a horizon of mountain ranges and peaks, by meadows and forests clinging to the slopes. In the immediate vicinity of the house, which gives the impression of being suspended in space, an almost overhanging wall of bare rock rises up abruptly. The whole, bathed in the twilight of an autumn evening, is grandiose, wild, almost hallucinating. The visitor wonders whether he is awake or dreaming. He would like to know where he is—whether this is the Castle of Monsalvat where lived the Knights of the Graal or a new Mount Athos sheltering the meditations of a cenobite, or the palace of Antinea rising up in the heart of the Atlas Mountains. Is it the materialisation of one of those fantastic drawings with which Victor Hugo adorned the margins of his manuscript of *Les Burgraves*, the fantasy of a millionaire, or merely the refuge where brigands take their leisure and hoard their treasures ? Is it the conception of a normal mind, or that of a man tormented by megalomania, by a haunting desire for domination and solitude, or merely that of a being in the grip of fear ?

" One detail cannot pass unnoticed, and is no less valuable than the rest for someone who tries to assess the psychology of Adolf Hitler : the approaches, the openings of the underground passage and the access to the house are manned by soldiers and protected by nests of machine guns. . . ."[1]

[1] Reprinted by permission of Hutchinson & Co. (Publishers) Ltd

But such high favours must be earned. And the general manager of the Hochtief Company, Eugen Vögler, has shown himself worthy of them. In 1938, he officially abandoned the Protestant Church. He might have said, like old Kirdorf at ninety, that he believed in Mathilde Ludendorff, the wife of the general, who founded a religion and claimed to have discovered the great secret of life. He might also have said that Wotan had appeared to him in a dream and that he had been converted to Germanism. As a matter of fact, he did nothing of the sort. One fine day Eugen Vögler wrote a business letter to his pastor. He explained, without any attempt to sugar the pill, that the interests of his firm required him to leave the Church. As the accredited contractor of the grandees of a regime which was hostile to Christianity, he owed it to himself and to his business to recant.

Such gestures are appreciated in Nazidom. They enable the regime to form an estimate of a character and to dominate a conscience. The Nazis encountered more resistance among the Catholics. But even in religious matters they utilise such traitors as they are able to enlist. The head of the " Catholic " section of the Gestapo at Berlin is an unfrocked priest.

The Catholic religion is still being persecuted. But, notwithstanding all his efforts, Hitler has not succeeded in breaking the spirit of the Church. The bishops stand firm. From the pulpit and in the confessional the clergy have sustained the resistance of their flocks. Despite some few cases of individual weakness, the Catholic Church will emerge stronger from its fight against the Nazi's neo-paganism and barbarity.

By his attacks on Catholicism, in particular in our

Rhenish regions, Hitler has reopened old wounds. Bismarck's Kulturkampf* had left painful memories. They were not finally surmounted till the last years. Catholics and Protestants did their duty to the Fatherland, shoulder to shoulder. At the time of the passive resistance in the Ruhr, the Catholics proved their unshakable loyalty to the full. The Cardinal Archbishop and the clergy of Cologne encouraged our patriotic action. Hitler is therefore a monster of ingratitude to persecute the Rhenish Catholics on the lying pretext that one cannot be a good Catholic and a good German at the same time. It is true, of course, that the Nazis have made it impossible.

I, like many other conservative Catholics, had hoped that the National Socialists would remain true to their programme and respect Christianity. I tried to exercise my influence in this direction. I suggested that Goering should appoint to the council of state Dom Hildefonse Herwegen, the Benedictine abbot of Maria Laach, one of the most venerable personalities of German Catholicism. Goering preferred to nominate Monsignor Berning, the Bishop of Osnabrück. But the fact that he did appoint a high cleric shows that at the beginning of the regime some of the Nazi leaders considered the Catholic Church as a positive factor in the new Germany.

The anti-Christian attitude of Rosenberg, Hitler, and Goebbels, and the immoral brutality of the whole National Socialist system, have ruined what possibilities existed after the concordat. The ignoble methods which the Nazis were not ashamed to employ and their hatred of all that is Catholic have revolted the Rhenish population. The wounds thus reopened are incurable.

* See Historical Notes at end of chapter, page 250.

A deep gulf has been opened between Catholic
Germany and the rest of the country. Never will the
Catholics tolerate a reversion to such methods. They
refuse to be treated by a Berlin government as if they
were second-rate citizens or bad Germans. I, for my
part, would never admit this. This anti-Catholic
mentality must be done away with once for all.

In my schooldays I protested against a teacher of
history who had insulted the popes. The teacher
replied that what he taught was in accordance with
the text-books. I rejoined that not everything contained in a Prussian history book was necessarily true.
I was severely punished for that remark. The
situation soon became impossible and my father had
to take me away from the school. But he had the
greatest difficulty in finding another Prussian college
that agreed to accept a Catholic pupil guilty of
rebellion.

During the last war I was attached as adjutant to
a general commanding a division on the western
front. One day, when we were riding together, the
general said to me, " I think a great deal of you, but
I have to be careful because you are a Catholic and
in the last resort you obey the Pope."

It was this Prussian distrust of Catholicism that lay
at the root of Bismarck's Kulturkampf. The Nazis,
who have invented the totalitarian state, have not
only retained this traditional Prussian hostility to
Catholicism, but they have made it worse.

This time, the cup is running over. The Rhenish
Catholics refuse to begin this painful experience all
over again. Since Berlin considers that our religion
is incompatible with patriotism and devotion to one's
country, we shall draw the logical conclusions.

Historical Notes

NIETZSCHE AND HIS SUPERMAN

National Socialism has attempted to falsify Nietzsche's work and to represent this great German philosopher as a precursor of the Nazi racial doctrine and the " Blood and Soil " theory. The truth is that Nietzsche found no greater object of scorn, in many of his works, than the inflated pan-Germanic mind. The " superman," as represented in his most famous work, *Thus Spake Zarathustra*, has quite a different aspect from the prospective " leaders " produced in the National Socialist leadership schools (*Ordensburgen*), Nietzsche's " superman " was the man living in solitude on the summit, because by his spiritual superiority he had overcome everything that Nietzsche considered to be prejudices and traditional nonsense.

THE SCANDINAVIAN EDDA

The collection of Germanic sagas which constitutes the basis of Germanic mythology. The Edda supplied Richard Wagner with his material for the *Ring of the Nibelungs*.

THE KNIGHTS OF THE TEUTONIC ORDER

A religious order of Prussian knights, which was established in order to spread Christianity in the territories east of Prussia. The Teutonic Knights colonised vast stretches in the Baltic regions, where they ruled with particular cruelty. They also penetrated into Poland and Russia.

THE CONCORDATS

" Concordat " was originally the name given to a treaty between the Papal See and the Emperors of Germany. In recent times, the concordats between the Vatican and

Prussia or Germany provided for the regulation of the rights of Catholics in Germany to profess their religion. They decided, in particular, upon the manner in which bishops and certain professors of Catholic theology are to be appointed in agreement with the Papal Court. Moreover, they regulated the exercise of canonic law and limited the freedom of preaching. The present Pope, Pius XII, when under his family name of Pacelli he was Papal nuncio in Berlin, succeeded in negotiating a concordat with Otto Braun, then Premier of Prussia. The agreement was faithfully kept as long as there was a democratic government in Prussia.

The Kulturkampf

This is the name given to the conflict begun by Bismarck in 1875, under the pretext that several measures taken by the Holy See represented interferences with the government's powers—in Germany in general and Prussia in particular. Since almost half of Germany's population was Catholic, Bismarck's step aroused widespread indignation. As the Catholics followed the leadership of their priests, the conflict gradually degenerated into persecution of the clergy. A few years later Bismarck was obliged to yield to Rome and make peace with the Church. However, the Kulturkampf has left its traces in Germany to this day, in the form of the Catholic Centre party, which was originally founded as a medium of self-protection, and which, after playing an essential part in the Reichstag opposition, became one of the most important government parties in post-war Germany.

PART FOUR

GERMANY AND THE FUTURE OF THE WORLD

CHAPTER ONE

FRAUDULENT NAZI FINANCE

The Exhaustion of Germany's Industrial Equipment

ONE day, when the time comes for concluding a peace, one of the not-so-easy problems will be the re-organisation of German economy. German propaganda must not lead us to the false belief that National Socialist economic practice has not been a complete failure. There is no integrated plan in Germany, as I have already pointed out in an earlier chapter. Hitler knows absolutely nothing about economic matters ; and he has always trusted those advisers whose counsel happened to be the most convenient at the time. All he has insisted on is getting the disposal of the large sums of money which he needed for his favourite plans, such as the arterial motor roads and re-armament.

Of course it is possible for a government to spend money for unproductive purposes. They may use, let us say, 20 per cent. of the revenue. But they must not swallow up 80 per cent., as they have done in

Germany. For after all such money as is not raised by taxation must be amortised. But in Germany no one thinks of such details.

It is also necessary that the most important economic questions should be freely discussed by people who know something about them. That includes, among others, the leaders of industry. So far as I can remember, this has been done properly only in a single and very minor case, namely the regulation of the druggists' trade. In that one instance Goering asked for the names of the three best pharmacists in Germany. These rendered an expert opinion, and as a result the matter was handled correctly. But when it came to more important things, to questions of fundamental economic significance, no such procedure was followed. In such cases the course chosen was always the one that seemed the simplest at the moment.

First of all, there was the question of inflation. One day the monstrous inflation which has long existed in Nazi Germany will become evident, and enormous difficulties will be the result. Above all, the peasants will realise that the money no longer has any value, and they will refuse to sell their products. At that moment everything will be finished. A Communistic solution would be possible only if, as in Russia, the peasants constituted 80 per cent. of the population. Since that is not the case in Germany, a Communistic system is not practicable at all. In Russia conditions are quite different. There the industrial workers, comprising 20 per cent., provide the remaining 80 per cent. of the people with the products which they very much need.

It is impossible to imagine how difficult it is for a manufacturer, in the circumstances existing in

Germany, to direct the management of his works. Obviously the day consists of a limited number of hours, and half of the owner's time is taken up in discussions with people who are ignorant of all the pertinent facts. Even Goering is without knowledge, although he occupies the position of supreme economic leadership in the Germany of to-day. All he knows is how to spend money. Dr. Hjalmar Schacht, as minister of economy, permitted himself to be driven much too far by the Nazi government's demands. Originally, no doubt, he organised the famous Stand-still Agreements with foreign countries in good faith. His definite intention was to pay back eventually the foreign credits which were thus suspended. But he had reckoned without his host. His first mistake was to prevent the German industrialists who had received private credits from paying their debts. For instance, the United Steel Works, with which I was closely associated, would undoubtedly have been able to meet their obligations if the government had not forbidden it. It was always assumed abroad that Schacht acted with the consent of German industry, but this was decidedly not the case.

The whole manner in which the Standstill Agree-ments were reached seems to me especially interesting, particularly for the lack of foresight shown by the leading economic circles—even before the Hitler regime. The first great mistake was to permit the General Credit Institution (*Allgemeine Kreditanstalt*) of Vienna to crash. Director General Vögler and I were at that time in Vienna as representatives of the foreign creditors. The Dutch administrator of bank-ing in Austria (representing the League of Nations) expressly warned both of us, and asked us to tell

Dr. Luther, the former chancellor, who was president
of the Reichsbank at the time, that the bank disaster
which happened in Vienna would be repeated in
Berlin. But Dr. Luther answered, " Nothing can
happen to us at all ; we have so much money."
Actually he had at that moment the very considerable
gold reserve of two billion marks. But when the
Darmstädter Bank got into difficulties because the
foreign countries demanded repayment of their loans
he surrendered by far the greater part of this gold
reserve.

The German bank crashes which followed were at
that time considered a consequence of Germany's
reparations obligations. This, however, was in no
wise the case. For in the meantime America, in
particular, had lent large sums to Germany which
were certainly not used for the payment of reparations. The debts in question were private debts
which had nothing whatever to do with reparations.

Immediately after the bank failures Germany
decreed the strict government control of foreign exchange. Under the conditions of this planned economy
all private business had to surrender its entire stock
of foreign specie. And as armament production ex-
panded, foreign money became progressively scarce
especially such funds as were available for foodstuff
and raw materials for non-armament industries.
still remember a time when ores were offered to
certain manufacturers. They applied to the Reichsbank, but were not given any foreign exchange
They therefore had to abandon the deal. Simila
difficulties were encountered in the procuring o
necessary credits. I know of a case where a credi
was granted, and part of it repaid. But after th

Standstill Agreement the Reichsbank no longer paid any attention to requests for permission to remit. There was simply a scarcity of foreign exchange, due to excessive armament production, and even the most urgent private obligations could no longer be honoured. Both industry and trade suffered ; branches so important to Germany as the fur trade could not get any foreign exchange at all. On the other hand the armament industry got all it wanted.

I remember, too, a case where a fairly large amount of scrap was purchased in the United States. The American firm dealt through a Jewish concern in London. The scrap had been promised, because it was not known in London that it was intended for Germany. When the Jewish dealers found it out they did not at first want to complete the deal ; but in the end prompt payment proved so attractive that the German armament industry obtained the merican scrap.

German conditions would probably have developed still more unfavourably, if the Nazis had not taken over from their predecessors very large industrial stocks, as well as a quite respectable gold reserve. Brüning, as chancellor, had pursued a deflationary policy which had made Germany a land of bulging inventories. The great flow of foreign loans into Germany at that time had the effect of inflating stocks. The dollars of the private loans of industry and banks went to the Reichsbank, while a corresponding sum in marks was credited to the owners. These marks were promptly used to lay in as many goods as possible. In this way Brüning prepared the situation very well for the Nazis—so well, in fact, that the Nazis ought to have honoured him with a

R

monument. Thus he became the pacemaker for the Nazis' spending policies. In addition, his deflationary policy led the country into a general economic crisis. In this way the above-mentioned economic processes were automatically augmented.

For my own factories I always executed ore purchases a year in advance. There was a depression in 1928-1929 and the question arose for us whether to buy ore and how much. In this case we thought we were cautious in buying 80 per cent. of the amount of the previous year. But employment fell to 25 per cent. with the result that very large unprocessed stocks remained. Similar conditions obtained in many concerns, in the iron and other industries. At the outset Nazi economy lived on these accumulated stocks.

It is legitimate to ask how Schacht could ever bring himself to tolerate so fraudulent an economy. Personally I do not doubt that originally he desired to manage with all honesty, and that he simply had no far-seeing conception of the economic development of the situation he found. His elimination from the government apparatus came when conditions developed to a point where he no longer felt able to assume the responsibility. Among other things the great industrial establishments had been burdened with expenditures which the state itself should have borne. As an example the I. G. Farben Industrie helped the Nazis a great deal—among other things by paying their propaganda agents abroad. That, by the way, was also done by many other private concerns. All of these expenditures were offset by corresponding mark credits in Germany, and thus the Nazis were able to make use of the large amounts in foreign currency which remained abroad. That, incidentally, is one of the reasons why foreign governments had such difficulty in discovering how Nazi propaganda was financed. Naturally all this meant a strain upon private balances which could not but lead to unbearable conditions in the end.

But when there was no other way out, payments were made with false bills of exchange. I am precisely informed about the matter because I was at the time president of the Bank of Industrial Obligations. We were approached with the demand to endorse a whole parcel of artificial bills. The management refused, declaring that this was not permissible under the by-laws of the bank, since the bank received no kind of equivalent for the bills. Thereupon the bank was served with a declaration from the minister of justice to the effect that the bank would not be called upon to be responsible for the bills. The government would discount them at the Reichsbank. We could sign with perfect peace of mind, we were told ; we would not be called upon, our signature notwithstanding.

The Bank of Industrial Obligations was a very powerful institution. Among other things it had loaned an enormous sum to agriculture. Its signature had always been honoured by industry as a whole. It had a very large capital. But its directors finally had no choice but to yield to the government's demand.

The bills, as I afterwards learned, were placed mostly with the savings banks and the state social insurance system. And that especially made the transaction so criminal. The poor people in Germany are, in general, trusting. The workman has a certain feeling of security ; he feels that nothing can happen to him in his old age. He is satisfied with a relatively small old-age pension. But he does at least want to be sure that in later life he is free from care. And it is just this class which has been made the victim; the people who blindly believe in their beloved Führer are the ones to lose their money.

The whole process is nothing less than the embezzlement of the minimum of four hundred marks which every German worker pays into the social insurance system of the Reich. In reality, therefore, it is the common people who pay the enormous expenses of the War. I am writing this with emphasis, in order to open the German people's eyes.

After the resignation of Schacht such methods were used exclusively. I consider the money as lost, and it is my opinion that the workers' insurance system will have to be reconstructed on a new basis. For when, one day, the people realise that they have lost their competence, they will be desperate. For this reason some of the employers have created private guarantees for their workmen. They have established savings banks at the factories. Here all the money paid in is paid back, and large reserves have been accumulated for these institutions in the course of time. For this reason many workmen are already very grateful to their employing concerns. They have begun to understand that the state has abandoned them, while it still protects their factory.

In the autumn of 1934 I went to Argentina for a few months. This was after the murders of Röhm and Schleicher, and I was anxious to breathe some purer air. I want to repeat here once again that the Röhm affair was rank bestiality. The leaders of the SA had been assembled by agreement with Hitler, and this same gathering was afterwards used as evidence of their treasonable plans. One must search widely and long in the records of history before finding so despicable an act. Shortly after the murder of Schleicher, by the way, I asked Goering just what had been the matter with Schleicher. Goering answered that it had been proved that he had been in treasonable intercourse with the French ambassador. At the same time, however, Hitler accused the general of connections with Stalin !

So I was glad to escape from this witches' cauldron for a while. I continued my travels until the spring of 1935, and in Argentina I came to understand—through a number of examples—the foolishness of the German commercial policy, which attempted to achieve self-sufficiency (or " autarchy ") for the Reich. I was received by the president of Argentina. He said, " Won't you do something to make Germany buy some of our Argentine meat ? " That was in reply to my request that Argentina should place some sizable orders with German industry. The president was willing enough, if Germany would only buy more meat in his country. For he was anxious to show the English that other people, too, buy Argentine meat. I reported this to Hitler when I returned to Germany. He agreed. But Darré, the minister of agriculture, rejected everything. He didn't want a single kilogram of meat from Argentina. This is a sample of the workings of the absurd Nazi government machine.

Later on I was again in the Argentine. By then a commercial agreement had become much more difficult to realise. We would have done better to buy the meat and throw it overboard, for at least we could have negotiated a better industrial agreement. But the most injured man in the whole business was the German worker, who did not get sufficient meat, while the English workers in normal times have got plenty of excellent meat. The fault lies, of course, with the whole principle of autarchy. Certainly a limitation of imports is necessary, but an idiotic autarchy such as Germany aspires to is impossible. That is the result of having blockheads like Darré in important posts.

The following considerations will show how wrong such a policy is. In all European countries fertilisation with animal dung is still necessary, and all peasants keep livestock to that end. It is therefore a first principle of any farming policy to provide the means of procuring cheap fodder. Plentiful cheap fodder cannot be had except by importing it from abroad. No wonder the peasants are disgruntled : once they got their chance, the whole Nazi swindle would be over in a week. As yet, however, the peasants dare not say a word, much less risk an overt act.

The famous barter agreements which Germany has been making with other countries for years (under which goods are exchanged for goods instead of money) have again and again proved to be nonsensical. In Italy, for instance, one may buy, for one mark, books which in Germany cost ten. But that is by no means the worst example. For instance, Germany exported books to Hungary in exchange for maize. But the Hungarians didn't want any books, so what did they do ? They raised the price of the maize they sent to Germany commensurately with the price they were charged for the books ! In Rumania, too, Germany had to pay double the price for maize in the barter trade. There are many other examples I might cite.

In the future economic order it will certainly not

be possible to let industry manage quite independently. The state will always have to exercise a measure of control. But on the other hand it is wrong to think that industry merely wants to earn profits. In reality we industrialists have just one worry : how to keep our factories busy. If prices are raised, the demand falls off. And production is more important than price. In the meetings of industrialists energetic words are often spoken in the interest of lower prices. Not, of course, because the industrialists are unselfish, or anxious to give their products away cheaply, but because they have learned that high prices are bad for business.

But as soon as there is overproduction there is an unhealthy fall of prices. For when there are too many factories, prices sink so low that wage and salary reductions inevitably follow, and thus starts the descending spiral which leads to depression. Many owners of industries, unfortunately, believe that all is well so long as their machines are occupied. But it is my opinion—and this will be of great importance for the future of Europe—that certain industries must make agreements among themselves, not only nationally, but internationally. I am a partisan of the great cartels, so as to eliminate exaggerated competition and enmity between concerns. What such competition can lead to is to be seen from the fact that from time to time steel rails have been sold cheaper than the price of pig-iron. Irrational lowering of prices is just as wrong as unjustified increase.

However, cartels are good only for large industries —the " heavy " industries, the chemical industry, coal mining, and textile manufacture. The worker is always inclined to believe that cartels are directed against him, but that is not true. Stability of wages can be achieved only when the price of the product is stable too. In general, however, the government is much less sensible than the workman. For the state would like to deprive business of everything—and that is true especially of the Nazi state. The worker, on the other hand, has understood that you have to leave to enterprise enough surplus for the development of its plant.

It must not be forgotten that Germany's industrial equipment has been almost completely used up, especially in heavy industry, where machines wear out much faster than, for instance, in textile mills. In the latter a machine may last twenty years, while in heavy industry the life of the average machine is limited to five. And especially so in certain kinds of shops, for instance the rolling mill.

Another thing to remember is that the Germans are still ignorant of the fact that many plants will have to be completely modernised. In the United States a veritable technical revolution has been at work. This is true, for instance, in the manufacture of tin plate. Here is a branch of industry with an enormous consumers' demand. American technicians have invented a new process. There are twenty-four tin-plate works in the United States ; only two exist in Germany. German tin-plate production requires five thousand workmen ; with the new process, the same production would require only five hundred. But the necessary modernisation will cost a great deal of money. Shops, such as exist in America, cost at least ten million dollars to build and equip. And if German industry does not switch to the new process, it will drop out of the race. For the tin plate produced in the United States to-day is of much better quality than ours.

Of course, one would have to treat with the displaced workmen and find them new jobs. In any case, careful deliberations will be necessary if a solution is to be found. It may be possible, for instance, to find places for superfluous labour in the automobile industry. But it will not be simple. There are districts in Germany, such as the Siegerland, where most of the workmen have their own houses and gardens. They are half factory-worker and half farmer. For such cases it might even be necessary to create a new industry, in order to avoid driving people from their bit of soil. But if nothing is done, the German tin-plate industry will be dead in five years.

All these questions are questions of the future ; but they are of the greatest importance for German economy. For the extreme regimentation of German industry under the National Socialists has completely ruined its factories through excessive exploitation. Some industrial improvements have, of course, taken place in Germany as well, but in comparison with America (where business men do not have our troubles !) this amounts to nothing at all.

Nevertheless, I have hope for the future development of Europe. I believe, too, that one may be hopeful for its future in a spiritual sense. There will surely be something like a resuscitation of democracy. But I am of opinion that it will have to be accompanied by a revival of faith.

The past century, it is well known, was largely an irreligious one. Scientists believed they could explain everything, both physical and metaphysical. Some time ago a Dutch writer named Huizinga wrote a very good book, in which he says that under the influence of the great discoveries the masses were taught that science could explain everything, and the masses believed in their scientists. Then, suddenly, came still more scientific discoveries. Man discovered that the smallest molecule, or electron, is a universe in itself. Einstein arrived with his theory of relativity. Suddenly people saw that we are further removed from truth than ever. Both Planck, the German physicist, and Huizinga believe that we must go back to faith. Planck, as is well known, is a friend of Einstein. To-day few scientists are convinced that man has succeeded in discovering all the basic secrets of the universe. Nothing remains, therefore, but to return to faith.

Among ordinary people this development, thus far, has had quite different results. After being assured that everything can be explained, and after being told that nothing remains to be explained, they no longer believe in anything. Thus, because they do not know what they are to believe, and because they still *want* to believe, they do not believe in Christianity and profess to believe only in a god whom they can see. And that god, in Germany, is Hitler.

As for me, I have no doubt whatever that a return to religion will come. For the German people will experience a great disillusionment with its god Hitler, who has not made war by reason of his genius, but because he slithered into it. War, in the last analysis, came because nobody knew any longer what to do next. Hitler believed he could impress the German people with his attack on Poland, and so force them into renewed admiration of their god.

CHAPTER TWO

GERMANY AT WAR: THE CHINKS
IN HER ARMOUR

WHAT I had feared, and what I wanted to avert at the eleventh hour by publishing my correspondence with the government of the Reich, has happened after all. The total war against European civilisation has begun, with all its devastating consequences for the west, including my own homeland, the region of the Rhine. The responsibility rests with the Nazi leaders, who are playing their last card. Their personal interest and the interest of their party are not identical with the welfare of Germany.

In so far as I could, I have always given my opinion openly, and I have always tried to throw my counsel into the scales against war. The public, however, imagines that heavy industry is always fundamentally in favour of a war because it makes good profits out of war. Nevertheless, I have maintained that the opposite is true. I was able to do this only because I was an industrialist and a Reichstag deputy at the same time. As an industrialist I would never have been permitted to utter my opinion. That I did it, therefore, is no merit of mine.

What I tried to point out, aside from the moral aspect, was that Germany was not prepared for war. Both for moral and political reasons I wished to avoid the war. But I believed, too, that in the given circumstances war was not justifiable from the German side. That is what I openly told General von Blomberg, then minister of defence, so my point of view was known exactly. In my last conversations with the powers that be I said : " If political facts of which I am ignorant make war inescapable, it is necessary to do everything that is humanly possible in order to postpone its outbreak." That was in July, 1939.

Even if one adopts Hitler's point of view, one must see that he committed a grave error, for he should never have carried out his war plans in less than five years, or even ten. This opinion of mine was shared by most of the higher officers of the army. They all wanted to proceed slowly with rearmament, and in the higher army circles the current view was that Germany should have waited at least another five years. The young lieutenants, however, were imbued with the gambling spirit ; they believed that the war against the great democratic Powers would be just as easy as the conquest of Poland proved to be.

But it is dangerous to lull the soldiers into false hopes : it is not enough to win a few battles ; one must win the war. One should remember what a change in the army's morale was caused by the last great offensive of 1918. Before this offensive the army's power of resistance was not shaken. After it, however, everything was changed, as if by a miracle. And the army of to-day is not the army of the World War of 1914–1918. Its general staff no doubt is very good. But the officers' corps and the non-commissioned officers are a different story. All of them to-day are even less educated than they were in 1918. And it is very doubtful whether they will be equal to the emotional shocks which are a foregone conclusion in case of a long war.

Germany's armaments, great as they may be in an absolute sense, are by no means complete. In certain parts they do not correspond to the ideas about them which are current in the world. I shall show this by a few examples.

To begin with, there is aviation. In this branch, no doubt, a great deal has been accomplished. It is incredible to me that other countries did not discover this. If they discovered it, they seem to have believed —until the last moment—that they could reach an understanding with Germany on a tolerable basis. Years before the war Hitler deceived England by asserting that he was prepared to make a limitation agreement to cover air forces and military strength in general. He proposed such a convention on the basis of an army of 360,000. This was publicly done. I believed from the beginning that this was a deception, but it was taken seriously both in Germany and in the Allied countries. Later on, again in public, he declared that the Allies had not even answered his proposal. As German propaganda, this was a tremendous success. Adolf Hitler was now considered to be completely justified if he continued to arm.

Industrialists did not have much influence, and, as I have related, I personally had been in conflict with the Reich government since 1935. The principal mistake was made by Dr. Hjalmar Schacht, for at this moment he was the strongest man, both for the party and the army. If at that time he had warned

that the Nazis' course was dangerous, the leading
buisness groups would have taken notice. Schacht
was by no means in agreement with the measures
which he knew the government was taking ; but he
thought that things could be still arranged before it was
too late. High officers' circles were deeply depressed.
They always felt that progress was made too fast, at the
cost of the quality which they deemed indispensable.

As late as the occupation of Austria these officers
had been able to observe the general confusion
which developed. Later on there were the general
manœuvres in the Eifel region, west of the Rhine.
At these manœuvres one general was quite desperate,
because everything went wrong.

When the National Socialists came to power
Germany had, perhaps, four military airplanes in all.
All the aviation factories were bankrupt. Only
Heinkel and Junkers were working. The founder of
the Junkers Works was not a really professional manufacturer. He was rather a very gifted professor who
was preoccupied with new models ; and his factories
were constantly being used for trying out the new
types which he constructed. That, of course, reacted
on the commercial capacity of his plants. The
Junkers Works always had to be subsidised by the
state, because the few existing airplane factories had
to be preserved.

Naturally, right from the start of the Nazi regime
the revival of aviation was a thing particularly close
to Captain—now Field Marshal—Goering's heart. He
had been a flier in the World War of 1914–1918.
Goering begged me to help him. So we attached to
him a gentleman who submitted plans to him on
a big scale. That was Herr Koppenberg, who was

placed in the technical department of the Junkers Works and who soon made the establishment hum. What he accomplished, from the ground up, in two years was really remarkable. Koppenberg had been in America and he applied to the Junkers Works the processes he had observed in the United States. In this way a genuine production plant was made out of the shop which had hitherto been only a sort of laboratory. But Goering never set foot in it, which made Koppenberg quite unhappy. He carried out his order, to produce mainly bombers, in brilliant fashion. Indeed, this had always been the hobby-horse of Junkers himself. To a large extent Koppenberg used Diesel motors for his planes.

One of the essential materials in making airplanes is wire. At the beginning this wire was imported from England. But one of the first things we did was to encourage the German wire industry to produce these airplane essentials at home. This was to a large degree successful, so that the wire imports from England stopped almost completely. The fact that no further orders for wire arrived in England must have considerably misled the English as to what went on in Germany.

This aeroplane wire has to be made of especially good steel, particularly the wires which are used for controls. By the end of 1934 the reconstruction of the Junkers Works was already so far advanced that moving belt production, on the American model, could be introduced. Then Koppenberg so re-arranged the Junkers production that special factories were erected for all important parts. The various parts were then assembled in a special assembly plant. This method is the secret of the American

manufacturers' success ; in this manner they are able
to continue production without interruption. To be
sure, America is noted for the quality of its materials
in Europe far too much is still being skimped. Without a doubt, however, German aviation manufacture
has gone very far ; it is most likely the farthest
advanced branch of German armament production.

But what good are aeroplanes without gasoline? And
here we reach a question that is most important for
the striking power of German arms. An American
periodical has published an estimate of how much
gasoline the German army consumes in a day. This
estimate is calculated from the consumption of oil
in the Polish campaign, and it takes the conditions
obtaining in Poland as a basis. In Poland sixty
German divisions were in combat ; at this writing
the general estimate places the German army at one
hundred more or less motorised divisions. In Poland
about 15,000 tons of gasoline were consumed per
day. Therefore the present consumption would be
25,000 tons per day. But that covers only the
motorised army. Beyond that the air force requires
6,500 additional tons. Altogether this makes a require-
ment of well over 30,000 tons per day. But German
oil production is only 10,000 tons a day, and all of
Germany's synthetic production is not suitable for
aviation. Accumulated stocks of aviation gasoline
do not exist. Up to the end of the Polish campaign
aviation gasoline production had not been provided
for. Special provisions should be made within the
synthetic oil industry for the production of gasoline
that can be used by planes. It is, of course, possible
to produce aviation gasoline from coal, but the plans
for this are still in their early stages.

Gasoline is produced from coal by a process patented by the I. G. Farben Industrie (Fischer-Drop). But the gasoline thus extracted is much too light. It is not even usable for automobiles, because of its lightness. The I. G. Farben process was originally based on the invention of Bergius. It produces gasoline with an octane content of only 800, while a 1,000-octane content is needed for aviation motors. The factory erected for synthetic gasoline production is very beautiful, but the section which is intended to produce aviation gasoline at this writing has been hardly begun.

Another important problem for the proper functioning of a flying corps is the personnel, i.e. the fliers. The training of German pilots has proceeded much too fast. Only in the year 1936 did Germany begin to build aeroplanes in large quantities. I once had a conversation with one of our best civil pilots. He said : " The training of a good bomber pilot requires from three to five years. I do not believe in the excellence of the training which has been given in Germany ; it is much too fast."

(The army has been much more cautious. The authorities were aware of the necessity of creating a technically well-trained officers' corps, all the more so because this time Germany lacked the great numbers of non-commissioned officers which were of decisive importance in the World War of 1914–1918.)

In the matter of aviation I should like to add that just as the chief of the *Luftwaffe*, Goering, always gave his attention to what suited him, and nothing else (I have already mentioned that he never visited the Junkers Works), so his first assistant, Air Marshal Milch, only bothered about airfields and nothing else. To create good airfields in Germany is no great art.

S

For money is no consideration here. The best land could be requisitioned for this purpose, regardless of anything. (On the other hand, the proprietors from whom land was bought for this purpose could make whatever conditions they pleased. For instance, my son-in-law retained the rights to the grass growing on the land, which he sells to the military administration.)

There are some good examples of the general wastefulness of the German military treasurer. In the city of Krefeld the parade grounds had become superfluous after the last war. They had been turned into a beautiful golf links. When the time came for Germany's rearmament, Krefeld was of course to become a garrison town again. So the parade grounds had to be restored. The army wanted particularly the golf links, whose landscaping would have to be transformed for drill purposes. So they built a new golf links next to the old one, gave it to the owner of the old golf links, and built the parade ground where it had been once before. That, of course, is crazy ; but money is no object, as I have often remarked before. Similarly, the riding academy of Hanover was simply moved to Berlin.

But not only in the matter of rearmament is money squandered. For instance, in Cologne the barracks of the cuirassier regiment had been reconstructed to make a very handsome museum. This museum lay just opposite the Cologne cathedral. On this spot, facing the great and venerable church, the Nazis have built—by way of spiritual competition, as it were—a huge party assembly hall. It didn't bother these people at all to tear down the museum, whose reconstruction had, of course, swallowed up a gigantic sum. All these are only examples from my immediate neighbourhood, which I was able to observe in detail.

Nevertheless there can be no doubt that the Nazis' greatest accomplishment is rearmament in the air. Much has been done, too, in motorisation of the army —the great slogan of recent decades. But what has been said about gasoline supply in connection with aviation is equally valid for armoured trucks and tanks. Before the war broke out, there was no previous actual experience to show how the motorised troops would function. In conversations with me one of our generals gave expression to certain misgivings in this regard. " At the beginning," he said, " no doubt all will go well. But what will happen later ? One great difficulty, in particular, arises from the supply of motorised troops with oil, since these troops advance at great speed. It might be necessary to send a column of oil-tank trucks after them, for secondary supply."

In any case it has not yet been ascertained to what degree so large an army as the German can be effectively motorised. What has been done has without doubt been done well. But it is my conviction that really great, wide-sweeping battles cannot be won by Panzer divisions alone. They are an excellent weapon for piercing a front, but when the breach is made, other troops must also be advanced in the proper order. And so I believe, too, that the weakness of an army which is 100 per cent mechanised lies in the high measure of its mechanisation. How is all this material to be kept in repair ? For so fully a mechanised army one should be able to maintain repair shops everywhere, to make sure of success. And the maintenance crews to serve these repair shops must comprise a very considerable number in

relation to the number of combat troops. Ideally
speaking, one ought to follow the example of Henry
Ford, whose repair shops are distributed over the
whole world, in Germany as well as in Brazil.

In contrast to aviation and motorised weapons,
German artillery is definitely bad. There are, of
course, large motorised cannon in considerable
quantity. But the commonly used Model 88 of the
field artillery is too heavy and too big. Five years
are not a long period for the design and production of
cannon. And the Germans have concentrated during
that time chiefly on anti-aircraft guns. But the last
war showed decisively the great importance of light
artillery. It is the artillery which gives to infantry the
necessary confidence in the field. Model 88 is excellent
for what it is ; it has a long range and great effective
power, but, as I said, it is too heavy for use in the field.

So far as I am acquainted with the facts, it was not
till 1938 that Germany began to make artillery
ordnance on the grand scale. In fact, this manufacture was not begun until the Nazis got control of
the Skoda Works of Bohemia, after the Czech crisis
of 1938. Already in the first World War the Skoda
Works were of great importance in the equipment of
the armies of Germany and its Austrian allies. The
mortars were never built by Krupp, but by Skoda.

In conclusion, I should like to say this about the
subject of German armament. Germany to-day
possesses a very good special steel, which can be
turned in the factories much faster than before. But
many essential machine tools are still lacking. They
should have been built before the outbreak of war, but
there was not time enough. This gap in German
armament production is probably the clue to the

Nazis' effort to make this a *blitzkrieg* throughout. The desire to apply to other countries the method of swift piercing and overrunning, which has been successfully carried through in Poland, has been amply shown. Purely external evidence of this is the fact that the German bomber squadrons were permitted to carry on their activity without any considerations of humanity, just as Goering has always wanted it to be done. To me the most frightful example is Rotterdam. This great commercial city has always stood in close relation to Germany, and many buildings there were German property. What has been perpetrated in the destruction of that city is indescribable. I cannot imagine that the French would ever have destroyed Strassburg in so ruthless a manner. All this simply shows the urge to get ahead quickly ; that is the reason for spreading terror on every side. No German in future will be able to show himself in the world without shame.

Some time ago, when Marshal Voroshiloff seemed to be a danger to the Stalin regime, the story went the rounds in Germany that Stalin would receive Voroshiloff only if he left his weapons outside. I don't know whether Hitler nowadays, when he receives his generals, has them searched for weapons before they are admitted. He is certainly no longer quite sure of them. In any case, Hitler is absurdly protected. No doubt the reader is familiar with the story which the former French ambassador in Berlin, M. François-Poncet, used to tell. The story is that during one of his visits to Hitler a flower-pot fell over. Instantly ten SS men appeared, rushing into the room through all the doors.

Whether true or not, the story illustrates how Hitler

has made himself safe. To-day Hitler can do anything he wants, without having to fear any opposition ; and so he has precipitated this war. But I am sure that he will not win the war, and the responsibility will be his.

Publisher's Note

It can hardly be questioned that an industrialist as eminent as Fritz Thyssen is in a good position to judge the state of Germany's armaments. Although a few things may have been going on in several branches of German war industry that were not brought to his knowledge, his statements are to be trusted in so far as the quality of German armaments is concerned. This quality, he says, is uneven ; and when the war began a number of economic pre-requisites, indispensable for the smooth functioning of the German war machine in case of a prolonged conflict, had not been fulfilled. However, the first stage of the war in the west has shown that opportunities, especially of an economic nature, have offered themselves to the German army in the course of the hostilities ; and these opportunities had been reckoned with by those political groups in Germany who thought it possible to use the methods applied in the Polish campaign in a war against the western democracies. That a war which decides the fates of millions should not be based on such speculations, need not be demonstrated at length. However, Adolf Hitler has actually been able to conquer Belgium and Holland in a *Blitzkrieg*, and to force France to sign a not very honourable armistice, all this with an army whose equipments were incomplete, as Fritz Thyssen has probably justly described them. These facts seem to corroborate the theory that so far Hitler's war in western Europe has been decided, not by the strength of arms but much rather by the unscrupulous pioneer work of Fifth Columnists and the treason committed by their allies in Belgium, Holland and France.

CHAPTER THREE

THE PLACE OF THE TWO GERMANIES IN A UNITED EUROPE

WHEN they declared war on Poland, Hitler and his adviser, Joachim von Ribbentrop, had not foreseen that this time France and Great Britain would take up their challenge. Even after the Polish campaign, to the very last moment preceding the attack in the west, Hitler hoped that he would be able to manipulate the two allied Powers by diplomacy and propaganda. But when he realised the futility of his efforts, he risked everything at one throw. Ignoring the most solemn engagements, he invaded three neutral countries in order to launch against the two great western Powers the most formidable attack known to history. "Total war" was unleashed with all its frightful consequences for western Europe, including my native Rhineland.

Hitler will lose this war; that is my conviction. But Nazi nihilism has not shrunk from this barbarous assault on European civilisation as a whole. Up to the moment when I published the documents containing my protest against the war, I had still a faint hope of being able to stop, if not Hitler himself, then

at least those who have not lost all sense of responsibility
—of halting them on the brink of that abyss where
the folly of the Nazi chief has taken a whole people.
But are there still people in Germany who think
about the future ? And if there are, what can
they do ?

The responsibility for this total war, this assault on
all the human and Christian values of Western
civilisation rests with the Nazi leaders and with them
alone. It is they who have staked the whole future
of Germany on one card. What they are concerned
about is their own personal interest, the interest of
their party, the upholding of their tyrannical domination, but not the good of the country whose government
they have usurped.

Still, I am obliged to admit that up to the present
no one has been able to hold them back. The
German army executes their will.

For my own part, this crime put an end to any
scruples that I might have had. Europe cannot
survive still another modern war. Everything must
be done to make war impossible henceforth. It is
the future of mankind itself that is at stake, for the
destruction and the ruin of western Europe would
dry up for ever the spiritual sources from which our
present civilisation has sprung and to which it returns
for sustenance again and again.

When he founded the empire, Bismarck compared
the German people to a rider : " Place it in the
saddle," he said, " and it will be able to ride." These
were the words of a bold statesman who had confidence
in the German people. But the founder's boldness
was combined with prudence and caution. For twenty
years he constantly watched his rider—showing him,

indeed, how to clear obstacles, but at the same time preventing him from stumbling and from straying into adventurous paths. At every turn Bismarck was conscious of the difficulty of providing a reasonable existence for the new empire within the European framework. Never would he have applied Nietzsche's maxim, to "live dangerously," to the policy of a great state. He had taken every precaution to assure the political stability of the Reich. He himself drafted its constitution. The Prussian monarchy was to support the weight of the composite state, but the federal form of government limited Prussia's influence within Germany, and compelled the emperor to take account of the interests of each of the individual states. In the federal upper house, the Imperial Council, the vote of the ruling princes of the several states balanced that of the king and emperor. On the other hand, the Reichstag, elected by universal suffrage, was designed to support and control the central government by the people's will. In comparison with a unified and centralised republic like France this kind of institution appears to be complicated in its functions. But it corresponded to the historical development and the diversity of Germany, the Germany which Bismarck's bold and successful manœuvre had united into a great modern state.

For twenty years, the new empire, under the guidance of its founder, seemed to justify the hopes which the latter had placed in it. In its foreign policy it effected a reconciliation with the Austro-Hungarian Empire, secured the friendship of the young kingdom of Italy, and imposed the respect for its power upon a France which had just been defeated, while carefully

avoiding all provocation. At the same time Bismarck
sought to secure the friendship of Russia. He avoided
alienating England in the naval and colonial fields.
In twenty years he had placed Germany in the saddle
and had taught her to ride. Germany progressed in
all fields of endeavour. She enriched herself by her
labour and became prosperous.

By forcing this great minister to resign soon after
the beginning of his reign, William II placed all this
in jeopardy. Dazzled by the splendour of his imperial
dignity, imbued with his own authority, he was
incapable of using the delicate constitutional instrument created by Bismarck. Under his reign, the
Prussian system, then foreign to the western and
southern parts of the country, extended its influence
to the whole of Germany. The German people,
forgetting its local traditions, attached itself to its
young emperor. Such sceptics as maintained a
reserved attitude were regarded as cranks with out-
moded ideas. Very soon the German people was no
longer mounted on its own steed, according to the
words of Bismarck ; it was content to follow the lead
of the brilliant imperial equestrian in his shining
armour and helmet, without inquiring whither he
was bound. The Kaiser's intentions were certainly
not bad. But like almost all Germans, he had no
head for politics. The various mistakes which he
had committed forced him one fine day to resort to
force, in order to save his face. This is the danger
that invariably accompanies a policy based on the
maintenance of prestige. Throughout his reign
William II never realised that politics were a question
of intelligence and that recourse to violence only
proved the lack of it.

The result of the unfortunate policy of William II was the war of 1914 with its disastrous consequences, not only for Germany, but for the world as a whole.

My greatest accusation against Hitler is that he has once again led Germany into a war. It would have been so easy to realise all his reasonable desires by means of a sensible policy. He had only to live and let live. Everyone would have agreed that the war of 1914 had been the sequel of a series of political mistakes. But this time Hitler brutally refused to consider any solution based upon sound policy, and he has wittingly thrust Europe into this new disaster.

I admit that Hitler, in *Mein Kampf*, revived the insane aspirations of the Pan-Germans. But not even the most Rightist circles in Germany ever took such hysterical ideas seriously. He was barking up the wrong tree.

The methods of the Hitlerian conquest in Poland, as described in the official documents, show that what we are witnessing is a relapse into barbarism in the midst of the twentieth century. The aggressions against Denmark, Norway, Holland, Belgium and Luxemburg afford further proof, if necessary, that, in the exercise of the right of the stronger, Hitlerite Germany, unrestrained by respect for the pledged word and the law, openly flouts the indignation and contempt of all civilised peoples. By extending the battlefield to Holland, Belgium, and France, the German army, under Hitler's leadership, has attacked some of the oldest and the most highly developed countries of Europe, possessing the oldest and the richest of spiritual traditions. All this is menaced by the total war, and the menace extends to my own Rhenish homeland.

It is my conviction that the attacks of the barbaric hordes in the west will eventually be broken. But a conclusion must be drawn from this new experience. The peace terms must be such as to make any further westward aggression impossible. None of the countries attacked harboured expansionist ideas ; none of them menaced the existence of the German Reich. The England of to-day, first among equals, is no longer the colonial conqueror of the earlier times. She is now a country like other countries, at the head of a commonwealth of free peoples in all parts of the world. She has adjusted herself quite naturally to the conditions of contemporary life and does not dream of abusing her industrial power by terrorising her neighbours. France has definitely renounced any ideas of conquest. Hitler's behaviour is the ever-renewed proof that anyone who harbours evil designs invariably suspects others of being like himself.

By extending the war to the west, by attacking small neutral nations which are defenceless in the face of the German colossus, Hitler has definitely disproved the prophecy of the founder of the empire. The German people has not justified the hopes of Bismarck. It has been unable to master its steed. Under Hitler, the existence of a Greater Germany has once more proved to be a mortal danger to the life of the free peoples of Europe. It would be folly to run the risk of such a perilous adventure for the third time.

Without as within, the Hitlerian regime, as demonstrated by Hermann Rauschning, most clear-sighted of analysts, is nothing but complete nihilism. Four months before the war one of Hitler's privy councillors, Secretary of State Wilhelm Keppler, after a dinner given by the President of the Reichsbank, said in my presence, " It is in our interest to maintain maximum disorder in Europe." This, as a principle of diplomacy, is monstrous. Leaders who are prepared to allow the policy of a great country to be guided by this principle are madmen and criminals, and deserve to be placed in a position where they can do no further harm.

But if one reflects on what has taken place, this Hitlerian maxim is indicative of the whole diplomacy of the regime. Ever since he has been in power, Hitler has endeavoured to spread disorder and strife between all states of Europe. For four years he made friendly overtures to Poland in order to facilitate the contemplated assault. For a long time he sought— successfully—to deceive England and France as to his real intentions. During the first eight months of the war he attempted to divide the two Allies. When he annexed Austria he gave formal assurances to Czechoslovakia. When by his blackmailing methods he got control of the Sudetenland, he promised to respect the independence of the remaining Czechoslovak territory. During the months before the war and since the outbreak of the conflict Hitler's Germany posed as the fiery protector of the neutrality of the small countries. Denmark, Holland, Belgium, Luxemburg, and Switzerland were given reiterated assurances and formal promises. Still further to mislead their future victims, the diplomats of the Reich remonstrated with them, accusing them of being not neutral enough. These Machiavellian tactics enabled Hitler to prepare his aggression systematically. He was thus able to avoid the establishment of an adequate line of defence in the west, which could only have been done by agreement among the smaller nations and by co-ordinating the moderate means at their disposal. Even the vaguest plans for a defensive alliance of military staff conversations between Holland and Belgium were regarded by the Nazi diplomats as a menace to the Reich !

The peace that will follow Hitler's defeat must guarantee Europe against a renewal of this nihilist policy. The countries of western Europe, great and small, are entitled to security. Born on the banks of the Rhine, I regard my Rhenish home as belonging to that western Europe which must be guaranteed against any new war-like incursion. Belgium has been invaded twice in twenty-five years notwithstanding the pledges given to her. France has for the second time become the victim of a ruthless and devastating modern war. Hitler attacked her despite the solemn word given by Foreign Minister von Ribbentrop in Paris in December, 1938.

Shortly after this Franco-German agreement, before all the workers and employees of the August Thyssen factories celebrating their twenty-five years' employment in the establishments founded by my father, I praised this pact in the following words, " It is a day of rejoicing for German mothers. There will be no more war between Germany and France." All applauded. Only some delegates of the Nazi party seemed none too pleased, but they were careful to make no comment. The Germans are a peaceful people. But they have never realised that other nations, too, are inspired by a will to peace. Propaganda has made them believe that France and England planned to attack them.

As shown above, the Hitler regime has attempted

to extend its nihilist grip over the souls and consciences of the people. A deep gulf has once more been fixed between the real Germany, that of the west, where Bismarck's Kulturkampf (his great and, possibly, sole mistake) has never been completely forgotten or forgiven, and the Prussianised Germany of the east. The enslavement of consciences and the attempt to destroy Christianity are the forms assumed by total war on the spiritual plane. What Hitler wants is the destruction of the soul. At the present moment the Catholic populations of the west are not in a position to rebel. But they will never forget the outrage committed upon their religion, their priests, their most sacred feelings, in particular at the time of the scandalous prosecutions for the alleged crimes of immorality of which the Catholic Clergy was accused. The abyss between the two Germanies can never be bridged.

What must be saved is the true Germany, the Germany of the west. She must continue to play her part in a civilisation to which she has largely contributed through the centuries, and which she will enrich by precious values in the years to come. The Germans of the west must be guaranteed those fundamental rights which are the patrimony of all peoples of the west, and that of freedom of conscience first of all. They must be able to defend themselves against a return of a foreign tyranny. Europe's security from war and the guarantee of freedom of conscience—these are the two great moral ideas which must form the basis of a just and stable future peace.

Germany's new status will not be a mere reversion to the past. It will not mean a return to a sort of German federation or Holy Roman Empire composed of tiny principalities. A modern state, to be independent and sovereign, must have a certain amount of territory. After Bismarck's Kulturkampf and after the anti-Catholic excesses of the Nazis, which were supported by Prussia proper, I can but see one solution and one guarantee against the return of such abuses—namely, that Catholic Germany should become a Catholic monarchy.

Return to a monarchical system would not be a mere attempt to revive a respectable historical tradition. Between the last war and the present one the German people has proved that it is incapable of adjusting itself to democratic institutions. It does not know how to employ them. Following a long series of mistakes, the Weimar Constitution, a model of its kind, paved the way for an authoritarian government which, in its turn, led to the dictatorship. It must not be forgotten that it was Chancellor Brüning who invoked the famous Article 48 of the Weimar Constitution and, against his will, ruled for a period of two years on lines contrary to the spirit of this Constitution, which was no longer workable.[1] A return to the monarchy would make it unnecessary to resort to such expedients in the future. Let us take the case of Belgium. For the last few years this country has had to grapple with serious domestic difficulties. Where would it be to-day, without the authority of a king being imposed on the parties, above which he incarnates the country as a whole?

Moreover, the re-establishment of two German

---

[1] *Author's Note :* Article 48 of the Weimar Constitution provided for full powers of the executive during a period of emergency proclaimed by the president. During such periods of emergency the government could enact decree-laws, to be ratified by the Reichstag at some later date.

monarchies, one in the west and the other in the
east, would enable each of the two states so constituted to develop a political " personality " of its own.
Western Germany, so rich in historic traditions and
so modern in spirit, would quite naturally return to
the traditions of the old Germany within the framework of Christianity. To its east, Prussia might once
more resume its own special character as a colonial
territory, established by the Brandenburg electors
and their successors, the kings of Prussia. Who
knows ? Once freed from that lust of conquest by
which it has been devoured, that country might
exercise a useful and pacific influence in eastern
Europe.

There is nothing Utopian in this suggestion. It
corresponds to a European necessity and to present
realities in Germany. The difference between the
two regions of Germany which I have just described
is insufficiently realised abroad. The unity achieved
by Bismarck was due to a deliberate act of force ;
though this, at least, was finally approved by the
populations concerned. The alleged definitive unifi-
cation of Germany which Hitler boasts to have
accomplished is, like all the acts of the regime, merely
a sham. The former German states have disappeared
in theory ; but in fact, they have been replaced by
the satrapies of the party. Certain Gauleiters are
more powerful in their districts than were ever the
reigning princes whom they have succeeded. To
call Austria the *Ostmark* (Eastern March) cannot
deprive that country of its political and regional
individuality. Above all, the fact that the name of
Bavaria has been " officially " abolished does not
mean that Bavaria has disappeared.

But what is new in Germany of to-day is the inner revolt of the Catholic conscience against the religious persecutions. During the sixteenth century, after the Reformation, Germany was torn asunder by religious wars. This finally led to the institution of a regime of tolerance and a certain freedom of conscience so far as religion was concerned. The modern form of intolerance invented by the National Socialists, and their encroachment upon the realm of personal conscience, are in complete contradiction to the German spirit and German historical tradition. Even in the Prussia of the eighteenth century, Frederick the Great was wont to say, " *Jeder soll nach seiner Fasson selig werden* " (" To every man his own Heaven ").

Rosenberg, the great " intellectual " of National Socialism, is an importation from Russia. He has not a drop of German blood in his veins. To him and his disciples Germany owes the methods of the " leagues of the godless "—the methods of Bolshevik Russia.

There is yet another aspect of National Socialism that has revealed the difference between the two Germanies. The absolutism of the leaders, their insistence upon passive obedience, the servility of the governed—even in the highest posts—are completely foreign to our Germany of the west. In former days the Rhenish carnival, with its gay disrespect of persons, had its own methods of correcting the somewhat too Oriental mentality of certain Prussian officials. The joyous laughter of the Rhinelanders has been stifled by the tyranny of the regime, or at best it has been enlisted in the service of official policy. But these populations of the west resent as an outrage to their personal dignity the suppression of all human rights—of freedom of conscience and liberty of opinion. The revolt is smouldering; it but awaits the opportunity of bursting into flame. On the other hand, it seems that in eastern Germany the population has adjusted itself more easily. The extension of Prussian military discipline to all phases of life (" *Parieren, nicht räsonnieren !* "—" Obey, do not argue ! ") has been quite naturally accepted as the necessary condition for the accomplishment of great plans of conquest.

" The Führer is always right "—that is the modernised form of " *Parieren, nicht räsonnieren!* " Is this servility, of which various instances have been given in these pages, a feature of the Slav character? I am inclined to believe it. It is certainly not European. Never in western Europe, even before the French Revolution, has there been such contempt of the individual man.

Reduced to essentials, the question is not that of dividing Germany into two parts, or the forcible creation of two Germanies. What is necessary is merely to re-discover the frontier between Europe of the west and Europe of the east—a line which Germany has sought to efface during a period of barely a century. The true Germany, with its western traditions, must be separated from Prussia, which belongs to the east.

This is not a task to be carried out by the Germans alone, and subject to their judgment alone. The war is a crime which will certainly bring its own punishment. But a purely military solution of the problem of security would in the long run prove to be as precarious after this war as after the last. The victorious Powers could not occupy foreign territory indefinitely. Opinion in the democratic countries will develop much as it did after the last war. In 1914, England went to war to destroy Germany's naval power. Twenty years later, England sanctioned the re-birth of the Germany navy and concluded with Hitler the naval treaty of 1935. Even France ended by admitting the re-militarisation of the Rhineland and the re-establishment of compulsory military service in Germany. Therefore, the victors would be unwise to reckon with the future maintenance of their present spirit of defence, since even Hitler succeeded in lulling it to sleep. What must be done is to devise a thoroughly effective system, capable of living by its own means.

Moreover, the proposed separation of Germany from Prussia should be undertaken in a new political spirit. In the Europe of to-day there is no place for disputes over questions of supremacy. Treaties of Westphalia are out of date. The maintenance of fortified garrisons on foreign soil has been a thing of the past these fifty years. To believe that a great country can for long be kept in a state of impotence is a dangerous delusion. The terrible hour of awakening that has just struck for Europe is a definite proof of the obsolete character of the Treaty of Versailles. What must be done to-day is to remove all obstacles to the future foundation of the United States of Europe.

The economic field may perhaps prove the most fertile in new solutions. A sound economy, permitting all the peoples of Europe to live and to prosper, is fundamentally of greater interest to them than the ambitions of dictators who first ruin their country by excessive armaments and finally plunge all peoples into misfortune, including their own.

SHORT BIOGRAPHICAL SKETCHES OF THE PRINCIPAL PERSONS NAMED IN THIS BOOK

OTTO BRAUN. Before the World War, he was Secretary of the Social Democratic Party. After the revolution, he became Minister of Agriculture in the Prussian State Cabinet. In 1920, he was made Prime Minister of Prussia, and remained in office with some short interruptions until June 20th, 1932, when he was removed by von Papen's *coup d'état*. He left for Switzerland on the day of the general election, March 5th, 1933. His merits are numerous, and he was a good servant to the Social Democratic Party.

COUNT BROCKDORFF-RANTZAU. Scion of an old aristocratic family, he was German Minister to Denmark during the first World War. A liberal-minded statesman, he maintained friendly relations with the German Social Democratic party. After the German Revolution, Chancellor Scheidemann appointed him minister of foreign affairs. In 1919 he refused to sign the Treaty of Versailles, after trying in vain to obtain the Allies' consent to admit Germany to the peace negotiations in Paris. After the signature of

the Rapallo Treaty between Germany and Soviet
Russia, he was appointed German Ambassador to
Moscow, where he died several years later.

HEINRICH BRÜNING.　As a member of the Catholic
Centre party, Brüning was close to the Catholic
labour movement. From 1921 to 1930 he was the
executive president of the German *Gewerkschaftsbund*—
the central organisation of the Catholic labour unions.
In the Reichstag he was entrusted with the annual
budget reports. In 1930, he was elected leader of the
Catholic party. In the same year, on March 31st,
President Hindenburg called upon him to form a new
cabinet. There is no doubt that Brüning took office
in the most difficult period possible, when unemploy-
ment had reached its peak, when German banks
declared themselves unable to fulfil their obligations
toward their foreign creditors, and when the National
Socialists were threatening the peace of the country.
He saw himself obliged to govern by emergency
decrees and by restricting the authority of the Reichstag, a policy which he based on the provisions made
by the Constitution (Article 48) for times of emergency.
Unwittingly he thus created a precedent for Hitler,
and enabled him to eliminate the parliament without
violating the Constitution. In 1932, President Hindenburg, won over to Papen's intrigues, asked Brüning
in a few curt words to resign his office.

DR. HEINRICH CLASS.　Class was a lawyer in May-
ence up to 1919, and was Chairman of the Pan-
German League. Under the influence of Class, the
League adopted an ever more radically nationalistic
policy which did not fail to influence the policy of
the Imperial Government, reaching its climax in the
Moroccan crises of 1908 and 1911. In 1913, Class

published a book under the pseudonym "Daniel Fryman" entitled *If I Were the Emperor : Political Truths and Necessities*. It is remarkable that many of Class's suggestions have been almost textually incorporated in the National Socialist Party platform, and carried out in detail by Adolf Hitler.

WILHELM CUNO. Under Kaiser Wilhelm II, he was Geheimrat in the Reich Treasury. Albert Ballin, founder and director general of the Hamburg-America Line, made him a director in this company ; and after Ballin's suicide in 1918, Cuno became his successor. In this capacity he attended the Geneva Conference as economic adviser to the German delegation. Cuno belonged to the German People's party until the Kapp Putsch of 1920 ; from then on he was non-partisan. In 1922, President Ebert appointed him Chancellor of the Reich, in which office he succeeded Chancellor Wirth. His cabinet showed little diplomatic skill when negotiating with the Allies on the question of war reparations. As a consequence, the Reparations Commission, in 1922, according to the reparation clauses of the Versailles Treaty, declared Germany to be in default, a decision which led to the occupation of the industrial districts of the Ruhr by French and Belgian troops. Cuno died January 1st, 1933.

MAJOR DÜSTERBERG. He was a member of the German General Staff during the World War. An intimate of General Ludendorff, he organised after the German collapse a league of German World War veterans, called the *Stahlhelm* (Steel Helmet). The Stahlhelm, a nationalistic organisation, played an important part in subsequent years. Düsterberg suffered a severe defeat as a candidate to the presidential elections in 1932. When Hitler became Chancellor of the Reich, Düsterberg had to resign his chairmanship of the Stahlhelm, owing to his partly Jewish origin.

FRIEDRICH EBERT. A saddler's assistant and later trade union official in Bremen, Ebert soon reached an important position both in the German labour union movement and in the Social Democratic party. After August Bebel's death he succeeded him as chairman of the Social Democratic party. When the revolution started in 1918, Prince Max of Baden, then Chancellor of the Reich, handed over the government powers to him. When the German Republic was proclaimed, Ebert became president of the provisional " Government of the People's Commissioners." This government, which included three representatives of each of the two wings of the Socialist Party, remained in office till the convening of the Legislative German National Assembly. The National Assembly elected Ebert President of the German Republic, and he remained in office until his death in 1925. During the last years of his life Ebert was the victim of repeated and malicious attacks by nationalistic elements, accusing him of having encouraged, in 1917, the strike of German munition factory workers and of having thus contributed to Germany's defeat.

CAPTAIN EHRHARDT. Ehrhardt was the leader of one of the most active German " Free Corps," i.e., one of the numerous illegal military formations founded all over Germany between 1918 and 1921 with the purpose of contravening the disarmament clauses of the Versailles Treaty.

MATTHIAS ERZBERGER. Before the first World War, Erzberger represented the Catholic Centre party in the Reichstag. During the war he made several trips abroad with a view to preparing possible peace negotiations. In 1917 he played an important part in bringing about the Reichstag resolution which induced the Pope to offer his good offices as peace mediator. This, and his violent criticism of the Imperial government's financial policy, earned him the hatred of the nationalistic groups. After the German collapse, he was sent by his government to negotiate the armistice terms with Marshal Foch in the forest of Compiègne, where he had to sign the terms dictated by the Allies. This not only increased Erzberger's unpopularity with the nationalists, but also meant that the republican government had made the mistake of burdening itself with the responsibility of losing the war. Erzberger was accused of selling Germany out to her enemies. Dr. Helfferich, a former Imperial secretary of state, even accused him of corruption. In 1920, a short time after his resignation as Minister of Finance, Erzberger was shot to death by several young nationalists while he was spending a short holiday in Württemberg.

WALTHER FUNK. Funk was editor of the economic section of the *Berliner Börsenzeitung*, a daily which was considered to be the political organ of the War Ministry. Funk's main function was to keep up the paper's social relations with high finance and industry, and he was official Economic Adviser of the Nazi Party for a considerable time before Hitler came to power. This very mediocre journalist succeeded Dr. Hjalmar Schacht as Minister of Economy in 1938, and as President of the Reichsbank in 1939

JOHANN GIESBERTS. He was a member of the Catholic labour unions who, in the years 1919–22, had reached the office of secretary-general of the German Catholic labour unions. As such, he exerted a great influence on the policy of the Catholic Centre party in the Reichstag, of which he had for long been a member. He was considered one of the principal representatives of the left, socialistically inclined, wing of the Centre and constantly endeavoured to maintain good relationships between his party and the Social Democrats. He was minister of postal communications in several cabinets. After Hitler seized the power, Giesberts was arrested by Storm Troopers and dragged in triumph through the streets. After being held for some time in a concentration camp he was at last set free, after terrible humiliations.

WILHELM GRÖNER. As chief of the Transport Division of the German High Command, Gröner distinguished himself during the first World War by organising military railway transportation. For some time he was Chief of the "Kriegsamt," a post somewhat approaching that of a Minister of Munitions. Being democratic in his spirit, Gröner successfully accomplished his task in collaboration with the leaders of the German labour unions and the Social Democratic party. He succeeded Ludendorff as General Quartiermeister and was thus, to all intents and purposes, Chief of the General Staff. He was one of the generals who advised the Emperor to abdicate. After the German collapse he was responsible for the good order in which the German armies returned to their homes. Gröner became minister of defence in Brüning's cabinet, and eventually also took over the ministry of the interior. While in charge of internal affairs he forbade the wearing of "political" uniforms, a measure aimed at the Nazi SA and SS organisations. Soon after, he was overthrown by the intrigues of General von Schleicher, his former subordinate in the ministry of defence.

MAX HOELZ. A Communist agitator, Max Hoelz played an important part in the labour revolt of 1921, which he organised in Central Germany, especially in Thuringia. This uprising was essentially an answer to the nationalistic revolt which had found an inglorious end in the Kapp Putsch. Hoelz, an idealistic adventurer, enjoyed for a short time a romantic reputation similar to that of the notorious *banditi* of the eighteenth and the early nineteenth centuries in Germany. The revolt being suppressed by the intervention of the army, Hoelz was captured and condemned to imprisonment for life. Freed by an amnesty of the Republican government, he went to Russia. Nothing further is known about him.

ALFRED HUGENBERG. Once a youth of literary pretensions, Hugenberg entered the Prussian civil service, developed his reactionary political tendencies, and married the daughter of the influential mayor of Frankfort-on-Main, Adickes. This speeded his career ; he became a *Geheimrat* and was of great help to the Kingdom of Prussia when its government expropriated the Poles living in the Prussian province of Posen. His success in this affair made him one of the most outstanding leaders of the anti-Polish movement in Germany. During the first World War, Herr Krupp von Bohlen und Halbach engaged him as an administrative official of the Krupp munition plants. After Germany's collapse Hugenberg entered the German National People's party, the reorganised party of the Prussian Junkers. Through his hands flowed the funds collected by German industrialists for the

purpose of combating the German Republic. Moreover, he founded the publicity firm ALA, which
gradually gained complete control over the distribution of industrial advertisements, both to German and
foreign papers ; and he created a series of press
agencies which sold news and editorials at low rates
to the then destitute National Socialist press. By and
by he became the head of a chain of newspapers,
which he bought during the inflation period, and to
which he gave a National Socialist twist. He exerted
a great influence upon the German publishing firm
of August Scherl, and practically owned the greatest
German motion-picture firm, the Ufa. Having become the absolute boss of the German National
People's party, he concluded an official alliance with
the National Socialists in 1932. Sure of his and his
party's position, and confiding in Hitler's promise to
give him the ministries of economy and agriculture,
he became one of the most active advocates of Hitler's
taking over power. Indeed, Hitler had engaged himself to President von Hindenburg not to change his
cabinet policy within the next four years without
Hugenberg's consent. Hitler " kept " his promises in
his usual manner, and forced Hugenberg to resign all
his offices on June 27th, 1933. Hugenberg's party
was outlawed along with all the others. Officially a
member of the Reichstag, Hugenberg is to-day one
of the numerous silent and disappointed old men
who made Hitler what he is.

DR. WOLFGANG KAPP. As director general of the
Agricultural Mortgage Bank in Königsberg, Kapp
founded during the World War the German Patriotic
party, whose programme opposed all endeavours for
peace and demanded vast territorial annexations in
France, Belgium, and Russia. Under a pseudonym
he published his views in an aggressive pamphlet.

After the proclamation of the German Republic, Kapp conspired with all the available nationalistic groups and, in March, 1920, he proclaimed the overthrow of the Coalition government, made himself "Chancellor" of the Reich and formed his own cabinet. After a few days, however, this coup, known as the Kapp Putsch, proved a failure, as the higher state officials refused to collaborate with the usurping "government," while the workers of all Germany proclaimed a general strike. The legally constituted government, presided over by Gustav Bauer, returned to Berlin from Stuttgart, whither it had fled, and resumed its leadership of German affairs.

ROBERT LEY. Ley is the head of the Nazi Party Organisation Department and of the German Labour Front to which all German workers are forced to belong. His strong addiction to alcohol earned him a bad reputation when he was a delegate to the International Labour Conference at Geneva. Once the publisher of a Cologne gossip paper, he enjoys to-day a position of unrestricted power. The German Labour Front has a membership of twenty million workers, whose annual contributions are used for the financing of various enterprises. Moreover, the Labour Front took over without compensation the "Bank of German Workers and Employees," which, before Hitler's rule, was the bank of the German labour unions. One of Ley's most profitable enterprises, the "People's Car," is dealt with in detail in this book. Dependent on the Labour Front also is the institution called Strength Through Joy, which enables its members to make cheap week-end and holiday trips, to attend theatres and concerts at reduced prices, and to take cheap cruises on steamers built for this express purpose, but which to-day are used by the navy for troop transports.

ERICH LUDENDORFF. Considered even before the World War one of Germany's best generals, Ludendorff proved his ability in the taking of the Belgian fortress of Liége. As Field Marshal Hindenburg's chief of staff, he is reputed to have won the battle of the Masurian Lakes, on the Russian front. When Hindenburg took over the High Command in 1916, Ludendorff was associated with him. Ludendorff's conduct of the war on the western front has been the subject of a wide controversy between military experts. When Hindenburg's last offensive of 1918 proved a failure, Ludendorff insisted that the government of Prince Max of Baden should ask the enemy for an armistice. Having expected a different course of events than that which took place, Ludendorff feared, after the establishment of the German Republic, that he might be made responsible before a court-martial, and fled to Sweden in disguise. But he discovered that his fears were unfounded, and soon returned to Germany, where he at first kept quiet, while busily writing his memoirs. Having moved to Munich, he re-entered public life by plotting with Kapp, by collecting funds for Hitler, and by participating in Hitler's Putsch of 1923. Although he was cleared of the charge of high treason, Ludendorff, it seems, began from then on to suffer from a mental ailment. He soon became entirely subjected to his second wife, Dr. Mathilde Ludendorff, who, although she was a specialist for mental diseases, founded a new " Aryan " religion which she called " The Well of German Strength." Ludendorff became her prophet and thus lost most of his former friends. When Hitler, with whom he had also had a quarrel, repeatedly offered him the command of the German armies, Ludendorff refused.

HERMANN MÜLLER. Müller began his career as a commercial traveller, but he became Editor of a Social Democratic newspaper and, later, a full time official of the Party. He was Minister of Foreign Affairs in the short-lived government of Gustav Bauer from June, 1919, to March, 1920. He was one of those who signed the Treaty of Versailles, and jointly with Stresemann, he endeavoured to establish friendly relations with the victorious countries and to make the treaty more bearable to the German nation. However, when he led the German delegation at the League of Nations Assembly in 1928, during Stresemann's first illness, his lack of diplomacy brought about a serious tension between him and Briand and Austen Chamberlain, a tension which Stresemann had to relieve later on. Müller was succeeded by Hermann Brüning in 1930, and died some time after.

GUSTAV NOSKE. For many years Noske was editor in chief of the *Volksstimme* in Chemnitz, Saxony, a moderate Social Democratic paper. Elected to the Reichstag, he criticised the High Command during the first World War and on the strength of this was appointed war minister by the republican government after the revolution. While in office Noske was a sharp opponent of the radical Socialists and the Communists, which earned him the hatred of both groups. On the other hand, he came more and more under the influence of the reactionary officers who were among his entourage in the War Ministry. He was destined to be disappointed in the confidence which he had placed in them, for they turned against the republic during the Kapp Putsch. When the democratic government returned to Berlin after the Putsch, Noske had to resign.

KARL RADEK. This Polish Social Democrat emigrated to Germany before the first World War. In Germany he collaborated on several social democratic newspapers. During the War, he went to Switzerland, where he became a c'ose friend of Lenin, whom he accompanied to Russia in 1917. After Germany's collapse, the Soviet government sent Radek to Germany as a Russian emissary. Back in Russia, Radek distinguished himself by his journalistic activities. In the Soviet purge of 1937, he was condemned to ten years' imprisonment.

ERICH H. A. RAEDER. A naval officer of long experience, Raeder was made admiral and appointed Chief of the Navy Command by the German government in 1928. In 1935, Hitler renewed his commission, and in 1939, he made him Grand Admiral (*Gross-admiral*). Since 1938 Raeder has been a member of Hitler's secret Cabinet Council.

HERMANN RAUSCHNING. For many years Rauschning was one of Hitler's younger men of confidence. Eventually, Hitler appointed him President of the Senate of the Free City of Danzig. After Rauschning had adhered to the National Socialist party for many years, despite its crimes and horrors, he suddenly fled from Germany and attempted to justify his conversion in several books. Of particular interest is his book, *The Voice of Destruction*, as it contains conversations with Hitler which, before the outbreak of the war, seemed to be artificial and not quite trustworthy, but the veracity of which has been confirmed by the events in Belgium, Holland, and France.

ERNST RÖHM. At the beginning of Hitler's career, Röhm, an officer of the former Imperial army, helped to finance the National Socialist party by making use of the treasury of the German army. After spending a few years in the Republic of Bolivia, where he was engaged in the reorganisation of the army, Röhm returned to Germany and began his intimate friendship with Hitler. Inspired by the more violent methods used in South American revolutions he reorganised the SA troops as a preparation for the coming internal struggle in Germany. After Hitler seized the power, Röhm widened the scope of his SA troops ; he thus met the opposition of the Reichswehr, whose officers accused him of planning to put the SA organisation above the regular army. Mysterious events led Hitler—certainly not without the influence of the army circles—to see a danger in the spirit that animated the Storm Troopers. On June 30th, 1934, Hitler hurried to Munich where, he was " told," Röhm was preparing a revolt. Adolf Hitler killed his friend, after having him waked from his sleep. It is known what horrors followed this murder ; numberless loyal National Socialists lost their lives only because some of their party comrades harboured vague suspicions, or had grudges against them.

DR. HJALMAR SCHACHT. Having studied national economy at the University of Berlin, Schacht made a rapid banking career and was appointed, despite his youth, director of the " National Bank for Germany," which was subsequently merged with the Darmstädter Bank. During the first World War he held an important post in the German bank administration in occupied Belgium. After the War he was one of the founders of the Democratic party and one of the stoutest advocates of democracy. Just after the inflation period the Reichstag entrusted him with the task of controlling Germany's currency. When the German Reichsbank was re-established as the powerful

U

Central Bank of Germany, thanks to the Dawes agreements, Schacht was made the president of this institution despite the opposition of high finance and the administrative board of the Reichsbank. Several years later Schacht quite unexpectedly resigned his Democratic party membership with the explanation that he opposed the party's decision to refuse compensation to the former German reigning princes for the funds they had left in Germany ; and that he, Schacht, in his quality as president of the Reichsbank, could not account to any foreign government for his party's declaration in favour of the confiscation of private property. In 1928, Schacht went to Paris, sent as an expert by the German government in order to take part in a conference at which an alleviation of Germany's reparations obligations was to be discussed. Schacht's attitude was so belligerent that the conference almost blew up. After the German government accepted the Young Plan, Schacht resigned from the presidency of the Reichsbank, but he was recalled to the post by Hitler in 1933. In 1934, he was entrusted with the ministry of economics. It was he who invented the subtle methods which enabled the Nazi regime to increase the scope of Germany's inflation without the German public realising it. He resigned from his post as Minister of Economics in November, 1937, and from the Presidency of the Reichsbank in January, 1939. His resignation was supposed to be due to his opposition to Marshal Goering, who then took over the leadership of the whole of German economy. Nevertheless Dr. Schacht is still at the service of the German government in whose interest he has made several trips abroad.

SCHLAGETER. The young man played an active role in several German " Free Corps " (*See* Ehrhardt).

During the occupation of the Ruhr he was accused of sabotage by the French authorities, and shot. Since then the National Socialists count him among their national saints.

DR. KURT SCHMIDT. He held for a short time the office of minister of economy in the National Socialist government ; he resigned because he did not wish to be responsible for the fact that under the Nazi regime the ministries had to take their orders from National Socialist party officials, in making political and economic decisions. After resigning he returned to his former position of director general in a large German insurance company.

HUGO STINNES. A prominent figure in the coal, iron, and steel industries in the Ruhr region. During the first World War he not only received huge orders from the army, but also managed to exercise a great influence on General von Ludendorff. He was particularly interested in the plan of annexing the Belgian industrial region of Campine. After Germany's defeat Stinnes became a member of the German People's party, in which he bitterly opposed Stresemann, its founder. After he had become convinced that the German government did not intend to stop the inflation by ceasing to print new banknotes, he decided to fight the German currency on a large scale and bought up all the enterprises he possibly could. Eventually he owned not only his original coal mines and iron and steel plants, but a chain of factories varying from paper mills to oil refineries and motion-picture industries. Moreover, he owned the *Deutsche Allgemeine Zeitung*, an important Berlin daily. After the German currency was stabilised he lacked sufficient capital to keep all his enterprises going. A sudden death helped him out of this embarrassment, the solution of which he left to his sons. They failed in their attempts to borrow the needed capital from various bankers, and thus the huge Stinnes concern collapsed.

GREGOR STRASSER. Born in Bavaria, Gregor Strasser settled in Munich, where he owned a pharmacy. He joined the National Socialist movement in its early stages and became one of Hitler's closest collaborators. In 1932, a disagreement arose between him and Hitler, because he disapproved of Hitler's intention to seize power without sharing it with any other party. Strasser began negotiations with General Schleicher with a view to entering Schleicher's cabinet and enabling the general to establish a government supported by all the elements of German labour. Strasser counted on a large following in case the National Socialist party should split. However, Hitler succeeded in isolating him and subsequently took his revenge on Strasser (who in the meantime had become the administrator of a large chemical concern) by ordering his murder on the night of June 30th, 1934.

JULIUS STREICHER. The name of Julius Streicher is associated with the *Stürmer*, a Nuremberg weekly founded in 1922 and notorious for its anti-Semitic and pornographic character. It also attacked every person whom Streicher suspected of republican sympathies. He was charged and sentenced more than once by Law Courts before the Nazis came to power. This, however, did not prevent him, as one of Hitler's most intimate friends, from being given absolute control over the Bavarian province of Franconia. The " Czar of Franconia " still publishes his blood-thirsty paper, which has the government's official sanction, and he is the leader of the German pogrom policy. His weekly is, of course, being widely distributed in the countries now occupied by Germany.

DR. GUSTAV STRESEMANN. Stresemann was a member of the National Liberal party which he represented in the Reichstag before the first World War. During the War he advocated unrestricted submarine warfare. In the last year of the War he changed his opinions, asked for political reforms, and fought the reactionary Prussian Junkers. After the German collapse the founders of the new Democratic party did not forgive him for his former attitude, and refused to give him a leading position in their party. This obliged him to found the German People's party. When the Ruhr occupation caused the total collapse of German finance and economy, Stresemann was called upon to form a new cabinet, which he did on the basis of a party coalition. Stresemann's foreign policy led to the Dawes agreements, the Locarno conference in 1925, and, in 1926, to Germany's admission into the League of Nations Council. He won the friendship of Austen Chamberlain and especially of Aristide Briand, which lasted until Stresemann's death. Having achieved more for Germany than any other single man, yet being opposed in his policy by the members of his own party, he succumbed to a severe illness and died in the fall of 1929.

ALBERT VÖGLER. In Imperial Germany, Vögler was already one of the most influential directors in the industrial region of the Ruhr. Subsequently he became director general of The United Steel Works, Inc., the most powerful and most extensive industrial enterprise in Germany, the president of which was

Fritz Thyssen. After the revolution that followed the first World War, he was elected to the Reichstag by the conservative German People's party and became a member of the Reich Economic Council. At all times he supported all the groups that opposed the republican cabinets. Nevertheless he was sent by the government, along with Dr. Schacht, to the preliminary discussions of the Young Plan, which took place in Paris. While the discussions continued, he suddenly returned to Germany to take council with his friends, the Ruhr industrialists, and resigned his mandate for the reason that he did not like the Paris proposals. In the subsequent deliberations in the Reichstag on the subject of the Young Plan, he was the leader of the nationalistic opposition which refused to accept the plan.

GUSTAV VON KAHR. He was the leader of the Bavarian federalist independence movement, which intended to put Crown Prince Rupprecht of Bavaria on the Bavarian throne. Being appointed Commissioner of the Bavarian State in 1922, his attitude encouraged the then incipient National Socialist movement in Munich. When Hitler, in common with Ludendorff, proclaimed his own government in a Munich beer hall (the " Bürgerbräu ") on November 9th, 1923, he was certain of having Kahr on his side. During that very night, however, Kahr recognised the danger and uselessness of the new movement, and he ordered the police to shoot at the National Socialists who, led by Hitler and Ludendorff, were solemnly marching to the Munich Feldherrnhalle. His *coup* having failed, Hitler was convicted of high treason and condemned to prison confinement in the Fortress of Landsberg. Hitler took his revenge and ordered the assassination of Kahr soon after he came to power.

FRANZ VON PAPEN. As German military attaché in Washington during the World War, Papen had a large share of responsibility in the notorious acts of sabotage throughout the United States, which contributed to America's entry into the war. After the war was over Papen acquired a large fortune by marrying the daughter of a rich industrialist of the Saar region. He was a member of the Prussian Diet, and when his and General Schleicher's intrigues overthrew the cabinet of his party colleague Brüning, in 1932, Papen became Chancellor of the Reich. Once in office he not only attempted to introduce a dictatorship in Germany, but also staged a *coup* in Prussia by deposing all the members of the Prussian government. During the short time he remained in office Papen was extremely successful in his foreign policy, for at a conference in Lausanne he secured the Allies' consent to the cancellation of German reparations after a final payment of one billion Reichsmarks in cash. Papen's government was heavily defeated in the Reichstag Elections, and was succeeded by General Schleicher. Several months later Papen took his revenge and caused the fall of Schleicher, who was succeeded by Adolf Hitler. On June 30th, 1934, when Röhm and many others were assassinated, armed troops penetrated Papen's office and killed his secretary. However, Papen himself remained in favour with Hitler, who employed him on several important diplomatic missions. As German ambassador in Vienna, Papen prepared the Austrian Anschluss ; subsequently, he became German ambassador in Ankara, Turkey.

KURT VON SCHLEICHER. Formerly a member of the General Staff of the Imperial army, he was given an important administrative post in the defence ministry of the German Republic. He was soon promoted to the rank of colonel, and then general. Being fond of politics, he favoured the so-called " Black Reichswehr "—the illegal army divisions whose existence he skilfully hid both from the Reichstag and the Allies. Schleicher was sympathetic to the National Socialist movement from its very beginning ; when General Gröner, minister of defence in the Brüning cabinet, forbade the wearing of uniforms to the National Socialist militia, Schleicher plotted the overthrow of General Gröner, his superior. When he had succeeded in overthrowing Brüning's cabinet Schleicher considered his time had not yet come, and used Franz von Papen as his " stooge." Papen was suddenly dismissed by President von Hindenburg under the influence of Schleicher's renewed intrigues. On the President's express wish, Schleicher openly entered the field of politics and accepted the formation of a new cabinet. Although he intended to govern dictatorially, he desired to give his regime an appearance of popularity by courting labour. His true intention, however, was to separate the labour unions from their affiliated parties. Simultaneously, he intended to provoke a split in the National Socialist party by drawing Gregor Strasser, one of its leaders, to his side. However, before these preparations could bring about the desired success, Schleicher was no longer Chancellor. Papen had taken his revenge ; he had turned President von Hindenburg against Schleicher by telling him that the general was planning an armed revolt against him and that troops were stationed in Potsdam, ready to march on Berlin. Schleicher was dismissed by the President and replaced by Hitler. On June 30th, 1934, Schleicher and his wife, who tried to protect him, were shot dead by a group of Storm Troopers. The semi-official explanation for his death was that he had conspired with the French ambassador, M. François-Poncet. In fact, François-Poncet, a friend of Schleicher's, had merely reported to Paris that it was practically certain that the army would make an end of the regime before the end of the year. Moreover, Schleicher was said to possess documents proving General Goering corrupt, and also the proof that Hitler had come into possession of the Order of the Iron Cross by irregular means.

INDEX

INDEX